CRITICS OF THE
ENLIGHTENMENT

CROSSCURRENTS

ISI Books' Crosscurrents series makes available in English, usually for the first time, new translations of both classic and contemporary works by authors working within, or with crucial importance for, the conservative, religious, and humanist intellectual traditions.

Titles in series

   Icarus Fallen, by Chantal Delsol, trans. by Robin Dick

Selected forthcoming titles

   Russia in Collapse, by Aleksandr Solzhenitsyn, trans. by Olga Cooke

   Equality by Default, by Philippe Bénéton, trans. by Ralph Hancock

   The Unlearned Lessons of the Twentieth Century, by Chantal Delsol, trans. by Robin Dick

   Tradition, by Josef Pieper, trans. by E. Christian Kopff

CRITICS OF THE
ENLIGHTENMENT

**READINGS IN THE FRENCH
COUNTER-REVOLUTIONARY TRADITION**

EDITED AND TRANSLATED BY
CHRISTOPHER OLAF BLUM

ISI BOOKS
WILMINGTON, DELAWARE

Library of Congress Cataloging-in-Publication Data:

Critics of the Enlightenment : readings in the French counter-revolutionary tradition / edited and translated by Christopher O. Blum.—Wilmington, Del. : ISI Books, 2003.

p. ; cm

Includes bibliographical references and index.
ISBN: 1-932236-13-9 (cloth)
ISBN: 1-932236-25-2 (paper)

1. France—Politics and government—1789–1799.
2. France—History—Revolution, 1789-1799. 3. Enlightenment.
I. Blum, Christopher O. II. Title.

DC142 .C75 2003   2003109727
944.04—dc22   CIP

Published in the United States by:

ISI Books
P.O. Box 4431
Wilmington, DE 19807-0431
www.isibooks.org

Cover design by Sam Torode
Book design by Kathryn Smith

Manufactured in the United States of America

CONTENTS

FOREWORD
PHILIPPE BÉNÉTON

The texts that Christopher O. Blum has chosen and elegantly translated will doubtless appear very strange or foreign to the American reader. The American nation was born modern; the French counter-revolutionary tradition was born anti-modern, in reaction against that singular, formidable, and extraordinary event that was the French Revolution. This tradition has fought a rear-guard action, and its light has dimmed with the triumph of modern ideas. Its history is, in the end, that of a failure, and a failure that, to some, gives the lie to its doctrine. Counter-revolutionary thought appealed to history and its wisdom against the revolutionary break from it, and, therefore, falls under its own condemnation because the course of history has not vindicated it.

Must we therefore read the texts of Maistre, Bonald, Le Play, and the others as the expression of a bygone era in the intellectual and political history of France? To a large extent, yes, certainly. Yet the interest of Christopher O. Blum's work does not end there. The texts that he has made available, most for the first time to an English audience, and that he has presented with care (texts generally forgotten, and sometimes even difficult to find in the French), are historically significant; some of them are also significant as literature. Thus Chateaubriand, who stands somewhat apart from the others and is difficult to classify, has strongly marked our literary history, while Maistre wrote with vigor and, at times, brilliance. Yet they are more than merely stylish. As the editor points out in his preface, these texts also raise questions of political and social philosophy that remain unanswered. More particularly, the counter-revolutionaries' critique of modern society is far from having lost all its relevance. On the contrary, the more the principle of the sovereignty of the individual is immoderately affirmed, the more their critique gains in importance. Put otherwise, if these texts are strongly dated, they are also, in certain respects and subject to qualifications, very much living ones. There is a good use for counter-revolutionary thought. What follow are my reflections upon what that use might be.

THE WEAKNESSES OF FRENCH
COUNTER-REVOLUTIONARY THOUGHT

In essence, the weakness would seem to be the following: counter-revolutionary thought cannot be upheld in the full extent of its traditionalism and consequent rejection of universalism. Its critique of theoretical reason and political voluntarism is too extreme. The counter-revolutionaries are too obdurately opposed to all of modernity taken as a unitary phenomenon; that is, they fail to make distinctions.

First, as to their traditionalism, the counter-revolutionaries, or European conservatives, praised tradition as being opposed to the *philosophes'* pretentious and unrealistic use of reason. Yet they only ever defended some traditions, those of old Europe. For a time, it is true, this traditionalism was their strength, for against those who had gone astray, they could point to the example of a long history. But as soon as history had taken a new path, and had stayed on it, they ran into an insurmountable difficulty. How does one set one history against another? How does one appeal to tradition while rejecting those which are forming and developing within modern regimes? In France, notably, the more time went by, the greater seemed the contradiction between an appeal to the continuity of history and the desire to restore the *Ancien Régime*. The counter-revolutionaries were thus led to mutilate history and to ossify tradition. The need to sort things out and to take stock of things piecemeal, therefore, condemns their own criterion.

Now counter-revolutionary thought might well respond by saying that we must distinguish between true tradition, which was forged by the experience of the ages, and the false or corrupt traditions born from a violent uprising of theoretical reason. This does not, however, by itself remove the difficulty. Traditionalism, even limited in this way, leads logically to a cultural relativism difficult to reconcile with what the counter-revolutionaries otherwise held. Must we, in the name of tradition, place barbarous practices on the same level as civilized ones? Were the ancient Romans who opposed Christianity in the name of tradition right after all? To Maistre and his disciples, traditionalism took a radical form thanks to their opposition to the abstract universalism of the *philosophes*. Counter-revolutionary thought, therefore, lodged itself too much in the particular to the detriment of the universal. It manifestly went too far: tradition only ever has conditional virtues. A substantial politics can never be founded without reference to nature.

Second, their anti-rationalism. Theory, said the counter-revolutionaries, wasn't worth the trouble. Men can rule themselves in the details, that is to say, in precise and concrete matters, but they are powerless to think of the political and social order as a whole. The realities are too complicated and too variable for human reason to be able to reduce them to general formulae. Those who wish to reform everything by reference to abstract principles are fools.

This counter-revolutionary critique of the capacities of reason, opposed as it was directly to the confidence of the *philosophes*, is, clearly, too radical. The right rule, it seems, is this: we must make distinctions. One might indeed argue that Condorcet was a fool, but one ought not treat Montesquieu or Madison in the same manner. Modern political experience speaks of a variety of things. It speaks of the deadly consequences of an ideological use of reason that takes itself for Providence and misunderstands the nature and condition of man. It also speaks of the success, at least considered with respect to its own objectives, of the moderate version of liberal modernity. The founding fathers of liberalism promised civil peace, liberty, and comfort for all. In the main, these promises have been kept. Political and social reason is not as powerless as the counter-revolutionaries claimed. It has, for instance, produced these fruits. Political power has been domesticated. In the West, politics continues to divide men but their disputes are kept peaceful and no one risks his life or his liberty should he displease the reigning power. Conventions that artificially separate men have been destroyed or attenuated: the aristocratic conventions of the *Ancien Régime*, prejudices founded upon race, nationality, religion. Man's recognition of his common humanity has progressed. The Christian Gospel has always acted towards this end, but not always historic Christianity. Consequently, and in certain respects (to which we might add the favorable effects of scientific and economic rationality), our world has become more human. The will to use reason can be beneficial. After a long period of resistance, the Catholic Church has taken note of this progress: "It is certainly true, that a more heightened sense of the dignity and unique character of the human person as well as the respect due to the workings of the individual conscience constitutes a real gain of modern culture" (John Paul II, *Veritatis Splendor*). The counter-revolutionary dichotomy between past and present in which the past is idealized and the present rejected en bloc misunderstands great swaths of reality.

There is, however, more to be said. Liberal modernity is not a simple unity. If in some respects it is more in conformity with nature, in others it has left her far behind. In the face of this development, a part of the counter-revolutionary critique can be vindicated.

ON THE HERITAGE OF
COUNTER-REVOLUTIONARY THOUGHT

Our liberal modernity has departed from nature by emptying its own principles—equality, democracy, and the rights of man—of all their substance. Why the rights of man? Not because of some common nature, but because individual wills are sovereign. Why equality? Not because the fact of being human carries with it some meaning, but because the humanity of man is reduced to his indeterminate liberty. Individuals are autonomous; they are sovereign. The principle has become almost official since the moral revolution of the 1960s, and it is unfolding logically before us. Against this principle and its consequences, counter-revolutionary thought offers some antidotes.

To the myth of autonomy, it responds that the man of the radical version of modernity, the perfectly autonomous man, is a fiction. The French counter-revolutionaries, after Aristotle, Saint Thomas, and Burke, ceaselessly insisted, with arguments difficult to refute, upon the social dimension of human existence. Man does not make himself by himself; he receives from others (his relatives, his contemporaries, past generations) much more than he gives. Man does not live alone; he has a deep, fundamental need for others because he is a being constituted by relations. He who would exercise autonomous judgment in fact relies upon a thousand things he takes on the authority of others: that the earth is round, that Napoleon existed, that his parents are his parents, and so on. He who would attempt to live in an individualistic manner leaves behind him ties that matter, particularly those of the heart. Full and complete autonomy is a dream and a pernicious one at that. The consequence of the dream has been that in the midst of modern society, strong ties among men have been discarded in favor of weak ones. Modern individualism loosens true social ties, which are ties of attachment, in favor of contractual and utilitarian relations. Solid attachments are those which are created in the midst of communities, whether they be familial, religious, local, political, or professional communities. A good society cannot be reduced to a collection of individuals.

More fundamentally, a radical autonomy founded upon an indeterminate liberty is at once unrealistic and dangerous. It is unrealistic because every man is supported by things that do not depend upon himself alone. Each of us is in some sense free to think that two and two make five, that he will never die, that the past did not exist, and that hatred is the most beautiful thing in the world, but what would such a liberty signify other than the liberty to free oneself from the human race? An indeterminate liberty is also dangerous because the political world cannot be given order simply by appealing to the human will. The counter-revolutionary critique frequently underscored the truth that power cannot be regulated unless it submits to principles that are anterior to it and come from religion or nature. In a world in which indeterminate liberty reigns, political power will oscillate between the extremes of libertarianism and despotism, or will combine features of both.

Counter-revolutionary thought also offers a response to radical modernity's myth that it constitutes a providential system. Men, this myth holds, are innocent, whatever their conduct may be, and a technique will suffice to solve their problems. This system—a political organization, a social mechanism, or a pedagogical technique—will dispense agents of any substantial obligation. Against this form of utopianism, counter-revolutionary thought recalls simple and essential truths: that if the system is perverse, it can in no way be providential; that we cannot obtain the Good without asking agents to behave well; that morals count, and that it takes time to create good morals. Politics cannot be reduced to a mechanism.

From this perspective, the counter-revolutionary thinker who best shed light on the limited nature of any political solution is Edmund Burke. Politics, he said, is always a random collection. It achieves equilibrium when competing social ends agree to accept limits. Thus Burke's critique of the Rights of Man has lost little of its force: the language of modern rights only poorly takes the measure of reality because it is too categorical (it speaks of all or nothing), while social life, except in extreme cases, must be thought of in incremental terms (in terms of the more and the less).

Counter-revolutionary thought, finally, responds also to the danger of abstraction present in modern thought. The counter-revolutionary thinkers tell us that modern thought tends to lose sight of the real man, the man of flesh and blood and bones. On the one hand, it tends to cut up the human subject into his social roles—as consumer, as subject to law, as aged or infirm—and thus tends towards ignoring man as a whole. The pure economist has a blind spot similar to that of the doctor who thinks of his patient as merely a collection of organs, or the jurist who cleaves to his own technique. On the other hand, modern abstraction tends to level everything in the name of its sacrosanct principle of equality. Vital differences are wiped away; merit loses its rights. The counter-revolutionaries doubtless went too far and misunderstood the political and social importance of equality for all men, but they usefully recall how much great example and great works mean to us, and how admiration helps us to live and to govern ourselves. The difficulty consists in holding together equality with inequalities. Here again, we must carefully proceed to look for a point of equilibrium.

Let us recapitulate. Counter-revolutionary thought had for its chief error the complete rejection of the modern world. The symmetrical error would be to reject all of counter-revolutionary thought. We must make distinctions. We must, as much as possible, sort out what is good in modernity and what is good in counter-revolutionary thinking. What we need to do, therefore, is to combine the following:

- The rejection of unconditional traditionalism but also radical constructivism. In other words, time is not necessarily right, but there are things that time alone can achieve. Political and social reason is not providence, but neither is it incapable of any good.

- The adherence to modern equality, inasmuch as it is the recognition of the honor of being human that belongs to all men, but the rejection of modern equality insofar as it is founded upon indeterminate liberty. There is a dignity, in part mysterious, proper to the human being as such, but it does not follow from this that all kinds of conduct are valid.

- The rejection of the sovereignty of the individual with the affirmation of the rights of conscience. Man is not and cannot be fully autonomous. It does not follow, however, that human communities have the right to be oppressive.

Put otherwise, the correct formula, or the least bad formula, is perhaps that of a conservative liberalism. In any event, it can only be a mixed formula, one that takes account of historical particularities. Burke and Tocqueville knew this. The French counter-revolutionaries insisted upon the weight of historical singularities, but, paradoxically, they were too attached to pure formulae.

INTRODUCTION

"The age of chivalry is gone. That of sophisters, economists, and calculators, has succeeded; and the glory of Europe is extinguished for ever."[1] Edmund Burke's righteous indignation was elicited by the insults dealt to Marie Antoinette in October of 1789, but his words were universal in intent, and they aptly summarize the changes brought to Europe by the Enlightenment. The French Revolution (1789–1815) was the Enlightenment in action, bringing a new order with Napoleon's conquering armies. Gone was the age of chivalry, with its centuries-old aristocracy, its monarchies dating to the Middle Ages, and its religion and common culture inherited from the Roman Empire. The Revolution was the birth pang of an egalitarian, secular, and commercial society, and this was neither a mistake nor an impersonal evolution. The principal actors in the drama were well aware that they were enacting the Enlightenment's plans for a new order. When Napoleon described his France as "thirty million people united by enlightenment, property, and

[1] Edmund Burke, *Reflections on the Revolution in France* [1790], with an introduction by Russell Kirk (Washington, D.C.: Regnery, 1955), 111.

[2] Napoleon speaking in 1802 to his Council of State, quoted in François Furet, "Napoleon Bonaparte," in *A Critical Dictionary of the French Revolution*, eds. François

commerce,"[2] he declared a program, not a statement of fact. His France was but tenuously united, and Europe has ever since been divided by the legacy of the Enlightenment and Revolution. Yet the changes wrought by the French Revolution and Napoleon were decisive. Like Burke, the far-seeing Joseph de Maistre knew he was living at the end of an age: "I die with Europe; I am in good company."[3]

What died with the French Revolution was not merely a political order, it was an entire way of life. Georges Bernanos was surely right to say that "the drama of Europe is a spiritual drama."[4] European history is not driven by a change in the tools of production, it is driven by men, and men are moved by their convictions. "Political developments," as Newman said, are "really the growth of ideas."[5] Knowing these truths, Maistre and his fellow critics of the Enlightenment sought something much more important than merely preserving or restoring the Old Regime. They knew as well as any that it had been rife with abuses. What they sought was to revivify Europe by returning to the traditions that had civilized her in the first place. Their writings were meant to vindicate principles they took to have timeless significance: monarchy, the union of throne and altar, and traditional culture based upon family, agriculture, and the customs, morals, and beliefs inherited from the Christian past. They sought nothing less than to preserve the spiritual inheritance of Europe.

It must, however, be said that this spiritual inheritance was not a disembodied spirit. The French conservatives of the early nineteenth century sought to vindicate the principles of the Old Regime

Furet and Mona Ozouf, trans. Arthur Goldhammer (Cambridge, Massachusetts: Harvard University Press, 1989), 279.

[3] Joseph de Maistre to the count de Marcellus, 9 August 1819, quoted in Richard A. Lebrun, *Joseph de Maistre: An Intellectual Militant* (Kingston and Montreal: McGill-Queen's University Press, 1988), 253.

[4] Bernanos, *La Liberté pour quoi faire?* (Paris: Gallimard, 1953), 192.

[5] John Henry Newman, *Essay on the Development of Christian Doctrine*, sixth edition (1878; reprinted Notre Dame, Ind.: University of Notre Dame Press, 1989), 43.

not for their own sake, as if it were an antiquarian matter, but because they were convinced that these same principles could, if followed, again give birth to the kind of noble and truly human civilization that Europe had been at its best. This is precisely the spirit in which these authors are presented in this volume. There is no question today of restoring thrones. Yet to go forward we must have some conception of our goal, the goal of a life well lived. The texts presented here can help us by raising issues that are rarely discussed by Anglo-American conservatives, and thus by challenging us to look deeper into some of the fundamental aspects of human society.

Although the French conservatives like Maistre were often inspired by Burke, they went further in their critique of the new institutions, beliefs, and customs and in their reasoned examination of the old ones. The Revolution never crossed the English Channel, although it threatened to do so, and without the profound transformation that Napoleon's armies brought, English society remained imbued with many of the manners and morals of the Old Regime for much of the nineteenth century. In France, however, the Revolution of 1789 to 1815 was only the first of a series of revolutions and political crises over the next century. France in the nineteenth century was like Germany and Russia in the twentieth: the workshop of history, the place where rival ideas most openly fought for dominance.[6] As a result, French political writing on both sides of the spectrum is much more radical than is Anglo-American thought during this period. The Left was not merely democratic or liberal, it was anticlerical and sometimes violently egalitarian. The Right was not cautiously conservative; it was robustly so. Such a polarization does not always bring wisdom to the fore, but it does bring into sharp relief the contrasting convictions of the opposing sides.

This volume contains selections from six of the leading representatives of the French counter-revolutionary tradition. The first three

---

[6] For a recent history that supports this view, see François Furet, *Revolutionary France, 1770–1880*, trans. Antonia Nevill (Oxford: Blackwell, 1992).

are the celebrated "prophets of the past."[7] Chateaubriand ranks with Hugo and Lamartine as one of the leading French Romantics. Maistre and Bonald are familiar to Anglo-American conservatives as Burke's French interpreters.[8] The last three writers are little known in the English-speaking world. Heirs to Chateaubriand, Bonald, and Maistre, these men were the leading members of the conservative school of social thought in the second half of the nineteenth century. Émile Keller was a prominent defender of Catholic interests in the French parliament and the author of an influential commentary on Pope Pius IX's *Syllabus of Errors*. Frédéric Le Play was one of the founders of sociology in France. Finally, René de La Tour du Pin, one of the architects of *Rerum Novarum*, was the last great expositor of the French counter-revolutionary tradition before the transformation of French political life caused by the Dreyfus Affair and the rise of *Action Française*.

FRANÇOIS-RENÉ DE CHATEAUBRIAND

Chateaubriand strode onto Europe's stage "with the *Genius of Christianity* in hand."[9] His timing was impeccable. The eloquent essay was put on sale in Paris on Good Friday, 1802. Two days later, on Easter Sunday, the Eldest Daughter of the Church was resurrected when Napoleon's concordat with Pius VII was announced with a *Te Deum* and solemn high mass at the Cathedral of Notre-Dame. For the first time in more than a decade, it was fashionable to be a Christian in France. Chateaubriand's fortune rose with the tide of emotion that followed the concordat. Soon his was a house-

---

[7] Jules Barbey d'Aurevilly, *Les Prophètes du passé*, 2nd edition (1851; Paris: Victor Palmé, 1880).

[8] See Yves Chiron, "The Influence of Burke's Writings in Post-Revolutionary France," in Ian Crowe, ed., *The Enduring Edmund Burke* (Wilmington: Intercollegiate Studies Institute, 1997), 85–93.

[9] Barbey-d'Aurevilly, *Les Prophètes du passé*, 128.

hold name, synonymous with the grandeur of the First Consul's rule.

Yet Chateaubriand's relationship with Napoleon was destined to sour, for he remained loyal all his life to the illustrious house his ancestors had served. His was an ancient family of Breton nobility, and one of his ancestors died on Crusade with St. Louis. By the eighteenth century, his family was impoverished. His father, after making a fortune as a privateer and slave trader, retired to the Breton countryside and bought a miserable landed property that he ruled from a gloomy medieval keep. François-René (1768–1848) inherited his father's wanderlust and romantic attachment to the family history, but not his money. As the younger of two brothers, he was required to make his own way in the world. His chosen career was the military, which he entered in the waning days of the Old Regime. In Paris, in July of 1789, he saw the mob parade the heads of the governor of Paris and his assistant around the city on the ends of pikes. When they approached the house in which he was staying, he lashed out at them: "You Brigands, is this what you mean by liberty?"[10] Thus began a stormy counter-revolutionary career.

Having left the army, Chateaubriand sailed for the New World, intent on discovering the Northwest Passage. This he had neither the resources nor the expertise really to attempt. Yet he did see much of the American back-country and gleaned many experiences with which to color the tale of Indian life that would first win him notoriety, *Atala: The Love of Two Natives in the Wilderness* (1801). While in rural Virginia, he chanced to see a newspaper detailing Louis XVI's flight to Varennes in the summer of 1791 and realized that his duty lay in France. By the next summer, he had joined the emigré army on the banks of the Rhine. With them he endured the insult of marching in the baggage-train of the Austrians into France, and then fleeing with them to the Low Countries when the invasion failed. He spent the next eight years in London, frequenting the

[10] Ghislain de Diesbach, *Chateaubriand* (Paris: Perrin, 1995), 59.

homes of sympathetic English and supporting himself by pasting together a rambling and intemperate *Essay on Revolutions* (1797), in which Voltaire and St. Augustine both served as authorities.

Like many of his generation, Chateaubriand had fallen under the influence of Rousseau, Voltaire, and the other "lights" of the eighteenth century. Yet some sort of change came over him during his last years in London and brought him back to the religion of his youth. By his account, the death of his mother in 1797, following upon the execution of his brother under the Terror in 1794, caused his conversion. But his attachment to the Christian religion was never particularly deep, and many have wondered whether the word conversion is the appropriate one to describe his change of heart. Indeed, while he penned the *Genius of Christianity*'s rhapsodies to conjugal fidelity and the virtue of chastity, he was hidden in Normandy in a lover's tryst, his lawful wife miles away. To his contemporaries, he was as famous, or infamous, a lover as he was a writer.[11]

For all its author's blemishes, the *Genius of Christianity* was an epoch-making book. It may not be an exaggeration to say that, so far as France was concerned, it was the pivot between the classicism of the eighteenth century and the romanticism of the nineteenth. The Enlightenment in France had championed both secular reason and secular taste: Christian art and customs were ridiculed as the childhood of art and life.[12] Soufflot's Pantheon was the architectural emblem of an age that saw Gothic churches stripped of their medieval decorations and the affective side of devotion downplayed. In opposition to the derision and disdain of Voltaire and his companions, Chateaubriand expressed a vibrant love for France's Christian past: her monuments, her customs, her beliefs. The cathe-

[11] This is the principal theme of André Maurois, *Chateaubriand: Poet, Statesman, Lover*, trans. Vera Fraser (1938; reprinted New York: Greenwood Press, 1969).

[12] See, for instance, Jean d'Alembert's comments on art in his *Preliminary Discourse to the Encyclopedia of Diderot* [1751], trans. R. N. Schwab (Chicago: University of Chicago Press, 1995), 61–62.

drals of Paris and Reims showed that "no monument is venerable lest its long history is, as it were, impressed upon its vaults, blackened by the ages." We cannot enter these Gothic churches, he wrote, "without a shiver and a vague sensation of the divine."[13] Like Burke, Chateaubriand had "discovered the value of culture in the experience of its loss."[14] He wrote of parish processions and church bells, Gregorian chant, and the superiority of the Bible to Homer. Thus he led the way for the continental Gothic revival, the rise of Christian romanticism in literature, and the rebirth of Gregorian chant at Solesmes. Yet his tastes were not purely medieval. In fact, one of the central themes of the *Genius of Christianity* was the excellence of the seventeenth century and its superiority to the eighteenth. The incredulity of the *philosophes*, he argued, had brought "abstract definitions, a scientific style, and neologisms: all fatal to taste and eloquence."[15] The century of Louis XIV was the century of true giants: La Fontaine and Pascal, Molière and Corneille, Racine and Bossuet.

The second edition of the *Genius of Christianity* followed close upon the heels of the first and bore a fulsome dedication to the first consul. Like many aristocrats and Catholics, Chateaubriand succumbed to the temptation to look upon Napoleon as the savior of France and the Church. He campaigned for a diplomatic appointment and was sent to Rome as the secretary to the ambassador, Napoleon's uncle, the cardinal of Lyon. He proved to be a poor subordinate and soon returned to Paris. While there, he learned of the murder of the duc d'Enghien. This was Napoleon's fiercest reprisal for the royalist agitations that had troubled his rule. Chateaubriand was later to see d'Enghien's murder as a chief cause of the usurper's fall, writing of it in his inimitable style: "the hair cut by Delilah was

---

[13] Chateaubriand, *Génie du Christianisme* [1802], ed. Pierre Reboul, 2 volumes (Paris: Garnier Flammarion, 1966), I: 400.

[14] Mark C. Henrie, "Edmund Burke and Contemporary American Conservatism," in Crowe, ed., *The Enduring Edmund Burke*, 198–212, at 206.

[15] *Génie du Christianisme*, ed. Reboul, II: 25.

nothing other than the loss of virtue."[16] Few interpreted d'Enghien's murder in such a colorful light, but then few followed his principled example of leaving Napoleon's service because of it. Chateaubriand exercised an understated opposition, the only kind possible for one who would remain free. During the waning months of the emperor's reign, however, he began to prepare for the crisis, and secretly wrote a manuscript that would denounce Napoleon as a Corsican usurper and call for the restoration of the House of France.

On Buonaparte and the Bourbons appeared on April 6, 1814. The Russians were already in Paris, and the Emperor had abdicated and attempted suicide at Fontainebleau. The pamphlet, then, did not precipitate the fall of Buonaparte (Chateaubriand employed the original, Italian spelling of the name as part of his campaign to brand the emperor as a foreigner). Yet it did sell ten thousand copies in a matter of days, and its popularity may have helped to convince Czar Alexander that a Bourbon restoration was feasible. Chateaubriand later claimed that Louis XVIII had said that the pamphlet had been "worth more to him than an army of a hundred thousand men."[17] This was an example of the hyperbole to which he was particularly prone when writing of his own achievements. Nonetheless, the pamphlet is one of the monuments of counter-revolutionary literature. Perfectly timed, sonorous, and righteously indignant, *On Buonaparte and the Bourbons* helped France to realize that she wanted an end to the Revolution.

The pamphlet is by no means uniformly critical of the Revolution. Chateaubriand retained a fondness for the men of 1789 and their liberties, particularly the liberty of the press.[18] Nevertheless,

---

[16] Chateaubriand, *Mémoirs d'Outre-Tombe* [posthumous, 1849-50], ed. Pierre Moreau, 6 volumes (Paris: Garnier, 1947), II: 327.

[17] *Mémoirs d'Outre-Tombe*, ed. Moreau, III: 285. It is unlikely that the king ever made such a statement. See Diesbach, *Chateaubriand*, 265–71.

[18] See Jean-Paul Clément, "Chateaubriand et la contre-révolution, ou la liberté sur le pavois," in Jean Tulard, ed., *La Contre-Révolution* (Paris: Perrin, 1990), 325–47.

On Buonaparte and the Bourbons deserves its prominent place in the literature of the counter-revolution for its one point, forcefully made: on balance, the French were better off under their old kings than under the Revolution. The scorn of the Enlightenment for the ancient House of France had given rise to a revolutionary rhetoric that equated kingship with tyranny. After the tumult of the 1790s and the decade and more of Napoleon's rule, it was plain to any dispassionate observer that the Bourbons had not been tyrants. And Chateaubriand was no dispassionate observer. Like Burke, he was angry that "all the pleasing illusions, which made power gentle and obedience liberal" had been stripped away.[19] He reminded his generation of their ancient patriotism, and that the rule of the kings of the House of France was a "paternal power . . . regulated by institutions, tempered by customs, softened and made excellent by time, like a generous wine born of the soil of the Fatherland and ripened by the French sun."[20] This monarchical patriotism waxed strong in France during much of the nineteenth and twentieth centuries.[21] As late as 1873, thousands of French would march in procession to Paray-le-Monial to pray to the Sacred Heart of Jesus to restore the Bourbons to their throne. It was also a reflective and at times self-critical patriotism. Chateaubriand and the legitimists who followed his example were often harsh critics of the abuses of the Old Regime and enlightened proponents of social reform.[22]

More important, however, than political restoration was the cultural restoration called for by Chateaubriand. At the height of the influence of the *philosophes* it had become unacceptable to praise Europe's Christian past. By the 1780s in France, d'Alembert's sneers, Voltaire's jibes, and Rousseau's sensuality had won the day.

---

[19] Burke, *Reflections*, 112.

[20] *On Buonaparte and the Bourbons*, below at page 28.

[21] See Jean-François Chiappe, *La France et le roi, de la Restauration à nos jours* (Paris: Perrin, 1994).

[22] See Steven D. Kale, *Legitimism and the Reconstruction of French Society, 1852–1883* (Baton Rouge, La.: Louisiana State University Press, 1992).

The *Genius of Christianity* made cultural conservatism socially acceptable. With *On Buonaparte and the Bourbons*, Chateaubriand showed that this conservative outlook could take the offensive and defend the restoration of tradition by an appeal to both sentiment and fact.

LOUIS DE BONALD

If Chateaubriand was the troubadour of the counter-revolution, then Bonald was its strategist. Neither his career nor his writings match the Breton poet's for panache. Where Chateaubriand dashed nimbly, Bonald strode ponderously. Yet both greatly influenced their own times and the century that followed. Together they were the leading minds of the Restoration and, for a time, they were among its leading politicians. Chateaubriand's great achievement was the Spanish expedition of 1823, when the "Hundred Thousand Sons of Saint Louis" crossed the Pyrenees and marched all the way to Cadiz to liberate Fernando VII from a liberal revolution. As foreign minister, Chateaubriand orchestrated the invasion with consummate flair, making it both a diplomatic advance and a public relations coup.[23] Bonald's achievement was less famous but more lasting: the repeal of legal divorce. He constantly taught that the family was the basis of society, and with the repeal of divorce, which kept divorce illegal in France until 1884, Bonald joined Chateaubriand in the ranks of those few theorists who have been able to put their ideas into political practice.[24]

---

[23] The classic account of the war in Spain is Chateaubriand's own: *Le Congrès de Vérone* [1838], ed. Guillaume de Bertier de Sauvigny (Geneva: Slatkine, 1979). For commentary, see Bertier de Sauvigny, *La Restoration* (Paris: Flammarion, 1955), 178–92; and Michel Bernard Cartron, *Louis XIX: roi sans couronne* (Paris: Communication de Tradition, 1996), 155–92.

[24] On Bonald's role in the repeal of legal divorce, see J.-J. Oechslin, *Le Mouvement Ultra-Royaliste sous la Restoration: son idéologie et son action politique* (1814–1830) (Paris: Librairie générale de droit et de jurisprudence, R. Pichon et R. Durand-Auzais, 1960), 174–76.

Louis-Gabriel-Amboise de Bonald (1754–1840) was born and died in Millau, the chief town of the Rouergue. Just west of the rugged upland of the Cévennes at the southern end of the Massif Central in southern France, the Rouergue in Bonald's day was home to poor shepherds, vintners, and farmers. The people of his region remained deeply divided by the legacy of the Reformation. What the Catholics called the "religion prétendue réformée" (the so-called reformed religion) had made great inroads there in the sixteenth century and for a time had succeeded in displacing the Catholic religion altogether. The Church returned with a vengeance, and religious strife smoldered throughout the reign of Louis XIV, eventually culminating in the Camisard rebellion of 1702, when Protestants in the Cévennes fought the crown with the help of English arms. When Robert Louis Stevenson took his *Travels with a Donkey in the Cévennes* late in the nineteenth century, he found a stark land whose inhabitants had long memories and fierce convictions. This background of religious division and political upheaval strongly marked Bonald's consciousness.

Bonald enjoyed a rare privilege among the provincial nobility: an education at one of France's leading schools. He was fifteen when he matriculated at the Collège de Juilly, which was directed by the Oratorians. There he found a mentor in Père Mandar, who had been a follower of Rousseau. It may have been Père Mandar's influence that led Bonald to welcome the French Revolution in its initial stages. At Juilly, Bonald's education was primarily in mathematics and philosophy. Unlike the Jesuits, who had retained their emphasis on classical education, the Oratorians had embraced the new learning, particularly Cartesian philosophy and the new empirical sciences. Indeed, Bonald's turgid prose style betrays the influence of his education. After Juilly, he entered the military, but he soon returned to his native country to take up the duties of the only son of one of the region's more important families.

Having established himself as a leading citizen, Bonald was elected to Millau's city council in 1782. Then, in 1785, he was named mayor by the province's royal governor. His tenure in the post was successful and popular, and he led his fellow citizens in several public celebrations of the early actions of the National Assembly in 1789. Among such actions was the change to election, rather than appointment, of certain local officials throughout France. This posed no obstacle to Bonald, who was retained as mayor by the citizens of Millau in an election held in February 1790 and then, later that year, was elected as a deputy to the departmental assembly. Throughout his municipal service, he showed himself to be a partisan of the increased independence of the nobility, and the locale they represented, from the government in Paris. He welcomed the French Revolution not for its liberal and anticlerical tendencies, but for its promise to restore what the nobility had lost to the central government over the past century. Accordingly, when the Revolution showed its true colors in the Civil Constitution of the Clergy, Bonald resigned his office in the departmental assembly. Fearing reprisals for his opposition to the Revolution, he emigrated to the Rhineland with his two eldest sons in October 1791.[25]

Like Chateaubriand, Bonald joined the army of emigrés. In the autumn of 1792 he marched with the duc de Bourbon as part of the Austrian reserves and was within earshot of the cannons when the French defeated the Austrians at Jemappes on November 6, 1792. But Bonald was destined to wield a pen, not a sword, and he soon devoted his life to intellectual combat. His exile from his family in Millau would last, in all, for more than a decade. While in the empire and Switzerland from 1791 to 1797 he wrote his *Theory of Political and Religious Power* (1797), an immense, rambling statement of his principles. Most of the copies of the book were sent to a bookseller in Paris and then seized and destroyed by the Directory.

---

[25] On Bonald's upbringing and early career, see David Klinck, *The French Counterrevolutionary Theorist Louis de Bonald (1754–1840)* (New York: Peter Lang, 1996), 13–46; and Henri Moulinié, *De Bonald: la vie, la carrière politique, la doctrine* (Paris: Félix Alcan, 1916; reprinted New York: Arno Press, 1979), 1–22.

The few who read the tome found Bonald's Latinate prose to be impenetrable.[26] After a brief reunion with his wife in 1797, he spent five years in a kind of internal exile in Paris, where, he reckoned, it was easier both to hide and to influence politics than in the countryside. While in Paris, he wrote three works that extended and refined his doctrine: *An Analytical Essay on the Natural Laws of the Social Order* (1800), *On Divorce* (1801),[27] and *Primitive Legislation* (1802). Napoleon seems to have admired the stern monarchism of Bonald's works and probably for that reason removed him from the list of proscribed emigrés in 1802. This allowed Bonald to return to Millau, from which he sent a steady stream of political journalism to the leading Paris reviews. In 1810, after having refused many offers of preferment from the emperor, he accepted a post on the Great Council of the University.[28]

Bonald returned to active political life under the Bourbon Restoration. From Louis XVIII he received numerous favors. The king retained him on the Royal Council for Public Instruction, made him one of the forty immortals of the *Académie Française*, and finally, in 1823, raised him to the peerage as hereditary viscount. In 1827, Charles X put Bonald, a convinced opponent of the freedom of the press, in charge of censorship. More important than these posts, however, was his role as a member of the Chamber of Deputies from 1815 to 1823. There he helped to lead the Ultra-Royalist Party and enjoyed his greatest success with the repeal of legal divorce in December 1815. He was also the guiding spirit behind other Ultra-Royalist policies, such as the attempt to restore trade guilds and the practice of primogeniture and entail for landed

---

[26] It seems that everyone who has read Bonald has found his style to be a stumbling block. See Michel Toda, *Louis de Bonald: théoricien de la contre-révolution* (Étampes: Clovis, 1997), 5–10.

[27] This is the only work of Bonald's to receive a complete English translation. See *On Divorce*, trans. Nicholas Davidson (New Brunswick, N.J.: Transaction, 1992).

[28] For a descriptions of this period in Bonald's life and of each of the works mentioned, see Klink, *French Counterrevolutionary Theorist*, 47–169.

property. With the Revolution of 1830, Bonald left political life. He spent his last decade looking after the family property, much of which he had managed to restore from the ravages and neglect caused by the Revolution.

The four selections from Bonald included here all date from the Restoration. He was at his best as a publicist. In his shorter pieces his considerable practical wisdom emerges, and his shortcomings as an overly systematic theorist recede to the background. The first essay is a long review of a biography of Jacques-Benigne Bossuet, the famous orator. Little known today, Bossuet (1627–1704) was effectively the spokesman for the Church in France under Louis XIV and thus became a chief target of the *philosophes* of the eighteenth century. Indeed, it is not much of an exaggeration to say that the Enlightenment in France was an extended argument against Bossuet.[29] Bonald accordingly took up the cudgels against the Enlightenment by championing Bossuet and the earnestness of the century of Louis XIV.

Similar in tone are many of Bonald's *Thoughts on Various Subjects* (1817). This volume includes some three dozen *pensées* from a total of several hundred. They are particularly valuable for illuminating Bonald's personality. A staunchly conservative, small-town nobleman, Bonald despised the new Parisian manners of the Revolutionary era. He agreed with Burke that "manners are of more importance than laws."[30] When he wrote that "lofty sentiments, lively affections, and simple tastes make a man," he was not merely mouthing platitudes. Instead, he was decrying a world dominated by fads and fascinations.[31] Bonald took a principled stand in defense

---

[29] Thus Peter Gay wrote that Bossuet's *Universal History* lay "across the philosophes' path, an obstacle, a problem." *The Enlightenment: An Interpretation*, 2 volumes (New York: Knopf, 1966), I: 75. For Jonathan Israel, the poles of the eighteenth-century debates were set out in the seventeenth century by Spinoza and Bossuet. See *Radical Enlightenment: Philosophy and the Making of Modernity, 1650–1750* (New York: Oxford University Press, 2001).

[30] Burke, *First Letter on a Regicide Peace* [1796], in *Select Works of Edmund Burke*, 3 volumes (Indianapolis: Liberty Fund, 1999), III: 126.

[31] On Parisian culture in the last decades of the eighteenth century, see Simon Schama,

of traditional, country manners and agreed with another counter-revolutionary, Jane Austen, that "we do not look in great cities for our best morality."[32]

The posthumous publication of Madame de Staël's *Considerations on the Principal Events of the French Revolution* provoked Bonald to write as elegant a statement of his principles as can be found. His *Observations . . .* (1818) present his central critique of the French Revolution. Both a crime and a mistake, the Revolution rejected France's natural institutions of monarchy, Church, and nobility in favor of a constitution that could only work in England. And, lest one be tempted to prefer a poor imitation of England, Bonald argued at length for the superiority of France's native institutions. Here we find the concise statements of his views on the political role of the nobility, his most original contribution to the theory of the counter-revolution. Burke defended prejudice, but Bonald gave a reasoned argument for the role of privilege. Nobility ought not to be reduced to wealth: it must confer rights because it is charged with duties. By making this argument, he was a reformer, for the French nobility had shown itself willing to jettison its duties in favor of the kind of freedom that would enable them, the wealthy, to dominate more effectively and without the hindrance of traditional strictures.

The final selection is Bonald's celebrated essay on the agricultural family. Here are to be found all of his most attractive ideas: the dangers of industrialization, the priority of the family within society, and the necessity for institutions to protect, rather than to destroy, traditional modes of existence.[33] The Revolution had struck mighty

Citizens: A Chronicle of the French Revolution (New York: Knopf, 1989) and the many works of Robert Darnton, especially *The Forbidden Best-Sellers of Pre-Revolutionary France* (London: Harper Collins, 1996).

[32] Jane Austen, *Mansfield Park* [1814], ed. James Kinsley (Oxford: Oxford University Press, 1990), 83.

[33] On these themes in Bonald, see Robert A. Nisbet, "De Bonald and the Concept of the Social Group," *Journal of the History of Ideas* 5 (1944): 315–31; and D. K. Cohen, "The Vicomte de Bonald's Critique of Industrialism," *Journal of Modern History* 41 (1969): 475–84.

blows at the family by secularizing marriage, legalizing divorce, and making obligatory the division of a family's property into equal shares at the death of the parents.[34] The Ultra-Royalists of the Restoration failed in their attempt to abolish civil marriage, but they did repeal legal divorce. They also sought to bring back the possibility of keeping a family's landed property intact through entail and primogeniture. The proposal was brought before the Chamber of Peers in 1826 but failed by a wide margin: the egalitarianism of the day was simply too strong. Nonetheless, Bonald's essay and political leadership helped to ensure that the counter-revolutionary movement would retain a strong agrarian element throughout the nineteenth century.[35]

JOSEPH DE MAISTRE

While Chateaubriand traveled the world in search of adventure, and Bonald tilled the soil in the provinces, Joseph de Maistre represented the king of Piedmont in the court of the czar in St. Petersburg.[36] The writings of each man matched his life. Where Chateaubriand was wild and romantic, and Bonald stodgy, Maistre was urbane. A native of Chambéry, which lies south of Geneva in the province of Savoy, then a part of the kingdom of Piedmont-Sardinia, Maistre (1753–1821) was sent to Turin to study law and then followed his father in the career of a regional advocate and jurist. He lived in Chambéry until the French Revolution annexed Savoy in 1792. He spent the next decade moving around southern Europe with his family and serving the king of Piedmont in various capacities. Then in 1803 he was sent to St. Petersburg as the repre-

---

[34] See Marcel Garaud, *La Révolution Française et la famille* (Paris: Presses Universitaires de France, 1978).

[35] See Kale, *Legitimism*, 210–60.

[36] For the details of Maistre's life, one should consult Lebrun's *Joseph de Maistre*, cited above in note 3.

sentative of the House of Piedmont, which was living in exile because of Napoleon's conquest of northern Italy. Maistre remained in St. Petersburg until 1817, shining in court circles as a brilliant conversationalist but spending a great part of his time reading and writing. The most important works that resulted from his prolonged sojourn in Russia were his *On the Pope* (1819), to be discussed below, and his posthumous *Soirées de St.-Pétersbourg* (1821). The *Soirées*, a dense and difficult philosophical dialogue, defies easy summary.[37] It was an uncompromising assault upon the deism of Voltaire and the Enlightenment. Both the *Soirées* and *On the Pope* enjoyed wide influence throughout Europe and were republished several dozen times over the next fifty years.

Maistre gained fame long before the two great works published at the end of his life. In 1797, while the Directory ruled in Paris, his *Considerations on France* appeared. In relatively short compass, he set out what would remain the central themes of his thought: the governance of human affairs by Divine Providence, the radical evil of the French Revolution, the centrality of the Christian faith to European society, the insufficiency of written constitutions, and the need to return to Europe's inherited institutions. He called for the return of the Bourbons, but he did so in a surprising way. The Terror, he explained, had been a providential means of purifying France from her errors and crimes, including her greatest crime, that of killing Louis XVI. Now that God had purified France, the rightful king could return with mercy rather than vengeance. He would need only to restore the proper order:

---

[37] Maistre described the work in this way (quoted in Lebrun, *Joseph de Maistre*, 254): "It does a turn, so to say, around all the great questions of rational philosophy, and can shock no one, except the ideologues and the Lockists. The work is designed to achieve the solemn wedding of philosophy and the Gospel." On the Soirées, see Stéphane Rials, "Lecture de Joseph de Maistre," in *Révolution et contre-révolution au dix-neuvième siècle* (Paris: Diffusion Université Culture, 1987), 22–40.

> The return to order will not be painful, because it will be natural and because it will be favoured by a secret force whose action is wholly creative. We will see precisely the opposite of what we have seen. Instead of these violent commotions, painful divisions, and perpetual and desperate oscillations, a certain stability, an indefinable peace, a universal well-being will announce the presence of sovereignty. . . . [T]his is the great truth with which the French cannot be too greatly impressed: the restoration of the monarchy, what they call the Counter-revolution, will be not a contrary revolution, but the contrary of revolution.[38]

Like Burke, Maistre thought that the customs and institutions of the Old Regime were, in large part, fitting and natural. Also like Burke, Maistre venerated the political compromise that emerged from England's Revolution of 1688. For France, a different political solution, in keeping with the needs of the age, would doubtless be required. Yet the essential character of such a solution would be its continuity with the institutions that had grown up in France over the centuries under the guiding hand of Divine Providence. The ideas of Rousseau and Robespierre were, therefore, the worst imaginable because they substituted abstract systems for providential design.

The first selection from Maistre in this volume is his little-known "Reflections on Protestantism in its Relations with Sovereignty." It was written in 1798, but only published in 1870 in a collection of his manuscripts.[39] The theme of the essay, that Protestantism necessarily leads to political revolution, had been a favorite of Bossuet and would be common coin among French traditionalists in the

---

[38] Maistre, *Considerations on France*, trans. Richard A. Lebrun (Montreal: McGill University Press, 1974), 169.

[39] Lebrun briefly mentions the circumstances of its composition in *Joseph de Maistre,* 160.

nineteenth and twentieth centuries.[40] In a thesis that has been recently revived in historical scholarship, Maistre linked Protestantism with the origins of the French Revolution.[41] The essay shows that Maistre was at times an intemperate writer, but it also displays his supple and strong style. The French, perhaps more than any other European people, are strongly moved by prose style, and while Maistre cannot be said to have supplanted Voltaire in the popular mind in the nineteenth century, it is true that his style won him followers. Many Catholics in nineteenth-century Europe learned from Maistre to see the Enlightenment and the French Revolution as upstart and foreign things, to be rejected with righteous indignation.

The other selections are from Maistre's most enduring work, *On the Pope*. As a contribution towards the declaration of papal infallibility at the first Vatican Council in 1870, *On the Pope* enjoyed an unparalled influence on Catholic intellectual life in Europe for almost a century. Yet Maistre's book was not merely an argument for the infallibility of the pope; it also presented a papal view of European history. For Maistre, the papacy was Europe's most important cultural institution. The popes had been the chief defenders of marriage, priestly morals (the safeguard of society's morals), and true liberty. This thesis went directly against the grain of the Enlightenment. For the *philosophes*, nothing could more menace human flourishing than authority in religious matters.[42] For Maistre, this very authority was the wellspring of civilization because it guaranteed the existence and continuity of the Christian religion. From this argument was born a fertile tradition of Catholic

---

[40] Thus, for instance, Jacques Maritain, *Three Reformers: Luther, Descartes, Rousseau* (1929; New York: Crowell, 1970).

[41] See Dale K. Van Kley, *The Religious Origins of the French Revolution: From Calvin to the Civil Constitution, 1560–1791* (New Haven, Conn.: Yale University Press, 1996). Van Kley, it should be noted, dismisses Maistre as a precursor to his own views, citing him as one of the proponents of the "rightist ideology's plot theory."

[42] The classic statement of this view may be found in Immanuel Kant's *What Is Enlightenment?*

historiography, including works such as the Spaniard Jaime Balmes's *Protestantism and Catholicity Compared in Their Effects on the Civilization of Europe* (1846) and, later, Christopher Dawson's *Religion and the Rise of Western Culture* (1950).

Maistre is, of course, the best known of the French traditionalist writers.[43] In recent decades, commentary on his thought has been sharply negative; it has even included the argument that his influence can be perceived in the origins of fascism.[44] One of the grounds for such an argument is the claim of Charles Maurras, the leading figure in *Action Française*, that Maistre was one of his "masters."[45] It may be debated whether *Action Française* is best described as fascist. It is true, however, that Maurras and his followers were, like the fascists, willing to resort to violent revolutionary activity in pursuit of their political ends. It has been argued that Maistre's discussions of the role of violence in human affairs, read out of context, provide some justification for this sort of activity. This is dubious, and, more importantly, such a reading would be strongly at variance with Maistre's contention that the counter-revolution must be the contrary of revolution, that is, a natural rather than a violent movement. More accurate was the reading given to the whole corpus of Maistre's work by his true heirs, the French Catholic traditionalists. They read him not as a prophet of violence, but as a champion of

---

[43] A well-known collection of excerpts from his works is Jack Lively, ed. and trans., *The Works of Joseph de Maistre* (New York: Macmillan, 1965). Since Lively's collection, Richard A. Lebrun has been steadily at work producing excellent translations of Maistre's works.

[44] See Isaiah Berlin, "Joseph de Maistre and the Origins of Fascism," in *The Crooked Timber of Humanity: Chapters in the History of Ideas*, ed. Henry Hardy (London: John Murray, 1990), 91–174, and Stephen Holmes, *The Anatomy of Antiliberalism* (Cambridge, Mass.: Harvard University Press, 1993), 13–36. For a response to Berlin's arguments, see Owen Bradley, *A Modern Maistre: The Social and Political Thought of Joseph de Maistre* (Lincoln, Neb.: University of Nebraska Press, 1999), especially pages xv–xix.

[45] On Action Française, see Eugen Weber, *Action Française* (Palo Alto, Calif.: Stanford University Press, 1962). On this point, see John C. Murray, S.J., "The Political Thought of Joseph de Maistre," *Review of Politics* 11 (1949): 63–86, at 86.

the Catholic faith and European traditions.[46] Thus Barbey-d'Aurevilly's 1851 popularization of Maistre claimed that his genius was the result of his excellent vantage point, that of "the historical revelation, the tradition."[47] At the head of the counter-revolutionary movement, the comte de Chambord consistently refused the use of violence in support of a restoration of the monarchy.[48] Moreover, leading Catholic figures in nineteenth-century France received inspiration from Maistre to devote themselves to the service of the Church.[49] Finally, Maistre, with Bonald, exercised an important influence on the restoration of the study of St. Thomas Aquinas in France.[50]

FRÉDÉRIC LE PLAY

With the July Revolution of 1830, the Bourbon Restoration ended, and with it the best hope of the counter-revolutionaries for

[46] See Stéphane Rials, "Fausses droites, centres morts et vrais modérés dans la vie politique française contemporaine," in *Révolution et contre-révolution*, 41–52, and Rials, *Le légitimisme* (Paris: Presses Universitaires de France, 1983).

[47] Barbey d'Aurevilly, *Prophètes du passé*, 63.

[48] See Marvin L. Brown Jr., *The Comte de Chambord: The Third Republic's Uncompromising King* (Durham, N.C.: Duke University Press, 1967).

[49] For instance, the Alfred de Falloux, sponsor of the 1850 law that won for Catholics freedom for religious instruction in secondary schools. See C. B. Pitman, trans., *Memoirs of the Count de Falloux*, 2 volumes (London: Chapman and Hall, 1888), I: 84: "I was in full tide of enthusiasm for the *Soirées de Saint-Petersbourg.*" The Oratorian Father Gratry was inspired by Maistre to attempt to reconcile modern science with Catholic theology. See Louis Foucher, *La philosophie catholique en France au dix-neuvième siècle* (Paris: J. Vrin, 1955), 199.

[50] See Foucher, *La philosophie catholique*, 265–66. Their influence in this direction was indirect. In philosophy, Bonald was strongly Cartesian, Maistre an eclectic mixture of ancient and modern. Yet their powerful arguments about the need for tradition and authority in philosophy led some of their followers back to St. Thomas.

repairing the social order ravaged by the Revolution. The remainder of the nineteenth century in France saw a variety of different regimes, but all were in some way beholden to the Revolution and the "Principles of 1789." Under the July Monarchy of Louis-Philippe d'Orléans (1830–48), political and economic liberalism was the order of the day. A property qualification kept the electorate small. Those who complained that they were not represented were told to "make themselves rich" so that they might qualify to vote. The overthrow of this crass regime in 1848 was welcomed both by conservative Catholics and by the new urban radicals, the socialists. Yet within three years, the Second Republic had gone the way of the first, and Napoleon III had declared himself emperor of the French. His authoritarian regime was initially friendly to the church, but it became anticlerical over time. During his reign (1852–70) many conservatives joined the Legitimist movement that supported the claim of the comte de Chambord, the grandson of the last Bourbon to reign, Charles X. To Chambord and many other conservatives, the sufferings of workers loomed large. The July Monarchy had brought France into the industrial age. With the factories came all the pathologies of the industrial order: urban poverty, unemployment, child labor, and socialist revolutionary movements. A remarkable generation of (broadly speaking) conservative thinkers grew up during the July Monarchy and rose to prominence under Napoleon III. Men such as Tocqueville, Montalembert, and Ozanam described themselves as liberals, but they sought to repair traditional European civilization. One member of this generation, however, was sufficiently counter-revolutionary in his teaching to earn the epithet "a rejuvenated Bonald": Frédéric Le Play.[51]

Le Play (1806–82) was born to a modest Norman family and trained in Paris to enter a career in mining.[52] He interested himself

[51] The phrase is from the literary critic Sainte-Beuve, as quoted in Robert A. Nisbet, *The Social Group in French Thought* (1940; reprinted, New York: Arno Press, 1980), 197.

[52] For Le Play's life, see Michael Z. Brooke, *Le Play, Engineer and Social Scientist: The Life and Work of Frédéric Le Play* (Harlow, United Kingdom: Longmans, 1970).

in social questions even as a youth. For a time, he lived with an uncle in Paris who was a confirmed royalist. Then, at the School of Mines, he befriended Jean Reynaud, a follower of the positivist Saint-Simon, and in the late 1820s took an immense walking tour in Germany with Reynaud to investigate mines. The Revolution of 1830 broke out in Paris while Le Play was recovering from a serious laboratory accident that left his hands damaged for life. Hearing of the tumult in the streets, and remembering his many conversations with Reynaud, Le Play determined that he would dedicate his life to the study of society in an attempt to heal its divisions and ills. Yet he would do so neither as a Saint-Simonian nor as a Catholic. He remained an independent and eclectic thinker and returned to the practice of the Catholic faith only at the end of his life, in 1879. What marked Le Play's thinking from his early years was a desire to observe and to describe human society.

Le Play spent the 1830s traveling Europe as a mining expert. In 1840, he returned to the School of Mines as professor, keeping this position until 1856. Also in the 1840s, he entered into the management of a large mining concern in the Ural Mountains of Russia. During these two-and-a-half decades, he spent much of each year walking the back roads of Europe. He spoke five languages and understood three others, and wherever he went he was keen to interview working families. He was particularly interested in the eastern European countries, where society was reminiscent of western Europe's Old Regime. From his extensive travels and studies he compiled a monograph, *The European Workers* (1855). This empirical study of fifty-seven mining families throughout Europe was his lasting contribution to what Robert Nisbet has called "the sociological tradition."[53] One of the keynotes of the volume was his discussion of the importance of family structure for human well-

---

[53] See Robert A. Nisbet, *The Sociological Tradition* (New York: Basic Books, 1966), 61–70. See also the introduction by Catherine Bodard Silver to her edition of selections from Le Play's writings: *Frédéric Le Play on Family, Work, and Social Change*, ed. Silver (Chicago: University of Chicago Press, 1982), 3–134.

being. His sociological studies were animated by his desire to discover a means of improving French society, and during the 1840s he met regularly to discuss social issues with some of the leading men of the day, including Dupanloup, Lamartine, Montalembert, Thiers, and Tocqueville.

Le Play had met Napoleon III in Russia during his travels in the 1840s, and from the early years of the emperor's reign he was active in political life. In 1855, he was brought in to save the Paris Exhibition, which was foundering because of poor management. The following year, Napoleon III asked him to join the Council of State, the Second Empire's principal legislative body. Over the next fifteen years, Le Play's official duties included numerous investigations of different industries as well as the management of the Paris Exhibition of 1867, a mammoth task that extended over a five-year period.[54] At the emperor's request, he published a statement of his prescriptions for society: *Social Reform in France* (1864). After the fall of the empire in 1870, Le Play spent most of his efforts founding and directing the Unions of Social Peace, an organization dedicated to healing France's political and social divisions through local study circles of leading men. He also remained the secretary-general of the International Society for Practical Studies of Social Economy, which he had founded in 1856. Through these organizations, his influence did reach some professional economists and sociologists; nevertheless, it was in conservative and Catholic circles that his ideas were most popular.

Two generous selections from *Social Reform in France* are included in this volume. The most complete statement of his reforming ideas, this work enjoyed modest success during Le Play's lifetime.[55] Émile Keller, the comte de Chambord, Albert de Mun,

---

[54] Fifteen million visitors came to the exhibition. For a description of it, see Alistair Horne, *The Fall of Paris: The Siege and the Commune, 1870–71* (Harmondsworth: Penguin, 1965), 21–33.

[55] It was printed eight times during his life. For a summary and discussion of the volume, see Nisbet, *Social Group in French Thought*, 197–221.

and René de La Tour du Pin all drew upon it for inspiration. Indeed, through its influence on La Tour du Pin, it can be said to have exercised an important contribution to the origins of Leo XIII's encyclical *Rerum Novarum*. What Catholics and other conservatives found congenial in Le Play's argument was his unflinching opposition to the "principles of 1789," and his recognition of the positive roles played by religion, private property, and a strong family in social reform.

Having ties neither to the Church nor the Bourbon family, Le Play was pragmatic in his political activity, even welcoming the Revolution of 1848. Nevertheless, his principles were strongly counter-revolutionary. Indeed, the introduction to *Social Reform in France* constitutes one of the more penetrating critiques of the social thought of the Enlightenment to be found in the nineteenth century. He rejected, in turn, belief in man's natural goodness, the inevitability of moral progress, the need for new moral doctrines, and theories of political and racial determinism. His central contention was that societies, just as the individuals that constitute them, are truly free. If a society exerts its moral capacities to overcome the human propensity towards evil, it will progress; if not, it will decline. For guidance as to how to carry this out, he recommended looking to the past and following the example of those societies that had functioned reasonably well. For this reason, he fought against the uncritical rejection of the past that the revolutionary school required. He did not envision returning to Old Regime privileges, and to that extent he was more progressive than Bonald. Yet like Bonald, in the end, it was a return to tradition that he recommended: "We should seek the true conditions of reform in the best practices of our fathers."[56]

That mothers too were important, and perhaps more important than fathers, is the chief burden of the selection from the third chapter of *Social Reform in France*, "On the Family." The selection makes two main points, both dear to Le Play. The first is that sup-

[56] *Social Reform in France*, below at page 222

port for ownership and inheritance of a family home is the chief means of social progress. Like Bonald, Le Play pointed to Europe's agrarian past as the model for strong families. To that end, he too campaigned for the repeal of the law forcing an equal division of inheritance among all the children of a family. The second point of the selection is that women are the chief agents of social progress. Here we find a theme well known to contemporary conservatives. What is noteworthy in Le Play's treatment is the way in which he develops this theme in relation to broader legal, political, and cultural matters. His proximate concerns, sadly, are no longer ours, for family life has so greatly declined since the mid-nineteenth century that what is at stake now is less its well-being than its very existence.

ÉMILE KELLER

Le Play and his generation were shaped by the failure of the Bourbon Restoration. They sought to restore the social and political stability of France within the framework of the liberal institutions brought by the July Monarchy. The fall of the July Monarchy and the ensuing June Days considerably diminished liberalism's prospects. For three days in June 1848, the streets of Paris were blocked with barricades as the Second Republic fought for its life against a revolt of the Paris workers. Some fifteen hundred died in the fighting, and three thousand rebels were subsequently executed by the victorious Republic. The ensuing regime would be a conservative one, and in 1851, when Prince-President Louis-Napoleon declared himself emperor, so great was the perceived threat of socialist revolution that even some liberals accepted his coup as necessary and good. For conservatives, the June Days and the events of 1848 throughout Europe demonstrated the need for a strong regime to withstand the danger of socialist revolution.[57] For some, however, there was an additional lesson: that

---

[57] See, for instance, the 1849 speech on dictatorship by the Spanish conservative Juan Donoso Cortes, in Béla Menczer, ed., *Tensions of Order and Freedom* (1952; reprinted, New

those who would preserve European liberties must address the plight of the industrial laborer, and must do so honestly and effectively.

One of the leading members of this new generation of conservatives in France was Émile Keller (1828–1909).[58] Born in Alsace, Keller was raised and educated in Paris. He spent most of his adult life there as a parliamentarian and leader in a number of Catholic institutions. Indeed, he was one of the most remarkable Catholic laymen of the nineteenth century. He came from a well-to-do Alsacian family and married a woman from the same circle. Of their fourteen children, three became Dominican nuns and a fourth became a Little Sister of the Poor. Keller was one of the leading members of the Society of St. Vincent de Paul for many years and then, in the 1860s, was one of the founders of Peter's Pence, the Catholic effort in France and other countries to support the papacy, then recently stripped of the greater part of its temporal dominion. Finally, in 1891, he was approached by a representative of Leo XIII and asked to found a Catholic political party in France, an offer he declined.

Keller also was notable as a patriot. Like many of his generation, he greatly admired the first Napoleon. In the wake of 1848, his concern was for the good of France and the good of the Church. He viewed Napoleon III suspiciously and considered him more an agent of revolution than counter-revolution. After Napoleon III's surrender to the Prussians at Sedan in 1870, Keller joined the French effort to keep Alsace and Lorraine from falling under Prussian domination. The effort failed, but only after much trooping around the hills of the Rhineland under artillery bombardment from the Prussians. Keller was made a colonel, a chevalier of the Légion d'honneur, and, in 1871, was elected to represent Alsace and Lorraine at the parliament held in Bordeaux under

Brunswick, N.J.: Transaction, 1994), 160–76; along with the commentary of Robert A. Herrera in *Donoso Cortes: Cassandra of the Age* (Grand Rapids: Eerdmans, 1995), 67–78.

[58] Details on the life of Keller are taken from Gustave Gautherot, *Un demi-siècle de défense nationale et religieuse: Émile Keller (1828–1909)* (Paris: Plon, 1922).

Prussian occupation. There he read the solemn protest of the Alsace-Lorraine deputation against the dismemberment of France. No fewer than five of his descendants would die during the Great War fighting to reunite Alsace and Lorraine to France.

As a politician, Keller's chief concern was to defend Christian society against the heritage of the French Revolution.[59] Elected to Parliament in 1859, he gained national attention for his courageous speech of March 13, 1861, criticizing Napoleon III for his role in allowing the Kingdom of Piedmont to conquer the greater part of Italy, including the bulk of the Papal State. For this, the emperor considered Keller his enemy and arranged his defeat in the next election, in 1863. Keller returned to Parliament in 1869 and kept a seat without interruption until 1881. His final term was from 1885 to 1889. During the 1870s and 1880s, he sponsored a number of measures to protect the Church and Christian society. In 1873, for instance, he fought for tougher penalties against factory owners who employed children. In 1879, when radical republicans sought to overturn the 1814 measure that had restored Sunday as a day of rest, he fought back, unsuccessfully, with an attempt to extend Sunday rest to railroads and the post office. Finally, when in 1884 the Republic repealed its prohibition on labor associations, he saw one of his primary goals accomplished.[60]

As a writer and thinker, Keller was strongly influenced by Joseph de Maistre and the other counter-revolutionary writers. His first book was a *History of France* (1858), in which he extolled the thirteenth century for its social harmony. In 1874, he published a biography of General La Moricière, the commander of Pius IX's army during the wars of Italian unification in the 1850s and 1860s. In

---

[59] He preferred the term "Christian society" to "counter-revolution." See Philippe Levillain, *Albert de Mun: catholicisme français et catholicisme romain du Syllabus au Ralliement* (Rome: École Française de Rome, 1983), 164 and 623.

[60] On Keller's involvement with Albert de Mun in the social legislation of the Third Republic, see Parker Thomas Moon, *The Labor Problem and the Social Catholic Movement in France: A Study in the History of Social Politics* (New York: Macmillan, 1921), 87–112.

1880, at the height of the Third Republic's anticlericalism, he compiled a massive document on the benefits brought to France by her monastic institutions, that is, by the ones then existing. His most important book, and the one from which our selections have been taken, was *The Encyclical of the 8th of December 1864 and the Principles of 1789, or, the Church, the State, and Liberty.*[61]

Keller's book needs to be read in light of the widely varied European reactions to Pius IX's encyclical of December 8, 1864, *Quanta Cura,* and the attached *Syllabus of Errors.*[62] With the encyclical and the *Syllabus,* Pius IX responded to more than a decade of revolutionary and anticlerical activity and legislation throughout Europe, especially in Italy. Thanks to the connivance of Napoleon III, the king of Piedmont had been able to conquer most of Italy between 1859 and 1861, and then, on March 14, 1861, had declared himself to be king of Italy. But King Victor Emmanuel was a Freemason, and his kingdom had openly persecuted the Church for years by confiscating land and closing convents. He was, therefore, promptly excommunicated by Pius IX. The encyclical *Quanta Cura* addressed these and other issues, and for its pronounced defense of Christian society it may be seen as the origin of the Church's many subsequent social encyclicals.[63] Most Europeans were so distracted by the pope's condemnation of "progress, liberalism, and modern civilization" in the famous proposition #80 of the *Syllabus* that they were unable to read either document with patience. Subsequent Catholic interpreters, particularly Bishop Félix Dupanloup of Orléans, were at pains to point out that the progress and civilization condemned by the Pope were only those

---

[61] For commentaries on Keller's *L'Encyclique du 8 décembre,* see Paul Misner, *Social Catholicism in Europe from the Onset of Industrialization to the First World War* (New York: Crossroad, 1991), 149–52, and Levillain, *Albert de Mun,* 163–74.

[62] For background on the pontificate of Pius IX and the *Syllabus of Errors,* see E. E. Y. Hales, *Pio Nono: A Study in European Politics and Religion in the Nineteenth Century* (London: Eyre and Spottiswoode, 1954).

[63] Roger Aubert, *Le pontificat de Pie IX (1846–1878)* (Paris: Bloud et Gay, 1952), 487.

that declared themselves to be inimical to the Catholic faith, such as the Masonic regime in Italy. For Dupanloup, the crucial distinction was to see that the pope was defending a Christian society as an ideal, and that while Catholics were bound to hold as the ideal or "thesis" the kind of society in which Church and state cooperate for the good of mankind, they could nevertheless tolerate a secular political arrangement.[64] Keller agreed with this distinction, but, as becomes evident in his preface, he thought that what was most important about *Quanta Cura* and the *Syllabus* was that they called for the wholesale renovation of society in accordance with Christian principles. It was not sufficient merely to say that Christian society was an ideal: the ideal must be sought by earnest practice.

The first of the three selections from Keller's *Encyclical of 8 December* includes both the author's brief preface and the introductory chapter. These admirably set out his response to Dupanloup. He argued that Catholics can welcome any number of aspects of modern society and tolerate many others, but that this flexibility must not become complacency. In this section, the influence of Maistre's *On the Pope* can be seen in Keller's assertion that the papacy is the beacon of European civilization. The second and third selections are from Keller's chapters about the social problem. Most significant here is his championing of workers' associations. The French Revolution had between 1789 and 1791 destroyed the old guild structure of master, journeyman, and apprentice, its campaign culminating in the Le Chapelier law of 1791 that prohibited all associations of workers of any kind.[65] Laborers would be free to work, but not free to associate. This paradox was at the heart of the social problem in France in the nineteenth century and would only be resolved, and then partially, by the legalization of trade unions in 1884. Bonald and many other counter-revolutionaries had called

---

[64] See Marvin R. O'Connell, "Ultramontanism and Dupanloup: The Compromise of 1865," *Church History* 53 (1984): 200–17.

[65] See William H. Sewell Jr., *Work and Revolution in France: The Language of Labor from the Old Regime to 1848* (Cambridge: Cambridge University Press, 1980).

for the return of the guilds because of their beneficent moral role in society. Le Play had opposed them on grounds that the liberty of labor was more important than freedom of association. With Keller's argument for the necessity of labor associations, the position is firmly grounded within the counter-revolutionary tradition. It would be taken up still more forcefully by René de La Tour du Pin, Leo XIII, and Pius XI.

RENÉ DE LA TOUR DU PIN

Keller's *Encyclical of 8 December* was greeted with a "conspiracy of silence" by the Catholic intelligentsia in Paris, his emphasis on the need for social reforms pleasing neither the liberals nor the reactionaries.[66] Yet the book enjoyed a vast influence through its effect on two young soldiers, Albert de Mun and René de La Tour du Pin. Interned together as prisoners of war in Aix-la-Chapelle in 1871, Mun and La Tour du Pin were given Keller's book by Father Eck, a German Jesuit. Mun later described the experience of reading it: "It was a precise, simple, and energetic exposition of Catholic truth and revolutionary error, of the principles of Christian society and the false dogmas of modern society. Reading it filled us with the most lively emotion. It seemed to us that in the shadows of our sorrow, a light had shined in our minds."[67] Inspired by Keller's stirring call for the French to devote themselves to furthering the cause of the pope and Christian society, Mun and La Tour du Pin would become the leaders of the counter-revolution in France for the next three decades.

Like Chateaubriand, René de La Tour du Pin (1834–1924) belonged to France's ancient nobility and descended from one who

---

[66] La Moricière wrote of the "conspiracy of silence" in a letter congratulating Keller for the book. Gautherot, *Un demi-siècle*, 132.

[67] Albert de Mun, *Ma vocation sociale: souvenirs de la fondation de l'Oeuvre des cercles catholiques d'ouvriers (1871–1875)* (Paris: Lethielleux, 1908), 13.

had fought on Crusade with St. Louis. He too had lost ancestors to the guillotine and was implacably opposed to the heritage of the Revolution. La Tour du Pin was raised on the ancestral property at Arrancy, near Laon, in the Champagne region northeast of Paris. His father instilled in him the belief that his aristocratic birth had conferred a calling upon him, instructing him to "remember that you are but the administrator of this land for its inhabitants." This sense of paternal responsibility for the villagers of the hamlet of Arrancy would for La Tour du Pin grow into a mission to serve France as a whole. Initially, his service would be in the army. After lengthy studies at several schools in the Paris region, he proceeded to active duty in the Crimean War, in the war against Austria in the Piedmont in 1859, in Algeria, and finally, on the Rhine frontier during the Franco-Prussian war. Then came the fateful internment in Aix-la-Chapelle and his friendship with Albert de Mun, like him a dutiful soldier from the conservative aristocracy. After their imprisonment, both Mun and La Tour du Pin returned to Paris, where they saw firsthand the horrors of the Commune of 1871. This quickened their resolve to work for the regeneration of the working class.[68]

Over the next twelve months, Mun and La Tour du Pin collaborated in founding the *Oeuvre des Cercles Catholiques des Ouvriers*, that is, the "Work of the Catholic Working-Men's Circles." For the next thirty years the *Oeuvre des Cercles*, or simply the *Oeuvre*, was the leading voice for the counter-revolution in France. It consisted of a central committee and a national movement of local circles. At the high-tide of its influence in 1881, the *Oeuvre* had some 550 local circles with a total membership of fifty thousand. Each of these circles brought together wealthy patrons with members of the working class in an organization that sought to improve the spiritual and material lives of the workers and to protect them from the propaganda of revolutionary socialism. One would not want to

---

[68] Biographical details are taken from Elizabeth Bossan de Garagnol, *Le Colonel de La Tour du Pin d'après lui-même* (Paris: Beauchesne, 1934).

overestimate the influence of a movement of fifty thousand in a nation with over thirty million inhabitants. Nonetheless, through Albert de Mun's fiery parliamentary oratory, the *Oeuvre* was known and even somewhat feared by left-leaning politicians.[69]

La Tour du Pin was the *Oeuvre des Cercles*'s theoretician. For many years he directed a group of leading members of the *Oeuvre* in the study of social theory and particularly economics. The group was remarkable for its breadth of vision. Not content only to read Bonald, its members took up St. Thomas Aquinas's *Summa Theologiae* for guidance on the theory of the just wage. Beginning in 1876, their findings were presented to the public when the *Oeuvre* founded its own journal, *Association Catholique*. The title was indicative of La Tour du Pin's central conviction: that the most damaging heritage of the Revolution was its individualism, and that this must be combatted by a new spirit of association or solidarity. He was inspired to this conviction by the leaders of the Catholic social movement in Germany and Austria, with whom he became familiar during his service as military attaché to the Austro-Hungarian Empire from 1877 to 1881. In 1884, he joined a group of leading Catholics for a series of seven annual congresses at Fribourg, Switzerland. The proceedings of these meetings were one of the sources for Leo XIII's encyclical *Rerum Novarum* of 1891. La Tour du Pin's central conviction was there upheld by the pope: that the plight of the worker was a question of justice, and not merely one of charity.[70]

In his later years, La Tour du Pin remained a firm partisan of the counter-revolution, even refusing Leo XIII's call to "rally to the

---

[69] On the *Oeuvre des cercles*, see John McManners, *Church and State in France, 1870–1914* (New York: Harper & Row, 1972), 81–93. On Mun, see Benjamin F. Martin, *Count Albert de Mun: Paladin of the Third Republic* (Chapel Hill, N.C.: University of North Carolina Press, 1978). For the context of the *Oeuvre*, see Paul Misner, *Social Catholicism in Europe*.

[70] See Robert Talmy, *Aux sources du catholicisme social: l'école de La Tour du Pin* (Tournai: Desclée, 1963). For a more brief account of La Tour du Pin's thought, see Charlotte Touzalin Muret, *French Royalist Doctrines since the Revolution* (New York: Columbia University Press, 1933), 200–16.

Republic." As a convinced monarchist and opponent of the rising socialist faction in French politics, La Tour du Pin could not fail to be attracted to Charles Maurras's *Action Française*. He joined the movement in 1905 and in 1907 allowed his articles to be collected by a member of *Action Française* and published under the title *Towards a Christian Social Order*. After the Great War, however, he left the *Action Française* movement.[71] His deepest principles were little in accord with those of Maurras. Maurras was a confirmed positivist who saw only the functional value of religion in society, while La Tour du Pin remained a pious Catholic whose admiration for the Christian Middle Ages was primarily spiritual.[72]

This sincere admiration for the Middle Ages is the keynote to La Tour du Pin's 1883 essay "On the Corporate Regime." In 1880, he had called for "a return not to the form, but to the spirit of the institutions of the Middle Ages."[73] That spirit was one of fraternal association. Like Bonald, La Tour du Pin championed intermediate associations, and following Keller, he called for a revival of the guilds, or corporations, of the Old Regime. Like the English Distributists of the early twentieth century, he sought to restore the ownership of productive property to as many people as possible.[74] In an industrial setting, this could take place through some form of profit sharing. Yet the restoration of the corporations was for a higher purpose than the merely material. He had harsh words for the credit union movement led by Schultze-Delitsch, who had insisted that the worker's plight was primarily an economic one and could therefore be solved

---

[71] Weber, *Action Française*, 76.

[72] On the contrast between Maurras and the Catholic counter-revolutionaries, see Jean-Christian Petitfils, "Postérité de la contre-révolution," in Tulard, ed., *La contre-révolution*, 387–99.

[73] La Tour du Pin to Joseph de La Bouillerie, 6 July 1880, quoted in Levillain, *Albert de Mun*, 671.

[74] See Dermot Quinn, "Distributism as Movement and Ideal," *Chesterton Review* XIX (1993): 157–73.

financially.[75] What society needed was thorough moral renovation, and this could only be accomplished through the restoration of the Christian family, the solidarity of workers and owners in a common corporate bond, and authentic national unity based on Christian principles. This renewed Christian society was to be a corporate regime.[76] The Enlightenment had given birth to liberalism and its contrary, socialism. Both had denied the social standing of the family and the intermediate association. La Tour du Pin's proposed corporate regime would restore these to primacy, and thus accomplish both the decentralization of power and the binding together of atomized and alienated individuals.[77]

CONCLUSION

The Enlightenment had sought to liberate man from the dead hand of tradition. His faculties once set free, Voltaire and his followers believed, man would soar to new heights of felicity. The French Revolution incarnated this desire and tore apart much of the social fabric of Europe. When the Church was despoiled, countless charitable and educational institutions across Europe were either suppressed or deprived of their financial basis. The end of noble privilege brought with it the centralization of politics and justice. With the destruction of the craft guilds and trade associations, the patrimony of the artisans was confiscated and working men were left unprotected from the ravages of unlimited competition. Nor did the Revolution spare the family: through the legalization of divorce and the enforcement of equal inheritance, the strong family struc-

---

[75] This was true of Schultze-Delitsch, but not of the credit union movement generally. See J. Carroll Moody and Gilbert C. Fite, *The Credit Union Movement: Origins and Development, 1850–1980*, 2nd edition (Dubuque: Kendall-Hunt, 1984), 1–18.

[76] On which see Matthew H. Elbow, *French Corporative Theory, 1789–1948* (New York: Columbia University Press, 1953).

[77] For commentary, see Robert Nisbet, *Social Group in French Thought*, 159–71.

ture of the Old Regime was replaced by an impoverished individualism. On top of all this, the vast cultural inheritance of Christendom was forcefully stripped away as the Revolution and then Napoleon's armies brought rampant iconoclasm, melting down church bells to make cannons, confiscating works of art and documents, secularizing the universities, and promulgating the culture of the Enlightenment. The French critics of the Enlightenment stood athwart all this progress and called for a return to the salutary traditions of European civilization. They were champions of piety towards family and local customs, fidelity towards kings, solidarity towards fellow men, and loyalty towards the Church.

The heritage of the French counter-revolutionary tradition in the twentieth century was a divided one. The French Right was hijacked by Charles Maurras and his *Action Française* movement in the wake of the Dreyfus Affair.[78] Maurras espoused a number of authentically counter-revolutionary measures, including the restoration of the monarchy and administrative decentralization. But his politics were riven with anti-conservative and altogether modern suppositions and practices. In addition to his positivist convictions, which led him to see the Church as a mere instrument of the state, Maurras employed a number of typically revolutionary political strategies, such as the manipulation of opinion through journalism and mass demonstrations, and even the use of organized violence. These tactics cannot be said to conform to Maistre's dictum that the counter-revolution is the contrary of revolution. Many of the professed counter-revolutionary political movements in Europe in the twentieth century were strongly influenced by Maurras and, like him, adopted revolutionary tactics in the service of conservative ends. From this combination stems the tragic aspect of conservative politics in Europe for much of the twentieth century. The Franco and Salazar regimes, for instance, both suffered from this problem,

---

[78] On this point, see Philippe Chenaux, *Entre Maurras et Maritain: une génération intellectuelle catholique (1920–1930)* (Paris: Cerf, 1999).

and what good was present in their ideals was compromised by their many moral defects.[79]

The authentic interpreters of the French critics of the Enlightenment in the twentieth century have generally been cultural figures. In France, the Catholic literary revival was much indebted to the writings of Chateaubriand, Maistre, Bonald, and their heirs.[80] Novelists and poets such as Claudel, Péguy, and Bernanos took up many of the theses of the counter-revolution and made them their own. Elsewhere, literary figures such as Hilaire Belloc and G. K. Chesterton, and scholars such as Christopher Dawson and Robert Nisbet, provided expositions of conservative thought that bear the imprint of the French tradition.[81] Today, for us, the term counter-revolution is problematic. With the end of the Cold War, it is not clear that there is a vibrant revolutionary tradition that needs to be opposed. Indeed, the liberalism of the French Revolution has itself been transformed into a kind of tradition.[82] Yet the French counter-revolutionaries spoke of general principles and not merely of the French political situation in the nineteenth century. For this reason, they have much to say to us. Moreover, the twenty-first century still faces the same task that the nineteenth failed to accomplish: the maintenance and rebuilding of the salutary cultural traditions of European civilization. By defending and articulating these traditions, the French critics of the Enlightenment contribute valuable resources for our endeavors.

---

[79] For an overview of the subject, see Tom Buchanan and Martin Conway, *Political Catholicism in Europe*, 1918–1965 (Oxford: Oxford University Press, 1996).

[80] See Richard Griffiths, *The Reactionary Revolution: The Catholic Revival in French Literature, 1870–1914* (New York: Ungar, 1965).

[81] See, for instance, Nisbet's *Conservatism: Dream and Reality* (Minneapolis: University of Minnesota Press, 1986), which includes numerous references to Maistre, Bonald, and Le Play.

[82] On which see Alasdair MacIntyre, *Whose Justice? Which Rationality?* (Notre Dame, Ind.: University of Notre Dame Press, 1988).

FRANÇOIS-RENÉ de

CHATEAUBRIAND

(Anti Napoleon)

ON BUONAPARTE AND
THE BOURBONS (1814)

No, I shall never believe that I write upon the tomb of France. I cannot be persuaded that the day of mercy will not follow the day of vengeance. The ancient patrimony of the most Christian kings cannot be divided. The kingdom whose birth was the dying Rome's last great work will not perish. The events we have witnessed were not the work of men alone. The hand of Providence is visible throughout. God Himself marches openly at the head of the armies and sits at the councils of the kings. How, without divine intervention, are we to explain the extraordinary rise and the still more extraordinary fall of him who quite recently had the world at his feet? It has not been fifteen months since he was at Moscow, and now the Russians are in Paris. All trembled under his laws from the columns of Hercules to the Caucasus, and now he is a fugitive, on the run, without asylum. His power overflowed like the incoming tide and, like the tide, it has receded.

How are this madman's sins to be explained? We do not yet speak of his crimes.

A revolution, prepared by our moral corruption and errors, breaks out amidst us. In the name of the law, we overturned religion and morality; we renounced experience and the customs of our fathers; we defiled the tombs of our ancestors, the only solid basis for any government, to found upon uncertain reason a society with neither past nor future. Wandering in our own folly, having lost all clear idea of the just and the unjust, of good and evil, we passed through the diverse forms of republican government. We called the populace to deliberate in the streets of Paris about the great objects that the Romans discussed in the Forum after they cast down their arms and bathed themselves in the waves of the Tiber. Then they came out of their dens, these half-naked kings, soiled and beaten down by poverty, mutilated and deformed by their work, their only virtue the insolence of misery and the pride of rags. Fallen into such hands, the fatherland was soon covered with wounds. What remains of our fury and our dreams? Crimes and fetters!

Yet at least our principle was noble. Liberty must not be accused of the faults committed in her name. True philosophy is not the mother of the poisonous doctrines spread by the false wise men. Enlightened by experience, at last we have come to see that monarchical government is the only one that suits our land.

What a claim!

It would have been natural to recall our legitimate princes, but we believed our sins too great to be pardoned. We did not dream that the heart of a son of St. Louis is an inexhaustible treasury of mercy. Some feared for their lives, others for their riches. Above all, it would have cost human pride too much to admit that it had been deceived. So many massacres, upheavals, and miseries, only to return to the point from which we began! Passions were still high, and pretensions of all kinds could not renounce the chimera of equality, the principal cause of our ills. Weighty reasons pushed us forward, petty ones held us back, and public felicity was sacrificed to personal interest, justice to vanity.

Thus we wished to establish a supreme leader who was a child of the Revolution, a leader with the corrupt law at his origins who would protect corruption and make an alliance with it. Upright judges, firm and courageous, captains renowned for their probity and talents, had arisen amidst our travails, yet they were not offered a power their principles would have prevented them from accepting. We despaired of finding among the French a brow that would dare to wear the crown of Louis XVI. A stranger stepped forward. He was chosen.

Buonaparte did not announce his plans openly. His character was revealed only by degrees. Under the modest title of consul, he first accustomed independent minds not to be alarmed at the power they had given him. He appeased the true French by proclaiming himself to be the restorer of order, law, and religion. The wise were tricked, the far-seeing duped. The republicans saw Buonaparte as their work and as the popular leader of a free state. The royalists believed that he would play the role of Monck,[1] and so were quick to serve him. Everyone placed his hopes in him. The brilliant victories of the brave French covered him with glory. Then he became drunk on success, and his tendency to evil began to show itself. The future will doubt whether this man was more guilty for the evil that he did than for the good that he could have done and did not do. Never did a usurper have an easier and more brilliant role to fill. With a little moderation he could have established himself and his line upon the greatest throne of the world. No one disputed the throne, for the generations born since the Revolution did not know our former masters and had only known travail and misery. France and Europe were spent. One only takes a breath after coming to rest; this rest we would then have purchased at any price. An adventurer had troubled the order of royal succession, made himself the heir to heroes, and profited in one day from the despoliation of genius, glory, and time; yet God did not wish that so dangerous an example be given to the world. Lacking the rights of birth, a usurper can only legitimate his pretensions to the throne through his virtues. In this case, Buonaparte had none in his favor but his military talents, and those were equaled, if not surpassed, by several of our generals. When Providence abandoned him and handed him over to his own folly, he was lost.

---

[1] George Monck (1608–70), a general under Oliver Cromwell, was the architect of the restoration of Charles II in 1660.

A king of France once said that if good faith had been banished from the company of men, it must be found in the heart of kings. This necessary quality of a royal soul was lacking in Buonaparte. The first known victim of the tyrant's perfidy was a royalist leader of Normandy. Monsieur de Frotté had the noble imprudence to attend a meeting to which he had been attracted by his trust in a promise. He was arrested and shot. A short time later, Toussaint l'Ouverture was similarly taken by treason in America and strangled in the castle where he had been imprisoned in Europe.

Soon a more famous murder disturbed the civilized world. Reborn were those barbarous times of the Middle Ages, those scenes found only in novels, those catastrophes that the civil wars of Italy and the politics of Machiavelli made known beyond the Alps. The foreigner, still not yet king, wished to have the bloody corpse of a Frenchman as a stepping-stone to the throne of France. And Great God, what a Frenchman! Everything was violated to commit this crime: the rights of men, justice, religion, humanity. The duke of Enghien was arrested in a time of peace on foreign soil and taken from the chateau of Offembourg. When he had left France, he was still too young to know it well. It was from the bottom of a post-chaise, then, between two gendarmes, that he saw the soil of his fatherland as if for the first time, and that he traversed the fields made famous by his ancestors only to go to his grave. He arrived in the middle of the night at the dungeon of Vincennes. By the light of torches, under the vaults of a prison, the grandson of the Great Condé[2] was declared guilty of having appeared on the battlefield: convicted of this hereditary crime,[3] he was immediately condemned. In vain did he demand to speak to Buonaparte (O touching and heroic simplicity!); the brave young man was one of the greatest admirers of his murderer. He could not believe that a captain could wish to assassinate a soldier. Worn out with hunger and fatigue, he was taken into the bowels of the castle. There he

---

[2] Louis II de Bourbon, the Great Condé (1621–86) was the victor at Rocroi in 1643.

[3] That is, the "crime" of having been a warrior like his fathers.

found a newly dug grave. He was stripped of his clothing and to his chest a lantern was attached so that in the darkness the ball might be guided to his heart. He wanted to give his watch to his executioners and prayed them to transmit the last tokens of his memory to his friends; they insulted him with base words. The command to fire was given. Without witnesses, without consolation, in the middle of his fatherland, only miles from Chantilly and several paces from those old trees under which the holy king Louis gave justice to his subjects, in the prison in which Monsieur the Prince was held, the young, the handsome, the brave, the last offspring of the victor of Rocroi fell dead. He died as the great Condé would have died, and as his assassin will not die. His body was secretly buried, and Bossuet will not be reborn to speak above his ashes.

It remained to the one who had lowered himself beneath mankind by this crime to affect to place himself above mankind by his designs, to give as an excuse for a sin reasons incomprehensible to the vulgar, and to make an abyss of iniquity pass for the heights of genius. Buonaparte had recourse to that miserable self-confidence that fools no one. Not being able to hide what he had done, he made it public.

When the death sentence was heard in Paris, there was open horror. One asked by what right a Corsican had spilled the most beautiful and pure blood of France. Did he think it possible to replace by his half-African line the French line that he had just extinguished? The soldiers groaned: this name of Condé seemed to belong to them alone and to represent the honor of the French army. Our grenadiers had encountered several times the three generations of heroes in the melee, the prince of Condé, the duke of Bourbon, and the duke of Enghien. They had even injured the duke of Bourbon, but the sword of a Frenchman could never exhaust this noble blood: only a foreigner could cut it off at its source.

Every nation has its vices. The French vice is not treason, blackness, or ingratitude. The murder of the duke of Enghien, the torture and assassination of Pichegru,[4] the war in Spain, and the captivity of the pope revealed in Buonaparte a nature foreign to France. In spite of the weight of our fetters, sensible to misery as well as to glory, we cried for the duke of Enghien, Pichegru, and Moreau,[5] we admired Saragossa, and paid homage to a pontiff cast in irons. He who stole the states of the venerable priest who had crowned him, he who at Fontainebleau dared to strike the venerable pontiff with his own hand and to pull the father of the faithful by his white hairs, which he believed to be another victory: he did not know that there remained to the heir of Jesus Christ that scepter of reeds and that crown of thorns that would triumph, sooner or later, over the power of the evil one.

The time is coming, I hope, when the free French will declare by a solemn act that they took no part in these tyrannical crimes, that the murder of the duke of Enghien, the captivity of the pope, and the war in Spain were impious, sacrilegious, hateful, and, above all, anti-French actions, and that the shame of them should fall only upon the head of the foreigner.

Buonaparte profited from the horror that the assassination of Vincennes thrust upon us to cross the last step and to seat himself upon the throne.

Then began the great debauch of royalty: crime, oppression, and slavery marched step by step with folly. Every liberty died. Every honorable sentiment, every generous thought became a conspiracy against the state. If one spoke of virtue, he was suspect. To praise a beautiful action was an assault against the prince. Words changed meaning. A people who fights for its legitimate sovereign is a rebellious people. A traitor is a loyal subject. France was an Empire of

[4] Jean-Charles Pichegru (1761–1804), a leading general during the early years of the Directory, joined the Royalists and was caught in the attempt to assassinate Bonaparte. He died in prison.

[5] Jean-Victor-Marie Moreau (1763–1813), also a general in the Revolutionary army, was arrested for his role in Pichegru's attempt on Bonaparte and exiled to America. He died in 1813 while serving in the allied army, fighting against Bonaparte.

lies: journals, pamphlets, discourses, prose, and verse all disguised the truth. If it rained, we were assured that it was sunny. If the tyrant walked among the silent people, it was said that he advanced among the acclamations of the crowd. The prince was all that mattered: morality consisted in devoting oneself to his caprice; duty was to praise him. Above all it was necessary to praise the administration when it made a mistake or committed a crime. Men of letters were forced by threats to celebrate the despot. They capitulated and praised him, and were happy when, at the price of several commonplaces about the glory of arms, they had purchased the right to emit a few sighs, to denounce a few crimes, to recall a proscribed truth! No book could appear without its ode to Buonaparte, like the stamp of slavery. In new editions of ancient authors, the censor removed all that he could find against conquerors, servitude, and tyranny, just as the Directory had corrected in the same authors everything that spoke of monarchy and kings. Almanacs were examined with care, and conscription was made into an article of faith in the catechism. There was the same servitude in the arts. Buonaparte had poisoned those ill with the plague in Jaffa, a painting therefore showed him touching these same plague-infested men with extreme courage and humanity. This was not the way that Saint Louis healed the sick who, with a moving and devout confidence, presented themselves to the royal hands. Do not speak of public opinion: his maxim is that the sovereign should arrange it each morning. The police, perfected by Buonaparte, had a committee charged with giving direction to minds, and at the head of this committee was a director of public opinion. Deception and silence were the two great methods employed to keep the people in error. If your children die on the battlefield, do you think that the police will tell you what has happened to them? They will conceal the events most important to the fatherland, to Europe, to the whole world. The enemies are at Meaux: you will learn it only by the flight of people from the countryside. They surround you with shadows. They play on your fears. They laugh at your sorrows. They disdain what you

9

feel and think. You wish to raise your voice, a spy denounces you, a gendarme arrests you, a military commission judges you. They crush your head, and you are forgotten.

It was not enough to shackle the fathers; the children must also be disposed of. We saw tearful mothers run to the ends of the Empire to demand the sons that the government had taken from them. These children were placed in schools where, to the sound of the drum, they were taught irreligion, debauchery, disdain for domestic virtues, and blind obedience to the sovereign. Paternal authority, respected by the most hideous tyrants of antiquity, was treated as a prejudice and an abuse by Buonaparte. He wanted to make our sons into some sort of Mamelukes, without God, family, or fatherland. It seems that this universal enemy tried to destroy France's very foundations. He more greatly corrupted men, and did more evil to mankind in the short space of ten years, than did all the tyrants of Rome together, from Nero to the last persecutor of the Christians. The principles that served as the basis of his administration passed from his government into the different classes of society, for a perverse government introduces vice in its people, while a wise government brings virtue to fruition. Irreligion, a taste for pleasures and expenses beyond one's means, a disdain for moral bonds, and a spirit of adventure, violence, and domination descended from the throne into our families. A little more time for such a reign and France would have been nought but a den of thieves.

The crimes of our republican revolution were the work of the passions and always left us with resources. There was disorder, but not destruction, in society. Morality was injured, but not destroyed. Conscience had its remorse. A destructive indifference had not mixed together the innocent and the guilty, and thus the evils of these times could have been quickly repaired. Yet how is one to heal the wound made by a government that posed despotism as its principle, that ceaselessly destroyed morality and religion by both its institutions and neglect, that did not seek to found an order upon duty and law, but upon force and police spies, and that took the stupor of slavery for the peace of a well-organized society faithful to the customs of its fathers and silently treading the path of its ancient virtues? The most terrible revolutions are preferable to such a government. If the civil wars produced public crimes, at least they gave birth to private virtues, talents, and great men. It is in despotism that empires disappear: by all kinds of abuses and by killing souls more than bodies, they lead sooner or later to dissolution and conquest. There is no example of a free nation that perished from a war between its citizens, and a state bent under its own storms has always arisen flourishing.

We have praised Buonaparte's administration. If administration consists in numerals, if, to govern well, it suffices to know how much a province produces in wheat, wine, and oil, what is the last penny one may levy as tax, the last man one may take, then certainly Buonaparte was a great administrator. It is impossible better to organize evil or to put more order into disorder. But if the best administration is that which leaves the people in peace, which nourishes their sentiments of justice and piety, which is frugal with the blood of men, which respects the rights of citizens, their properties and their families, then certainly the government of Buonaparte was the worst of governments.

And there were still more faults and errors in his own system! An extravagant administration swallowed up half the revenues of the state. Armies of customs collectors and receivers devoured the tolls they were charged to raise. There was not a single bureau chief who did not have five or six commissioners beneath him. Buonaparte seemed to have declared war on commerce. If some branch of industry were born in France, he would seize it, and it would immediately dry up in his hands. Tobacco, salt, wool, colonial goods, all were the object of his hateful monopolies as he made himself the sole shopkeeper of his empire. For absurd reasons, or rather by a decided distaste for the navy, he succeeded in losing our colonies and destroying our shipping. He built great vessels that rotted in our ports, or which he disarmed in order to serve the needs of his land army. A hundred frigates spread throughout the seas would have done considerable harm to our enemies, trained sailors for France, and protected our merchant vessels, but such commonsensical notions did not occur to him. We must not attribute the progress of our agriculture to his laws, for it was due to the division of the great properties, and abolition of feudal rights, and to several other causes produced by the Revolution. Every day this restless and bizarre man fatigued a people who needed only rest by his contradictory and frequently impossible decrees. In the evening he broke the law he had made in the morning. In ten years he devoured fifteen billions in taxes, which surpasses the sum levied during the seventy-three years of the reign of Louis XIV. The spoils of the world and fifteen hundred millions in revenue did not suffice for him; he was busied only with swelling his treasury by the most iniquitous measures. Every prefect, subprefect, and mayor had the right to augment the tolls for entering a town, to levy additional pennies on the towns, the villages, and the hamlets, and to demand arbitrary sums from landowners for such-and-such supposed need. All of France was opened to pillage. Sickness, poverty, death, education, the arts, the sciences: all paid tribute to the prince. Have you a maimed son, both legs amputated, incapable of serving? The law of conscription will oblige you to give fifteen hundred francs to console you for your misfortune. Sometimes the ill recruit died prior to the examination of the recruiting captain. Do you suppose the father to be exempt from paying the fifteen-hundred-franc penalty? Not at all. If the declaration of infirmity had been made before the death had taken place, the conscript being alive at the time of the declaration, the father would have been obliged to count out the sum upon his son's grave. Should the wretch wish to give some education to one of his children, he must count out eighteen hundred francs to the university, plus a payment towards the master's salary. If a modern author cited an ancient author when the works of the latter had fallen into what was called the public domain, the censor required five sous per page of the citation. If you translated while citing, you would pay only two sous-and-a-half per page, because then the citation would be in the mixed domain, half belonging to the work of the living translator and half to the dead author. When Buonaparte had food distributed to the poor in the winter of 1811, it was believed that he took such generosity from his thrift, but he took the occasion to levy additional centimes and earned four millions on the soup of the poor. Finally, we saw him seize the administration of funerals. It was worthy of the destroyer of the French to levy a tax upon their cadavers. And how could one demand the protection of the laws, for it was he who did it? The *corps législatif* dared to speak once and it was dissolved. One article alone of the new code radically destroyed property. A regional administrator could say to you: "Your property is regional or national. I am provisionally sequestering it: go and plead in the courts. If the region is incorrect, we will return your property." And to whom do you have recourse in this case? To the ordinary tribunals? No, these cases were reserved to the examination of the *Conseil d'État* and pleaded before the emperor as both judge and party.

If property was uncertain, civil liberty was still less secure. What was there more monstrous than that commission named to inspect the prisons, under the authority of which a man could be detained his whole life in a cell, without instruction, trial, or judgment, put to torture, and shot at night or strangled between two bars? Amidst all this, Buonaparte each year had named commissioners for the liberty of the press and individual liberty: Tiberius never toyed with mankind to this extent.

He crowned his despotic works with conscription. Scandinavia, called a human factory by one historian, could not have furnished enough men for this homicidal law. The code of conscription will be an eternal monument to Buonaparte's reign. In it are united all that the most subtle and ingenious tyranny could imagine to torment and devour the people. It truly was an infernal code. The sons of the French were harvested like trees in a forest. Each year eighty thousand young men were cut down. Yet these scheduled deaths were not all. The conscription was often increased by extraordinary levies. It devoured its future victims in advance, just as a dissolute man borrows against his future income. They finished by taking without counting. The legal age and the qualities required to die on the field of battle were no longer considered, and the law showed a marvelous indulgence in this regard. They went backwards towards infancy and forwards towards old age. Those who had already served were taken again, and those who had paid the indemnity were forced to march, like the son of one poor artisan, redeemed three times at the price of his father's small fortune. Sickness, infirmity, and deformity were no longer reasons for exemption. Mobile columns traversed the provinces as if they were enemy territory in order to take the people's last children. Should one complain of their ravages, the response was that these mobile columns were composed of good gendarmes who would console the mothers and return their sons to them. In place of the absent brother, they would take the brother who was there. The father answered for the son and the wife for the husband: the responsibility extended to the most distant relations and even to neighbors. Villages united in defense of their native sons. Garrisons were established on a peasant's lands, and he was forced to sell his bed to nourish himself until they had found the conscript hidden in the woods. The absurd was mixed with the atrocious. Often they demanded the children of those who were happy enough not to have had a posterity. They employed violence to discover the one who carried a name that existed only in the lists of the gendarmes, or for a conscript who had already served for five or six years. Expectant mothers were put to torture so that they would reveal where the firstborn of their wombs were hidden. Fathers brought in their son's cadavers to prove that they could no longer provide a living son. There still remained a few families whose richest children had been redeemed. These were destined one day to form the judges, administrators, savants, and landowners so useful to the social order of a great land: by the decree of the guards of honor they too were enveloped in the universal slaughter. We arrived at such a point of disdain for the lives of men and for France that these conscripts were called *prime matter* and *cannon fodder*. Those purveyors of human flesh even once batted around the question of how long a conscript would last, some holding out for thirty-six months, others for thirty-three. Buonaparte himself said: *My revenue is three hundred thousand men.* In the eleven years of his reign, he caused more than 5 million French to die, which surpasses the number killed in our civil wars over three centuries, under the reigns of Jean, Charles V, Charles VI, Charles VII, Henri II, François II, Charles IX, Henri III, and Henri IV. In the past twelve months, without counting the national guard, Buonaparte has raised 1,330 thousand men, which is more than one hundred thousand men per month. And someone dared to say that he had only spent our excess population.

It was easy to foresee what has arrived. Every wise man said that by exhausting France, the conscription would expose her to invasion as soon as she was seriously attacked. Bled white by the executioner, this corpse, emptied of blood, could make but a feeble resistance. Yet the loss of men was not the greatest evil done by conscription. It plunged us and all of Europe into barbarism. Conscription destroyed the trades, the arts, and letters. A young man who must die at eighteen years cannot devote himself to any study. To defend themselves, the neighboring nations were obliged to employ the same methods, and thus they abandoned all the advantages of civilization. And all the peoples, falling upon one another as in the century of the Goths and Vandals, saw the miseries of those times reborn. By sundering the ties of the whole society, conscription also annihilated those of the family. Accustomed from their cradle to see themselves as victims sentenced to death, children no longer obeyed their parents. They became lazy and debauched vagabonds, waiting for the day when they would go loot and devour the world. What principle of religion or morality would have had time to take root in their heart? For their part, the fathers and mothers in that class of people no longer attached their affections or gave their care to children they were prepared to lose, who were no longer their wealth and support, and who had become only a burden and an object of sadness. Thence that hardening of the soul, that loss of all natural sentiments which leads to egoism, carelessness about good and evil, and indifference towards the fatherland, which extinguishes conscience and remorse, which subjects the people to servitude by taking away their horror of vice and their admiration of virtue.

Thus was Buonaparte's administration of French affairs.

Let us examine the march of his government abroad, those policies of which he was so proud, and that he defined thus: *Politics is a game of men*. Well then! He lost everything in this abominable game, and France must cover his losses.

To begin with his continental system, this child's or fool's system was not the real goal of his wars, it was but the pretext for them. He wanted to be the master of the earth, while speaking only of the liberty of the seas. This insane system: did he do what was necessary to establish it? By the two great faults which, as we shall say hereafter, made his projects fail in Spain and Russia, did he not also fail to close the Mediterranean and Baltic ports? Did he not give all the colonies of the world to the English? Did he not open to them Peru, Mexico, and Brazil, a more considerable market than the one he hoped to close to them in Europe? Oh how true: the war enriched the people that he sought to ruin. Europe uses only a few of England's superfluities. The principal European nations find enough to suffice their chief necessities in the produce of their own manufacturing. In America, however, the people need everything, from the first to the last article of clothing, and 10 million Americans consume more English merchandise than 30 million Europeans. I do not even mention the importing of silver from Mexico and the Indies, of the monopoly on cocoa, quinine, cochineal, and a thousand other objects of speculation that are become a new source of wealth for the English. And when Buonaparte would have succeeded in closing the ports of Spain and the Baltic, then he would have had to close those of Greece, Constantinople, Syria, and the Barbary coast, which would have been to attempt to conquer the world. While he was busy with these new conquests, the conquered nations, unable to exchange the produce of their soil and their industry, would have thrown off the yoke and reopened their ports. Impossible by virtue of their gigantic size, his schemes were a failure of reason and good sense, the dreams of a fool and a madman.

As to his wars and his conduct with the cabinets of Europe, the least examination destroys their prestige. A man is not great because he attempts, but because he executes. Every man may dream of the conquest of the world: Alexander alone achieved it. Buonaparte governed Spain like a province from which he pumped blood and gold. He was not content with this. He wished personally to reign upon the throne of Charles IV. What then did he do? His evil policy was to sow the seeds of division in the royal family. Then he abducted the family, in disdain for all human and divine laws. He suddenly invaded the territory of a faithful people who had just fought for him at Trafalgar. He insulted the genius of a people, slaughtered their priests, injured the pride of the Castilians, and raised up against himself the descendants of El Cid.[6] As soon as Saragossa celebrated her own funeral mass and was buried under her ruins, the Christians descended from the Asturias and the new Moor was chased out. This war rekindled the spirit of the peoples in Europe, gave France one more frontier to defend, created a land army for the English, brought them back, after four centuries, into the fields of Poitiers, and handed them the treasures of Mexico.

If, instead of having recourse to these ruses worthy of a Borgia, Buonaparte had, by a more skillful but still criminal policy, under some pretext declared war upon the king of Spain, announced himself the avenger of the Castilians who were oppressed by the Prince of Peace, caressed the Spanish pride, and handled the religious

[6] Rodrigo Diaz del Vivar, El Cid (ca. 1043–99), the Castilian champion of the Reconquista, most famous for his conquest of Valencia.

orders, it is probable that he would have succeeded. "It is not the Spanish I want," he said in his fury, "it is Spain." Well then! the land rejected him. The burning of Burgos produced the burning of Moscow, and the conquest of the Alhambra led the Russians to the Louvre. A great and terrible lesson![7]

He made the same mistake in Russia. If in October 1812 he had stopped at the banks of the Duna, if he had been content to take Riga and to stay the winter there with his army of six hundred thousand men, to organize Poland behind him, with the return of spring he might perhaps have put the empire of the czars in peril. Instead, he marched to Moscow by one road, without stores and without resources. He came. The victors of Pultawa embraced their holy city. Buonaparte slept for a month amidst the ashes and ruins. He seemed to have forgotten the return of the seasons and the rigors of the climate. He let himself be amused by offers of peace. He was sufficiently ignorant of the human heart to believe that a people who had burned their own capital in order to escape slavery would capitulate over the smoking ruins of their homes. His generals cried out that it was time to retire. He left, swearing like an angry child that he would soon return with an army whose *vanguard alone would be three hundred thousand soldiers.* God sent out a breath of His anger: all was lost, and only one man returned to us!

Absurd in administration, criminal in politics, what then did he have to seduce the French, this foreigner? His military glory? Well then! he was stripped of it. He was, it is true, a great winner of battles. But beyond that the least general was more skillful than he. He listens to nothing of retreats or of the tricks of terrain. He is impatient, incapable of awaiting a result that would come only as the fruit of a long military calculation. He knows only how to advance, to charge, to run, to win a victory by *blows of men,* to sacrifice every-

---

[7] Chateubriand here echoes the first line of Bossuet's celebrated Funeral Oration for Henriette-Marie de France (1669): "He who reigns in heaven and who lifts up empires, to whom *alone* belong glory, majesty, and independence, is also the only one who glorifies himself by making laws for kings and by giving them, when it pleases him, great and terrible lessons."

thing for a success, and to kill half his soldiers by marches well beyond human power without worrying about a defeat. It mattered little: did he not have conscription and *prime matter*? Many believed that he had perfected the art of war, yet it is certain that he made it retrogress towards the infancy of the art. The masterpiece of the military art for a civilized people is to defend a large country with a small army, to leave many millions of men in peace behind sixty or eighty thousand soldiers so that the laborer who cultivates his furrow barely knows that they are fighting several miles from his farm. The Roman Empire was guarded by fifty thousand men, and Caesar only had a few legions at Pharsalia. Let him now defend us in our homes, this conqueror of the world! What, has all his genius suddenly abandoned him? By what enchantment is the France that Louis XIV surrounded with fortresses and that Vauban had walled in like a lovely garden now invaded from all sides? Where are the frontier garrisons? There are none. Where are the cannons on the ramparts? They are disarmed, even the vessels of Brest, Toulon, and Rochefort. If Buonaparte had wished to leave us defenseless against the forces of the coalition, if he had sold us, if he had secretly conspired against the French, would he have acted any differently? In less than sixteen months, two billion in cash, 1,400 thousand men, all the material of our armies and our forts were swallowed up in the forests of Germany and the deserts of Russia. At Dresden, Buonaparte committed mistake after mistake, forgetting that if crimes are sometimes punished in the other world, mistakes always are in this one. He displayed the most incomprehensible ignorance of what went on in the cabinets, refused to remain on the Elbe, was beaten at Leipzig, and refused the honorable peace that was offered him. Full of despair and rage, he left the palace of our kings for the last time, and with a spirit of justice and ingratitude, went to burn the place where these same kings had the misfortune to nourish him,[8] opposed his enemies with activity lacking all plan, suffered a final reverse, fled again, and at last delivered the capital of the civilized world of his hateful presence.

[8] Brienne, where he had studied in military school from 1779 to 1785.

The quill of a Frenchman will not refuse to paint the horror of his battlefields. An injured man was but a burden to Buonaparte: so much the better if he died, then we were rid of him. Piles of mutilated soldiers, thrown pell-mell into a corner, sometimes remained days and weeks until their wounds were dressed. No hospital is large enough to contain the wounded of an army of seven or eight hundred thousand men, nor are there enough surgeons to care for them. The executioner of the French took no precautions for them. Often there was no pharmacy, no ambulance, sometimes not even the instruments to cut off smashed limbs. In the Moscow campaign, for lack of cloth, they dressed wounds with hay. When the hay was gone, they died. Six hundred thousand warriors, the conquerors of Europe, the glory of France, were seen to wander amidst the snows and wastes, holding themselves up with branches of pine because they had not the strength to carry their arms, and their only coat was the bloody skin of the horses that had been their final meal. Old captains, their hair and beards bristling with icicles, abased themselves to the point of rubbing to keep warm those soldiers who had some food in order to obtain the smallest part, so much were they straitened by the torments of hunger! Whole squadrons, men and horses, were frozen during the night, and in the morning these phantoms could be seen standing amidst the chill. The only witnesses to the sufferings of our soldiers in these wastelands were the bands of crows and the packs of half-savage white hounds that followed our army to devour their leavings. In the spring, the emperor of the Russians made a search for the dead: more than one hundred sixty thousand cadavers were counted; twenty-four thousand were burned in one fire alone. The military plague, unknown since wars had been fought by only a small number of men, returned with conscription and the armies of a million men and the waves of human blood. And what did the destroyer of our fathers, our brothers, and our sons do when he had harvested the flower of France? He fled! He came to the Tuileries to say, while rubbing his hands at the fireplace: "The weather is better here than on the banks of the Beresina." Not a word of consolation to the wives and tearful mothers who surrounded him, not one regret, not one display of emotion, not a single admission of his folly. The Tigellins[9] said: "What was fortunate about this retreat is that the emperor lacked for nothing. He was always well nourished, sheltered in a good carriage. Indeed, he suffered not at all, and that is a great consolation." And amidst his court he seemed happy, triumphant, glorious, adorned with the royal mantle, his head covered with Henri IV's cap. He gloated, brilliant upon his throne, striking all the royal poses that Talma[10] had taught him. Yet this pomp only made him more hideous, and all the diamonds of the crown could not hide the blood that covered him.

Alas! This horror of the battlefields has come to us. It is no longer hidden in the wastes, we see it amidst our homes, in that Paris which the Normans besieged in vain almost a thousand years ago, and which prided herself on not having been conquered since Clovis became her king. To open a land to invasion: is this not the greatest and most unpardonable of crimes? We saw the rest of our sons perish under our own eyes. We saw troops of conscripts, old soldiers pale and disfigured, holding themselves up by the sides of the roads, dying of all sorts of wounds, barely holding in one hand the weapon with which they had defended the fatherland, and begging alms with the other hand. We have seen the Seine full of barges and our streets clogged with carts full of the injured lacking the first dressing upon their wounds. One of these carts, leaving a trail of blood behind, broke open upon the boulevard. Falling from it were conscripts without arms, without legs, pierced with balls and blows of the lance, crying out, and praying the passers-by to finish them off. These miserable youths, taken from their farms before they had reached their manhood, led with their farming clothes and bonnets onto the battlefield, placed as *cannon fodder* in the most dangerous places to use up the enemy's fire: these unfortunate ones, I say, were seized by tears, and when they fell, struck by the cannon balls, they

[9] A reference to Ofonius Tigellinus (died A.D. 69), Nero's fawning advisor.

[10] François-Joseph Talma (1763–1826), a popular actor during the Revolution, was one of Napoleon's favorites.

cried out: Oh my mother, my mother! a heartrending cry that marks the tender age of the child just torn from domestic peace, of the child fallen at once from the hands of his mother into those of his barbarous sovereign! So much slaughter, so much sorrow, and for whom? For an abominable tyrant, a Corsican, a foreigner who was wasteful of French blood precisely because he did not have a drop of it in his veins. *(mud blood?)*

Oh! Louis XVI refused to punish a few guilty men whose death would have secured his throne and spared us so many evils. He said "I do not wish to purchase my security at the price of the life of a single one of my subjects." He wrote in his testament: "I commend my son, should he have the misfortune to become king, to reflect that he should devote himself entirely to the happiness of his fellow citizens, that he should forget all hatred and resentment, and notably those which have to do with the evils and trials that I undergo; and that he can only work for the happiness of his people by reigning according to the laws." Then he pronounced these words upon the scaffold: "Men of France, I pray God that He will not avenge upon the nation the blood of your kings that will be spilled." Here is the true king, the French king, the legitimate king, the father and leader of the fatherland!

Buonaparte showed himself too mediocre in his misfortune for us to believe that his prosperity was the work of his genius. He was only the son of our strength, and we believed him the son of his works. His greatness came only from the immense forces that we placed in his hands at the time of his elevation. He inherited all the armies formed under our most skilled generals, led to victory so many times by all those great captains who have perished, and who will perhaps die even to the last man, victims of the fury and jealousy of the tyrant. He found a numerous people, enlarged by conquests, exalted by triumphs and by the movement that revolutions always give. He had but to strike his foot against the fertile ground of our fatherland and it produced treasures and soldiers for him. The peoples he attacked were tired and divided. He conquered them one by one by spilling upon each of them in turn the waves of the population of France.

When God sends to the earth the executors of his heavenly chastisements, everything is leveled before them: they enjoy extraordinary successes with mediocre talents. Born amidst civil discord, these exterminators draw their principal power from the evils that have given birth to them, and from the terror that the memory of these evils inspires. Thus they obtain the submission of the people in the name of the calamities they have survived. It is given to them to corrupt and to weaken, to destroy honor, to degrade souls, to soil all that they touch, to desire all and to dare all, to reign by lies, impiety, and fear, to speak all languages, to fascinate all eyes, to trick even our reason, to make themselves pass for great geniuses, when they are but common scoundrels, for excellence in everything cannot be separated from virtue. Dragging after them the nations they have seduced, triumphant through the multitude, dishonored by a hundred victories, with torch in hand and with their feet in blood, they go to the ends of the earth like drunken men, pushed on by the God they disown.

When, on the contrary, Providence wishes to save an empire and not to punish it, when he employs his servants and not his scourges, when he intends an honorable glory, not an abominable renown, then far from making his servants's route easy like Buonaparte's, he opposes them with obstacles worthy of their virtues. Thus one can always distinguish the tyrant from the liberator, the ravager of the people from the great captain, the man sent to destroy and the man come to repair. The former is master of all, and makes use of immense means in order to succeed. The latter is master of nothing, and has but feeble resources. It is easy to recognize in the first traits the character and mission of the one who devastated France.

Buonaparte is a false great man: the magnanimity that makes heroes and true kings was lacking in him. Thus no one quotes him saying one of those phrases spoken by Alexander or Caesar, Henri IV or Louis XIV. Nature formed him without feelings. His head was large enough, but it was the empire of shadows and confusion. All ideas, even good ones, could enter it, but they left just as quickly.

The distinctive trait of his character was an invincible stubbornness, a will of iron, but only for injustice, oppression, and extravagant systems. He quickly abandoned the projects that might have been favorable to morality, order, and virtue. Imagination dominated him, reason did not rule him at all. His plans were not the fruit of profound reflection, but the effect of a sudden movement or hasty resolution. Changeable, like the men of his country, he had something about him of the clown and the actor. It was all an act, even the passions that he did not have. He was always on stage. In Cairo, he was a renegade who boasted of having destroyed the papacy. In Paris, he was the restorer of the Christian religion. Today he is a visionary, tomorrow a philosopher. His scenes were prepared in advance. A sovereign who could take lessons from Talma so as to strike a royal pose will be judged by posterity. He wanted to seem original, and was almost always an imitator. Yet his imitations are so poor that they immediately recall the object or the action that he copies. He always tries to say what he thinks will be a great phrase, or to do what he presumes will be a great thing. Affecting the universality of genius, he spoke of finances and of spectacles, of war and of fashion, governed the fate of kings and toll commissioners, dated from the Kremlin a ruling on theaters, and on the day of a battle, arrested several women in Paris. Child of our Revolution, he has striking resemblances to his mother: intemperance of language, a taste for low literature, and a passion for writing in newspapers. Under the mask of Caesar and Alexander, we perceive a small man, and the child of a base family. He had sovereign disdain for men because he judged them according to himself. His maxim is that they do nothing except for their interest, and that probity itself is mere calculation. Thence the system of fusion that was the basis of his government, employing both the bad and the honest man, mixing vice and virtue by design, and always taking care to place you in opposition to your principles. His great pleasure was to dishonor virtue, to soil reputations: he would touch you only to stain you. When he had made you fall, you would become *his man*, according to the vulgar expression, and you would belong to him by right of shame. He would love you a little less, and you would disdain him a bit more. In his administration, he wanted only results to be known and never to be embarrassed by the means. The *masses* before him were everything, the individuals nothing. "The youth will be corrupted, but then they will obey me better. This branch of industry will be extinct, but for the moment I will obtain a few millions. Sixty thousand men will die in this affair, but I will win the battle." Thus lay the course of all his reasoning; thus are kingdoms destroyed!

Born to destroy, Buonaparte carried evil in his belly just as naturally as a mother carries her fruit: with joy and a kind of pride. He had a horror for the happiness of men. He said one day: 'There are still several happy persons in France; these are the families who do not know me, who live in the country, in a chateau, with thirty or forty thousand pounds in rent; I will know how to reach them.' He kept his word. Seeing his son play one day, he said to a bishop who was present: "Monsieur Bishop, do you believe that this has a soul?" Everything that distinguished itself by a certain superiority appalled this tyrant. Every reputation bothered him. He was jealous of talents, of intelligence, of virtue. He did not even love the sound of a great crime, were this crime not his work. The most disgraceful of men, his greatest pleasure was to injure those who approached him, without thinking that kings never insult anyone because one cannot take vengeance upon them, without reminding himself that he spoke to the nation most delicate of its honor, and to a people formed by the court of Louis XIV and justly renowned for the elegance of its customs and the grace of its manners. In the end, Buonaparte was but the man of prosperity. As soon as the adversity that makes virtues shine touched this false great man, the prodigy vanished: in the monarch could be seen only the adventurer, and in the hero, the newcomer to glory.

When Buonaparte chased out the Directory, he addressed this discourse to them:

"What have you done with that France that I left you so brilliant? I left you with peace, I come back to find war; I left you with victories, I come back to find defeats; I left you with the millions of Italy, and everywhere I have found confiscatory laws and misery. What have you done with one hundred thousand Frenchmen I knew, all my companions in glory? They are dead."

"This state of things cannot last. Before three years they will have led us to despotism. But we want a republic, a republic established on the bases of equality, morality, civil liberty, political tolerance, and so on."

Today, miserable man, we take you at your word and interrogate you with your own speech. "Tell us, what have you done with that France so brilliant? Where are our treasures, the millions of Italy, and of all of Europe? What have you done, not with one hundred thousand, but with five million Frenchmen, all of whom we knew, our parents, our friends, our brothers? This state of things cannot endure. It has plunged us into a hideous despotism. You wanted a republic, and you brought us slavery. We wanted the monarchy established on the bases of equality of rights, morality, civil liberty, and political and religious tolerance. Have you given it to us? What have you done for us? What do we owe to your reign? Who was it that assassinated the duke of Enghien, tortured Pichegru, banished Moreau, fettered the sovereign pontiff, seized the princes of Spain, and fought an impious war? You. Who was it that lost our colonies, destroyed our commerce, opened America to the English, corrupted our morals, took the children from our fathers, devastated our families, ravaged the world, burned more than a thousand villages, and filled the earth with horror for the name of the French? You. Who was it that exposed France to plague, invasion, dismemberment, and conquest? Again, you. Here is what you could not ask the Directory, and what we ask you today. How much more guilty are you than those men whom you found unworthy to reign! Should a legitimate and hereditary king have burdened his people with the least part of the evils that you have done to us, he would have imperilled his throne; and you, usurper and foreigner, you became

Henri IV still makes French hearts tremble and fills our eyes with tears. We owe the best part of our glory to Louis XIV. Have we not called Louis XVI the most honest man of his kingdom? This family sheds tears in exile, not for their misfortunes, but for ours. That young princess whom we persecuted and made an orphan lives in foreign palaces, but every day she regrets having left the prisons of France. She could have received the hand of a powerful and glorious prince, but she preferred to unite her destiny to that of her poor, exiled, and outlawed cousin because he was French and because she would not separate herself from the sufferings of her people. The whole world admires her virtues. The people of Europe follow her when she appears in the public promenades and cover her with benedictions; and we, we were able to forget her! When she left the fatherland where she had been so unhappy, she looked back and cried. We who have been the constant object of her prayers and her love hardly knew that she existed. "I sense," she once said, "that I will have no child but France." These touching words should make us fall at her feet with tears of repentance. Yes, the duchess of Angoulême will become fruitful on the fertile soil of her fatherland! The lily grows naturally in our land: they will be born again more beautiful, watered with the blood of so many victims offered in expiation at the foot of the scaffold of Louis and Antoinette!

The brother of our late king, Louis XVIII, who should first reign over us, is an enlightened prince who is inaccessible to prejudice and a foreigner to vengeance. Of all the sovereigns who could at present govern France, he is the one that best fits our position and the spirit of the age, just as of all the men whom we could have chosen, Buonaparte was the least fit to be king. The institutions of a people are the work of time and experience; to reign one must first have reason and regularity. A prince who has in his head but two or three commonplace but useful ideas would be a more fitting sovereign to a nation than an extraordinary adventurer, ceaselessly giving birth to new plans, dreaming up new laws, believing himself to reign only when he troubles the people and changes in the evening what he had created in the morning. Not only does Louis XVIII have the fixed ideas, moderation, and good sense so necessary to a monarch, he is also a prince who is a friend to letters, instructed and eloquent as many of our kings have been, with a broad and enlightened mind and a firm and philosophical character.

Let us choose between Buonaparte, who returns to us carrying the bloody code of conscription, and Louis XVIII, who comes forward to heal our wounds with the testament of Louis XVI in his hand. At his consecration he will repeat those words written by his virtuous brother:

"I pardon with all my heart those who have made themselves my enemies without my having given them any cause for it, and I pray God to pardon them."

The count of Artois, of a character so frank, so loyal, so French, distinguishes himself today by his piety, mildness, and goodness, as in his first youth he made himself noticed by his great air and royal graces. Buonaparte flees, struck down by the hand of God but not corrected by adversity. As he retires from the land that thus escapes his tyranny, he drags behind him unfortunate victims bound in chains: it is in the prisons of France that he will exercise the final acts of his power. The count of Artois arrives alone, without soldiers, without support, unknown to the French to whom he shows himself. Immediately he speaks his name the people fall to their knees. They kiss the hem of his garment, they embrace his knees, and they cry out to him through a flood of tears: "We bring you only our hearts, for that is all that the monster left us with!" From this manner of leaving France, and this manner of returning, recognize on one side the usurper and on the other the legitimate prince.

The duke of Angoulême appeared in another of our provinces. Bordeaux, the second city of the kingdom, threw itself into his arms, and the land of Henri IV, transported by joy, recognized in him the heir to the virtues of the Béarnais.[11] Our armies have hardly seen a knight more brave than the duke of Berry. The duke of

[11] On March 12, 1814, Bordeaux declared itself for the restoration of the Bourbons by welcoming the duke of Angoulême, who had come north from Spain with Wellington.

Orléans proves, by his noble fidelity to the blood of his king, that his name is still one of the most lovely of France. I have already spoken of the three generations of heroes, the Prince Condé, the duke of Bourbon; I leave it to Buonaparte to name the third.

I do not know whether posterity will be able to believe that so many princes of the house of Bourbon were outlawed by a people that owes all its glory to them, without having been guilty of a single crime and without their misery having come to them from the tyranny of the last king of their line. No, the future will not be able to understand why we have banished such good princes, princes who were our compatriots, to place at our head a foreigner and the most evil of all men. One can to some extent imagine the republic in France: in a moment of folly a people can change the form of its government and no longer recognize a supreme leader. Yet if we return to a monarchy, it is the yoke of shame and absurdity to wish for it outside of the legitimate sovereign, and to believe that it can exist without him. We may modify, if we wish, the constitution of this monarchy, but no one has the right to change the monarch. A cruel, tyrannical king, who violates all the laws and deprives a whole people of their liberties, may be disposed by a violent revolution, but in this extraordinary case, the crown passes to his son, or to his closest heir. Now, was Louis XVI a tyrant? Can we put his legacy on trial? By virtue of what authority did we deprive his line of a throne that belonged to it by so many titles? By what shameful caprice did we give the heritage of Robert the Strong to the son of a bailiff from Ajaccio? This Robert the Strong seems to have descended from the second line, which in turn was attached to the first. He was count of Paris. Hugh Capet brought to the French, as a Frenchman himself, Paris, his paternal inheritance, his wealth and his immense domains. So small under the first Capetians, France grew wealthy and large under their descendants.

To replace this ancient line, we have had to seek a king, as one senator said, in a people whom the Romans would not take as slaves. It is in favor of an obscure Italian, who made his fortune by despoiling the French, that we have overturned the Salic law, the *palladium* of our empire! How different were the sentiments and maxims of our fathers from our own! At the death of Philippe-le-Bel, they decided that the crown belonged to Philip of Valois to the prejudice of Edward III, king of England. They thought it better to condemn themselves to two centuries of war than to let themselves be governed by a foreigner. This noble resolution was the cause of the glory and the grandeur of France. The oriflamme was torn on the fields of Crecy, Poitiers, and Agincourt, but its tattered shreds at last triumphed over the banner of Edward III and Henry V, and the cry of *Montjoie Saint-Denis* silenced all the factions. The same question of heredity presented itself at the death of Henri III. The Parlement[12] then gave the famous edict that gave Henri IV and Louis XIV to France. Yet those were no ignoble heads: Edward III, Henry V, the duke of Guise, and the infante of Spain. Great God! what has become of the pride of France! She refused sovereigns as great as these to preserve her French and royal line, and she has made the choice of Buonaparte!

In vain do some pretend that Buonaparte is not a foreigner. He is, in the eyes of all of Europe and in those of all unprejudiced Frenchmen. He will be to the judgment of posterity. It will perhaps attribute to him the best part of our victories, and charge us with a part of his crimes. Buonaparte has nothing French about him, neither in his habits, nor in his character. The very traits of his visage betrays his origin. The language he learned in his cradle was not our own, and his accent, as well as his name, shows his homeland. His father and mother lived half their lives as subjects of the republic of Genoa. He himself was more sincere than his flatterers: he did not see himself as French. He hated and disdained us. Several times the words escaped from him: *This is how you are, you French.* In one discourse he spoke of Italy as his fatherland and of France as his conquest. If Buonaparte is French, it must necessarily be said that

---

[12] The parlements were the regional legal courts in the Old Regime. Of these, the Parlement of Paris took precedence and had the widest jurisdiction.

Toussaint L'Ouverture was more so: for in the end he was born in an old French colony, under French laws, and the liberty that he enjoyed gave him the rights of a subject and citizen. And a foreigner raised by the charity of our kings occupies the throne of our kings and burns to spill out their blood! We take care of his youth, and in gratitude he plunges us into the abyss of sorrow! Just dispensation of Providence! The Gauls sacked Rome, and the Romans oppressed the Gauls. The French have often ravaged Italy, and the Medici, the Galigai, the Mazarins, and the Buonapartes have laid waste to us. France and Italy should at last recognize one another and renounce one another forever.

How sweet it would be to rest at last from so much agitation and misery under the paternal authority of our legitimate sovereign! We have had a time to be the subjects of the glory that our arms poured out upon Buonaparte; today, now that he has stripped himself of that glory, it would be too much to remain a slave to his crimes. Let us reject this oppressor as all the peoples have rejected him. Let it not be said of us: they have killed the best and most virtuous of their kings; they did nothing to save his life, and today they spill the last drop of their blood, they sacrifice the rest of France to uphold a foreigner they detest. By what reason does unfaithful France justify her abominable fidelity? It must then be admitted that it is faults that please them, crimes that charm them, tyranny that suits them. Oh! if in the end the foreign nations, tired of our stubbornness, would consent to leave us this madman. If we were so base as to purchase by a part of our territory the shame of preserving in our midst the germ of the plague and the scourge of humanity, we must flee to the heart of the desert, change our name and our language, try to forget and make forgotten that we have been French.

Let us think of the good of our common fatherland. Let us reflect that our future is in our hands. One word can give us glory, peace, and the esteem of the world, or plunge us in the most frightful and the most ignoble slavery. Let us raise up the monarchy of Clovis, the heritage of Saint Louis, the patrimony of Henri IV. Today, the

Bourbons alone suit our miserable condition. They are the only doctors who can heal our wounds. Their moderation, paternal sentiments, and their own adversities suit a kingdom that is worn out by convulsions and suffering. Everything becomes legitimate with them; everything is illegitimate without them. Their presence alone will give birth to an order whose very source they are. They are brave and illustrious gentlemen and more French than we are ourselves. These lords of the Fleurs-de-Lys will be celebrated for their loyalty for all time. They hold so strongly to the root of our customs that they seem to be a part of France itself, and France misses them as it would air or sunlight.

If all would become peaceful with them, if they alone can put an end to our too-long Revolution, the return of Buonaparte would plunge us into frightful evils and interminable travails. Can the most fertile imagination represent what this monstrous giant would be if bound up within strict limits, no longer having the treasures of the world to devour and the blood of Europe to spill? Can we envision him closed up in a ruined and branded court, exercising his rage, his vengeance, and his turbulent genius upon France alone? Buonaparte has not changed at all. He will never change. He will always invent projects, laws, and absurd, contradictory, and criminal decrees. He will always torment us. He will make us forever uncertain of our lives, our liberty, our properties. While awaiting the chance to overturn the world again, he will busy himself with the care of overturning our families. The only slaves in a free world, the object of the disdain of other peoples, our most grievous misfortune will be no longer to sense our abasement and to sleep, like a slave of the Orient, indifferent to the cord by which the Sultan binds us when we awaken.

No, it will not be like that. We have a legitimate prince, born of our own blood, raised among us, whom we know, who knows us, who has our customs, tastes, and habits, for whom we have prayed to God in our youth, whose name our children know as well as that of their neighbors, and whose fathers lived and died with our own.

Will France be a forfeited estate because we have reduced our former princes to being exiles? Must a Corsican retain it by squatter's rights? Oh! for God's sake, let us not be found so disloyal as to disinherit our natural lord and to give his bed to the first fellow who asks for it. If we do not have our legitimate masters, to have the least Frenchman reign over us would be preferable to Buonaparte. At least let us not have the shame to obey a foreigner.

It remains only for me to prove that if the reestablishment of the house of Bourbon is necessary to France, it is no less necessary to Europe as a whole.

THE ALLIES

To consider at the outset only the reasons specific to Buonaparte, is there a man in the world who would ever wish to rely upon his word? Was it not a point of his policy and a penchant of his heart to be skilled at trickery, to regard good faith as foolishness and the mark of a small mind, and to make jokes about the sanctity of oaths? Did he keep a single one of the treaties that he made with the various powers of Europe? It was always by violating some articles of these treaties in a time of peace that he made his most lasting conquests; rarely did he evacuate a place that he had agreed to cede; and today, even now that he is beaten, he still possesses several fortresses in Germany as the fruit of his many rapes and the witnesses to his lies.

Will we bind him so that he will not be able to begin his ravages again? And would you weaken France by dismembering her, by placing occupying soldiers within her frontiers for a number of years, obliging her to pay considerable sums, and forcing her to have but a small army, and to abolish conscription? All this will be in vain. Again I say: Buonaparte has not changed. Adversity can do nothing to him because he is not above his fortune. He plans his vengeance in silence. All at once, after a year or two of repose, when the coalition has dissolved and each power has returned to its states, he will call us to arms, profit from our newly matured sons, rise up, free the fortresses, and fall again upon Germany. Even today he speaks only of burning Vienna, Berlin, and Munich. He cannot consent to leave his prey. Will the Russians return quickly enough to save Europe a second time? Will this miraculous coalition, the fruit of twenty-five years of suffering, be able to renew itself when all of the ties that bound it are broken? Did not Buonaparte find the means to corrupt ministers, seduce princes, awaken ancient jealousies, and even place in his debt several peoples blind enough to fight under his banners? Finally, will the princes who reign today all be upon their thrones? Might not a change in reigns lead to a change in policies? Will the powers, so often deceived, be able immediately to take up the vigilance that they have set aside? What! will they have forgotten the pride of this adventurer who treated them so insolently, who prided himself to have had kings in his antechamber, who sent signed orders to sovereigns, established his spies in their very courts, and said openly that before ten years were out his *dynasty* would be Europe's eldest? Will the kings parley with a man who committed outrages against them that even a private individual would not tolerate! A charming queen was admired by Europe for her beauty, her courage, and her virtues, and he hastened her death by the most base and ignoble outrages. The holiness of kings as well as decency prevents me from repeating the calumnies, the grossness, and the ignoble pleasantries that he uttered again and again to the kings and ministers who today dictate the law to him in his own palace. If the powers personally overlook these outrages, they cannot and must not overlook them for the interest and majesty of their thrones. They must make themselves respected by their people, break the sword of the usurper, and forever dishonor this abominable right of force on which Buonaparte founded his pride and empire.

After these considerations, we come to other, loftier ones, which alone should determine the coalition of powers no longer to recognize Buonaparte as sovereign.

It is imperative for the repose of the peoples and for the security of crowns, to the lives as well as to the families of the sovereigns, that a man who leaves the inferior ranks of society not be allowed without punishment to seat himself upon the throne of his master, to take his place among the legitimate sovereigns, to treat them as *brothers*, and to find in the revolutions that have elevated him enough force to balance his claim to the legitimacy of his line. If this example is given to the world but once, no monarch can count upon his crown. If the throne of Clovis can be given, in a civilized time, to a Corsican, while the sons of St. Louis are abroad in the land, then no king can be sure today that he will reign tomorrow. Let them beware: all the monarchies of Europe are more or less daughters of the same customs and the same time, all the kings are truly like brothers united by the Christian religion and the antiquity of our memories. This beautiful and great system, once broken, with new lines seated upon the thrones where they will make other customs, other principles, and other ideas reign: this is the end of the old Europe. And in the passage of several years, a general revolution will have changed the succession of all the sovereigns. The kings should therefore take up the defense of the House of Bourbon as they would that of their own family. What is true from the point of view of royalty is also true from the natural point of view. There is not a king in Europe who does not have the blood of the Bourbons in his veins, and who should not see in them illustrious and unfortunate relatives. We have already too much taught the people that they can shake thrones. It is for the kings to show them that if these thrones can be shaken, they can never be destroyed, and that it is for the good of the world that crowns do not depend upon the success of crime and games of fortune.

It is still more imperative to Europe that France, who is its soul and heart by her genius and her position, be happy, flourishing, and peaceful. This she can only be under her former kings. Any other government would prolong among us those convulsions that have made themselves felt to the ends of the earth. Only the Bourbons, by the majesty of their line, by the legitimacy of their rights, and by the moderation of their character, will offer a sufficient guarantee to treaties and heal the wounds of the world.

Under the reign of tyrants, all moral laws are suspended. Thus in England, during times of trouble, they suspend the act on which the liberty of citizens rests. Each knows that he does not do right, that he walks in a false path, but each submits and lends himself to oppression. We even have a kind of false conscience in vice, scrupulously fulfilling the orders most opposed to justice. The excuse is that better days will come when we will return to the ways of liberty and virtue, and that the time of iniquity must pass, just as bad weather must pass. Yet, while waiting for this return, the tyrant does as he pleases. He is obeyed. He can drag a whole people into war, oppress them, demand everything from them without being refused. All this is impossible under a legitimate prince. Under a legal scepter the whole world enjoys its natural rights and the exercise of the virtues. If the king wishes to surpass the limits of his power, he finds obstacles on every side. All the corporations make remonstrances; all the individuals speak out; we oppose him with reason, conscience, and liberty. This is why Buonaparte as master of only one village in France should be more feared by Europe than the Bourbons with France extended to the Rhine.

Besides, can the kings doubt the opinion of the French? Do they believe that they could have gained the Louvre this easily if France did not hope to find liberators in them? Have they not seen the manifest signs of this hope in all the villages they have entered? What have we heard in France for the past six months but these words: *Are the Bourbons here? where are the princes? do they come? Oh! if only we might see the white flag!* On the other hand, the horror of the usurper is in every heart. It inspires so much hatred that in our warlike people it has even balanced what is hard about the presence of the enemy, and we would rather suffer a momentary invasion than be threatened with keeping Buonaparte for all our lives. If the armies are defeated, let us admire their courage and deplore their sufferings. They detest the tyrant as much and more than the rest of

France. Yet they have taken an oath, and the French grenadiers will die, victims of their oath. The sight of the military standard inspires fidelity. From our fathers the Franks to ourselves, our soldiers have made a holy pact and are, so to speak, married to their swords. Let us not then mistake the sacrifice of honor for the love of slavery. Our brave warriors only await to be set free from their word. Let the French and the allies recognize their legitimate princes, and at once the army, freed from its oath, will range itself under that spotless flag, the witness of our many victories, of our few defeats, and of our constant courage, but never of our shame.

The allied kings will find no obstacle to their design if they wish to follow the only party that can secure the repose of France and Europe. They should be satisfied with the triumph of their arms. We the French should only consider these triumphs as a lesson of Providence, who chastises us without humiliating us. We can say to ourselves with confidence that what would have been impossible under our legitimate princes could only have been accomplished under the reign of an adventurer. The allied kings should henceforth aspire to a more solid and lasting glory. Let them come with their honor guard to *the site of our revolution*; let them celebrate a solemn funeral on the same place where the heads of Louis and Antoinette fell; let this council of kings, their hands on the altar, amidst the French people on their knees and in tears, recognize Louis XVIII as king of France. They will thus offer the world a greater spectacle than it has ever seen, and pour out upon themselves a glory that the centuries will not be able to erase.

Yet already one part of these events is accomplished. Miracles have given birth to miracles. Paris, like Athens, has seen foreigners enter her walls who, recalling her glory and her great men, have respected her. Eighty thousand conquering soldiers have slept among our citizens without bothering their sleep, without being carried to the least violence, without even making one song of triumph heard. These are liberators and not conquerors. Immortal honor to the sovereigns who have given the world such an example

39

of moderation in victory! What injuries do they have to avenge! Yet they have not at all confounded France with the tyrant who oppressed them. Thus they have already met the fruit of their magnanimity. They have been received by the inhabitants of Paris as if they had been our own kings, like French princes, like the Bourbons. We will soon see the descendants of Henri IV. Alexander has promised them to us. He remembers that the marriage contract of the duke and duchess of Angoulême is deposited in the archives of Russia. He has faithfully kept the last public act of our legitimate government. He has brought it to our archives, where we will in our turn keep the account of his entry into Paris as one of the greatest and most glorious monuments of history.

However, let us not separate from these two sovereigns who are today among us from that other sovereign who made the greatest of sacrifices to the cause of kings and the repose of peoples: may he find as monarch and as father the recompense of his virtues in the tears, the gratitude, and the admiration of the French.

Men of France! Friends, companions in misfortune, let us forget our quarrels, our hatreds, our errors, in order to save the fatherland. Let us embrace among the ruins of our dear land. Let us call to our help the heir of Henri IV and Louis XIV, who comes to wipe away the tears of our children, to make our families happy once more, and to cover our wounds with the mantle of Saint Louis, half torn by our own hands. Let us consider well that all the evils we have suffered, the loss of our goods, of our armies, the miseries of invasion, the massacre of our children, the troubles and the disarray of all France, and the loss of our liberties are the work of one man alone, and that we owe the contrary benefits to one man alone. Let us then hear from all sides the cry that can save us, the cry that our fathers made to resound in misfortune as well as in victory, and that will be for us the sign of peace and happiness: _Long live the king_!

LOUIS-GABRIEL-AMBOISE de

BONALD

(Anti - industry)

ON JACQUES-BENIGNE BOSSUET, BISHOP OF MEAUX (1815)

At last the eagerly awaited *History of Bossuet* by Monsieur de Bausset has appeared, and it shall not be long in finding its place on our shelves next to his *History of Fénelon*.

It is a fine thing to write the lives of the two prelates who have most greatly honored their country, their religion, and the world of letters by all the virtues of their estate and all the gifts of genius. It is also a fitting monument for a bishop to raise to the glory of his Church and his nation. Bossuet and Fénelon were perfect models of the mind's force and grace; and the former's forcefulness did not lack grace, while the latter's sweetness and eloquence were not wanting in force. Both lived at court and attached themselves to illustrious friends; both educated heirs of kings; both were involved in religious affairs of the highest importance. Long united, and, in the end, pitted against one another in a theological debate, they deployed—in a controversy their names have made famous—all the resources and richness of their minds, the one to justify the pious illusions of a beloved soul and an exalted imagination, the other to dissipate this vain phantom of perfection.[1] It was the strong and luminous reason of Bossuet that triumphed, but the vanquished

[1] Bonald here refers to the Quietist controversy of the late 1690s.

honored his defeat, and his religious docility has made his adversary's success be forgotten. Fénelon, early removed from the theater of ambition and grand affairs, withdrew to his episcopal duties. Bossuet, favored to the end by the court and the great, and, still more, esteemed by them, made decisions of great moment on the strength of his genius and renown.

This is Monsieur de Bausset's tale; and in the histories of these two celebrated men, he has presented well-attested facts with a devout fidelity that interrogates all testimonies, calls upon all traditions, consults all the contemporary writings, and always allows the subject to speak, adding only those details he could not have told or taught us.

After admiring this authorial conscience—the first duty of a historian and a merit all-too rare in our day—let us speak of Monsieur de Bausset's style. His is a model of biographical style, or rather of historical style, for the lives of great men go beyond them to history itself. His style is true, grave, elegant, correct, supple, and above all, natural. He alternates with ease between simplicity and a lofty tone as his subject demands. This style of his—it is the author himself, with all the qualities of mind and heart that have made friends of all who know him, and admirers of all who appreciate him. Never has Buffon's maxim, "The style is the man himself," been more fittingly applied.

And we who honor the esteem and friendship he accords us, if we may dare join our voice to the public's, declare that these two works, these masterpieces of biography, are perfected. We could praise them no better than to say that in our literature, where there are so many histories to be rewritten, these are works that no one will rewrite.

When one wishes to write the story of a public man and celebrated writer there are two possible methods. One may follow chronological order for the literary works as for the events of the subject's life, accepting that the similar works written in different periods will require frequent repetitions of facts. Or, one may abandon chronological order entirely and apply himself solely to the nature of the works, but then we see the writer, the orator, the savant rather than the man, and the author has written only a literary history.

Monsieur de Bausset wisely has pursued the two methods simultaneously. He recounts by date the personal and public circumstances of Bossuet's life, and he includes all that he can collect of the great man's writings on similar themes, regardless of their date, and thus he has written the history of Bossuet and of his writings.

A general reflection comes to mind when one has read the history of Bossuet: it is less the story of the private man than the moral history of the age in which he lived. And in this connection, we can say that Bossuet's life is the century of Louis XIV put on stage.

In truth, this work enables us to judge the importance that the public and the government then attached to the moral life, with what respect and what gravity they treated all related matters, and the place that the doctrine and ministers of religion occupied in society. Louis XIV, twenty-three years old and beset by all the temptations of youth, of court, and of power the reins of which he had just taken, hears Bossuet in the pulpit for the first time. The king's great sense divines the genius of the man who will make his reign famous, and he has a letter written to the *father of the young orator so as to congratulate him on having such a son*. Today we are confounded with astonishment when we see the most famous names of a brilliant court renounce the hopes or illusions of youth, birth, fortune, and beauty to seek the obscurity of the cloister, with the weaker sex embracing the more austere rule. Worldly fame and genius humbled themselves before the sublime dogmas and severe morals of Christianity. Racine expiated his dramatic masterpieces by the long silence of his pen, just as La Vallière expiated her weaknesses in retreat and mortification. Corneille punished himself for having written *Polyeucte* and *Cinna* by translating the *Imitation of Christ* into humble verse.

Men highly distinguished by birth and position but tangled in the brambles of life came to Bossuet to clear up their doubts or correct their errors. "The women most celebrated for their minds," as Bossuet's biographer tells us, "made the most serious discussions the object of their studies, and gained from them a wisdom that honored their intelligence as much as their zeal. At that time, one was ashamed to listen to discourses that excited violent debates and led to important results without seeking to know, at least to some extent, the reasons and authorities presented by the defenders of the opposing opinion."

It must be understood that this was a more solid nourishment for the mind than what is sought today in frivolous and culpable reading. The reason that governs the affairs of private individuals as well as those of nations, strengthens itself by works. Even if these lofty discussions do not always result in very distinct ideas, they leave serious and salutary impressions in the heart.

Religious disputes were affairs of state in the century of Louis XIV. I am aware of the aspersions that have been cast upon these deplorable quarrels in which stubborn innovators and weak administrations too often caused irritation or trouble, more than once pulling governments outside their bounds and minds far from moderation. Religious controversies are an evil, but religious indifference is a still greater one. The hard and fierce fanaticism of the Wars of Religion caused infinite evils to France over two centuries; this I know. Yet the most voluptuous doctrines, the most attractive moral lassitude and disdain or forgetfulness of religion in a society whose only care is pleasure—in a word, games, favors, and laughter—have brought us in less than fifty years to the most complete delirium, the most bloody revolution, the total upheaval of society, and the general disorganization of Europe—all because we wanted to treat serious things lightly and to make frivolous things important affairs.

In the age of Bossuet, however, there was an earnestness in thought, work, and even in manners. Politeness was ceremonious, and even in the bosom of families, there was tenderness without over-familiarity. The different classes of citizens carefully preserved their vices and their virtues, without contaminating the latter by the former. There did not yet exist that communication among the different professions which destroyed them by inspiring the inferior classes with a disdain for their lower position and a taste for the ruinous vices and the luxury that is one of the duties of high station, while the great themselves, forgetting their position in the social order, descended to easy vices, shallow pleasures, and to duties that would not impinge upon their private lives.

Bossuet was born in an honorable family of the judiciary, then still a sort of priesthood as decent and as serious as the other. "We are well aware," says Monsieur de Bausset, "how in those days these two bodies were considered by educated men, and how they lent natural support to the defense of religion and public morals. Confined to the duties of their estate, the majority of magistrates and of ecclesiastics remained strangers to the changes and frivolity of the world, in which their presence would have seemed out of place."

The spectacle of the morals, the occupations, and the habits of these respectable families struck Bossuet as soon as he was able to see them. Woe to the society that does not see this first instruction by example as one of the most powerful means for the direction of a man's youth, even of his whole life!

Monsieur de Bausset, who has carefully gathered all that might shed light on the life of his hero, has made use of the family book in which Bossuet's father and grandfather inscribed the birth of their children and wrote several pious words expressing a touching sensibility, and often prophecies (or perhaps merely their wishes) about the destiny that awaited them. Christian families faithfully observed this custom and in this way handed on from generation to generation the tradition of religious sentiments and the memory of paternal affection. Bossuet's birth was marked by these prophetic words from *Deuteronomy*: "The Lord has deigned to serve as guide to him; he has led him by many paths; he has instructed him in his law; he has preserved him like the apple of his eye."

Bossuet studied first at the Jesuit school in Dijon, then in Paris at the College de Navarre. Today, the highest class of society pretends to give its children a more liberal education by keeping them in the paternal house amidst all the distractions of the world and, at great cost, confiding them to the cares of a philosophical tutor who, after having given them a smattering of ancient literature and a more extensive familiarity with modern works, and after having taken them on the obligatory tour of Switzerland and Italy, throws them into the world, lacking both knowledge and principles.

Back then the great sent their children to colleges where they were educated with the children of other citizens. These first school friendships, the most lasting of all, had no small influence on the reciprocal sentiments of the different classes of society. The great Condé was raised at the College of Bourges as if he had been the son of a simple gentleman, without any other distinction than a carriage a bit larger than that of his fellow students.

"When reading the history of the College of Navarre," Monsieur de Bausset tells us, "one is struck by the long train of princes, the great, and lords who were sent there to receive the first smattering of the sciences and letters, without the splendor of their titles and the elevation of their rank being able to free them from the institution's strict and severe regime. They did not then know all those premature distractions that parties, spectacles, and the misguided tenderness of parents have hurried to offer to the youth."

Bossuet's education and its results give rise to some further observations.

In the era when Bossuet and all the great men of his day began their careers, only colleges directed by religious existed in France. Bossuet and his illustrious contemporaries were formed in provincial monastic institutions where only Greek, Latin, and religion were taught. These true philosophers studied no other philosophy than that scholasticism in which our modern ideology has seen nothing but useless and unintelligible abstractions.

The literary models were the ancient writers, sacred or profane. The works that the century of Louis XIV created—those works, as classic to us, and perhaps still more classic than those of the ancients, because they are written in our own language and with our thoughts—then existed only in the genius of their authors, and studious youths were reduced, for the moderns, to several lines of Malherbe, or to the writings of Montaigne, whom the best minds of this century disdain for his cynicism and his vain and skeptical philosophy.

And we, with the help of literary institutions then unknown, with academies, atheneums, public and private instruction, and academic prizes multiplied more by vanity and private interest than by true interest in letters, we who with a deeper understanding of antiquity (or at least a longer enjoyment of its masterpieces) and the benefit of the *Grand Siècle*'s immortal works, how is it that we have been so unworthy of its authors? Are our minds weaker? Is nature worn out? No, society has changed. Nature, if the comparison be permissible, is the father of the mind, but society is its mother and nourishes its talent. The seeds that she receives from nature she develops with greater or lesser success, and she gives them a direction more or less happy, according to her own disposition and temperament, and according to the mind that directs her. Under Louis XIV, society was occupied with religion and morals, with lofty and serious things, and thus it offered substantial nourishment to good minds. The sacred books, the Fathers of the Church, and several authors of antiquity were sufficient to produce the writers, orators, philosophers, moralists, and poets who adorned this beautiful era of the human mind, and that literature, so earnest even in the most common genres and the least substantial subjects.

The society that succeeded it—dissipated, scornful, irreligious, frivolous, and occupied only with intrigues, pleasures, and money—had all the models of antiquity as well as the masterpieces of the previous century, yet was only able to make geometers, physicians, and naturalists. For, while the century of Louis XIV had its geometers and physicians, and the eighteenth century its celebrated writers, it is the eloquence of poetry that distinguishes the seventeenth century from all others, while the progress of the physical sciences is the most glorious title of the succeeding century. And if we count as belonging to the century of Louis XIV those men and works of the eighteenth century that still belonged to it (those who lived before 1740), those that remain are not above righteous reproach. Voltaire, in the last part of his literary life, was a dangerous and culpable wit. Jean-Jacques Rousseau was a sophist who fought the whole world as well as himself. Montesquieu would have been less indulged in Louis XIV's age than in our own, and his style would not have earned pardon for his errors. Should these same men have been born into the century of Louis XIV and raised in that strong society, they would have marched as the equals of the best geniuses of that era; but their misfortune, or our own, was that they wished to make themselves doctors of morals and politics in a society that could only produce experts in physics. With the morals and the mind of the century of Louis XIV, we too should raise up Bossuets and Corneilles. Nature is inexhaustible and always fertile, but either society does not assist nature, in which case good minds are wasted, or she acts to the contrary, and there appear dangerous talents who destroy the womb that bears them.

But I have strayed from Monsieur de Bausset.

A good work on useful men or necessary things is a benefit to society, and we owe this and many other benefits to the restoration of a king to whom truth is no reproach, nor history satire.

The *History of Fénelon* appeared at the beginning of the tyranny; a while later and it would have been banned, and the *History of Bossuet* would never have seen the light of day. Be that as it may, it is a happy portent for the century of the Restoration, that it open under the auspices of Bossuet, with his history beginning a new era and his biographer reminding us of his good moral doctrines and true literary principles. Although his lessons have long been neglected, when Bossuet reappears in our midst it seems that the interval that separates us from the great man disappears, and that we hear him once more address the heads of nations with those prophetic words that he spoke in vain upon the burial of the Queen of England: *Et nunc, reges, intelligite, erudimini qui judicatis terram.* "And now, o kings, take heed. Instruct yourselves, you judges of the earth."

It is difficult to make an extract of a historical work that is itself an extract, and that offers us neither a system to discuss, nor a criticism to explain. Monsieur de Bausset wished to make Bossuet known in all his facets, to complete the picture of him whom men of the world and even literary types regard simply as the most eloquent of our orators, thus admiring only that part of his writing to which Bossuet himself—well above all the weakness of intellectual pride or the failings of self-love—attached the least importance, and which he did not even take great care to publish. Today, as we publish his orations even for schoolchildren, it is well to recall that Bossuet did not publish his funeral orations, and that the majority of these works appeared only after his death. I will therefore imitate the historian's example, and, in order to make known Bossuet's works, I will make known the hero. As to the style, it is nearly everywhere so easy, clear, elegant, and noble that I am sorely tried by the difficulty of too many choices. I am tempted to transcribe whole passages rather than to cite small bits. I resign myself to the sad task of scraping only a few commas and periods from this great and worthy work.

Nothing better proves the secret and necessary attachment of religious and political society, of the analogy that exists between their constitutive principles and the influence that they exert on one another, than to see the innovators of the sixteenth century forced to reform in politics at the same time as they reformed in religion. The exigencies of political controversy made Bossuet a publicist in spite of his wish to be only a theologian.

It is not our place to discuss Bossuet's merits as a theologian; or, rather, it is no one's place. Bossuet has been judged. His contemporaries proclaimed him, while he was alive, to be a Father of the Church, and this title, which he shares with so many marvelous intellects, has been confirmed by the general sentiment of Christian Europe.

Yet in political matters, where Bossuet has the same genius, he does not hold the same authority. He belongs to that class of writers whose opinions can be examined by those who have particularly studied the constitution of societies.

Bossuet loses nothing even under such scrutiny. Politician or theologian, he is always Bossuet, just as profound, concise, and luminous in his reasoning as he is fertile, majestic, and captivating in his oratory. This great man seems to me to have united what might be called the two extremes of the human mind: the most earnest dialectic and the most animated eloquence.

If Bossuet's polemical theology has aged and is in some ways outdated because of the silence of his adversaries and because the most recent variations of their doctrine are now a century old, his political thought is timely. We may even say that he fought against a political style, for when nations have been unable to retain their habits, they replace them by styles, ceaselessly changing them as they seek for what they have lost.

Thus Bossuet is no less profound as a publicist as he is great as a theologian. Eternal teacher of society, after having taught religion to his own century, he can teach politics to our own.

When the Reformation had freed the peoples from all exterior and visible religious authority by attributing to each of the faithful the right and ability to interpret the books that are the deposit of our religious and moral doctrine, it necessarily incited the peoples against political authority by attributing to each subject the right and power to be a part of the sovereign. For if man need not recognize any authority over his thoughts other than one his reason may judge, why should he submit to any authority over his actions other than his own will?

Germany propagated the new religious doctrines in the north of Europe and even in France. They penetrated England, where a constitution that had been popular for a long time was marvelously fitted to the popular principles of the new religions. England, in her turn, spilled forth onto the Continent the new political principles, and Buchanan's *Jus regni* in Scotia and Hubert Languet's *Junius Brutus* established these as dogmas:

"That the people makes the sovereign and grants sovereignty."

"That it is contrary to reason that a people subjects itself to a sovereign without some contract, and that if it did the treaty would be null because contrary to nature."

"That the people does not stand in need of reasons to validate its acts."

According to Bossuet, these are "principles so excessive that they were detested by the most able men of the Reform." Yet from them have the philosophers of our century, less able and less moderate men, made the new code of societies.

"[Bossuet's] fifth *Admonition to the Protestants*," says Monsieur de Bausset, "is perhaps the most beautiful treatise of politics that has ever been offered to the meditation of statesmen and to all those who, without aspiring to that preeminence of opinion and renown, love to listen to the voice of reason and those eternal maxims hallowed by the experience of centuries for the repose of societies."

"The *Admonition* concerns one of the greatest questions that has ever been disputed among men: what form of government does Providence ordain? Bossuet undertakes to examine whether the foundation of empires reposes on the authority of kings or, as the Protestants claim, on the will of the people."

Monsieur de Bausset does not say enough, for Bossuet does not place the foundation of society on the authority of kings. He declares this authority to emanate from the very will of God, for kings are the lieutenants and ministers of God, accountable only to Him for the use they make of their power. Thus the question is whether we seek the foundation of power in the sovereignty of God over man, or in the sovereignty of man over his fellows.

In the fifth *Admonition*, Bossuet opposes the idea of the sovereignty of man or of the people (an idea of which we have had such a terrible experience) with such genius and ability that when one compares what the philosophers of our day have written in favor of this view, one is embarrassed for one's own century and nation. One is ashamed that cleverness has triumphed over genius, and passion over good sense.

Bossuet defended the independent power of kings in all of his works, believing this form of government most fit to assure the happiness of peoples and the stability of states. This is not surprising. Nourished from infancy by the truths of religion, he was accustomed to seek the model of social perfection in the sacred books, where he also found the true model of oratorical perfection. He saw the Decalogue as the source of all laws, and the accidents of Hebraic society, constituted by God himself, as an example for all societies. The account of society's origin found in the books of Moses he took to be true because it conforms to both reason and experience. Mankind descended from a first family. Families multiply themselves, are held together by descent and by community of locale and needs, and form tribes in which an elder, under the modest title of judge, settles differences, unites the wills, and directs the powers. Tribes, eventually joined together through alliances, treaties, and sometimes by conquest, become nations. In this final stage of society, monarchical government arises as the only government that can preserve the tribes and that retains in this last development of the social body all the independence of the paternal power that existed at the beginning.

To these sentiments, or, if you wish, to these prejudices in favor of the independence of the monarchical power, Bossuet joined accusations against popular government, accusations rendered stronger by recent events that have filled Europe with horror and fright. All were then aware of England's troubles, especially the judicial murder of Charles I by political institutions wracked by sectarian fury. Bossuet had made an eloquent meditation upon them in the funeral oration of the spouse of this unfortunate prince and could not but dread the form of government that permitted a people thus to act against its king. He dreaded "that principle of rebellion hidden in the heart of the people, that cannot be uprooted except by entirely removing, at least from the individuals, however many they may be, all thought of relying upon force, or of any remedy against the public power other than prayers and patience."

"It is a great error," he said, in that style at once so simple and so strong, "to believe that sovereign power may be limited only by placing another sovereign power above it. What you wish to render incapable of doing evil will thus be made incapable of doing good, and, rather than limit the power by the force that you place over it, the most natural way to prevent it from oppressing you is to make it be concerned with your salvation."

Bossuet's noble genius seems to have perceived this beautiful ideal—the eternal support of courageous souls and lofty minds—uniquely in the simple and natural ideas of a divine and paternal royalty whose power consisted in mildness and force, obedience, affection, and respect, and for whom to govern was a duty and to be governed a right.

Yet if Bossuet spoke to the people of their duties towards their kings, he spoke no less forcefully to kings of their obligations towards Him from whom they held their power: "I do not call majesty," he said,

> that pomp that surrounds kings, or that exterior splendor that dazzles the low-born. This is the reflection of majesty, and not majesty itself. Majesty is the image of God's grandeur in the prince. The prince, as a prince, is not regarded as a private individual, but as a public person. The whole state is in him, and the will of all the people is contained in his own. So much grandeur for one man! The power of God makes itself felt in an instant from one end of the world to the other; the royal power acts at the same time throughout the kingdom. It holds the whole kingdom in its estate, just as God holds the whole world. Let God pull back his hand, and the world will return to nothingness. Let authority cease

in the kingdom, and everything will be in confusion. Bring together all that is greatest and most august; see an immense people united in one person; see this sacred power, paternal and absolute; see the hidden reason that governs the whole body of the state contained in one sole head: here you see the image of God and you have an idea of the majesty of royalty. Yes, God has said it: You are Gods. Yet O gods of flesh and blood, O gods of mud and dust, you will die like other men! O kings, boldly wield your power, for it is divine and good for mankind, but wield it with humility, for it is given to you from elsewhere and, in the end, it leaves you weak, it leaves you mortal, and it charges you before God with a greater task.

Now, in declaring himself for the independent power of kings, Bossuet did not, his historian tells us, "examine in a general manner what is the best form of government, nor did he censure or condemn any of the forms of government that ordered the ancient or modern nations." I believe it: such political discussions did not enter into Bossuet's plan, and they had not yet become necessary. The example of England tempted no nation, and, in spite of the germs of democracy spread around Europe by the concessions won by the Reform at the treaty of Westphalia, religious ideas about the authority of kings still had great force, even in England. Nevertheless, it must not be believed that Bossuet remained indifferent to these great questions. In his *Discourse on Universal History*, while speaking of the political institutions of Greece, he said: "I do not examine whether these institutions were as wise as they are falsely said to have been. . . . [I]n the end, Greece led a charmed life." Thus he said clearly enough that he found them more fair-seeming than truly reasonable. In the fifth *Admonition*, he said: "I avenge the rights of kings and of all sovereign powers, for they are all equally attacked, if it is true, as one pretends, that the people everywhere rule, and that the popular state, *which is the worst of all,* be the basis of all states." Elsewhere he proves that the most common, the most ancient, and the most natural government is monarchy. Consequently we may believe that Bossuet would have ranged the diverse degrees of goodness of political institutions between democracy, the worst of all states, and monarchy, which seemed to him the best, according to whether they approached or distanced themselves from one or the other of these two extreme forms of government.

Monsieur de Bausset adds: "We may suppose that if Bossuet had been born in a republic, he would have been the most zealous citizen, just as he was the most obedient subject of the monarchy." A man of the Church, Bossuet would have been a peaceful citizen even in a popular state, if it be possible to be peaceful in a state that is not. I believe that it is, but I dare not affirm it of Bossuet. If he were a statesman in a popular state, I believe he would have felt himself hemmed in. Vulgar men, who do not have enough moral force to govern alone, nor enough moderation to remain in their place, form a party in order to dominate together, just as timid travelers do to cross a forest; this is what is done in all republics. Yet men of strong mind and character do not consent to live in a popular state except to make their power prevail, and, if circumstances favor them, to restrict that of others. Like Caesar, Cromwell, and so many others, if they flatter the people, it is to make them servile. Cicero himself, to whom experience gave sentiments that he might not otherwise have found in himself, became so disgusted with popular government that he said: *"Mihi nihil unquam populare placuit."*[2]

Be that as it may, when all the governments want constitutions (I do not say written ones, but outdated ones), they require stronger administrations, and the weaker are men's temperaments, the more severe must the regime be. A constitution is order in things, but an administration is order among men. The more men multiply, the more points of contact there are among them, the more difficult it becomes for administrations to conciliate so many interests and to

---

[2] "Nothing popular ever pleases me."

contain so many passions. Now, without speaking of the general or local causes which tend to increase the population in Europe and to keep people there, let me say that modern people are in a particular position in this regard and that it constitutes a difference between them and the people of antiquity that has yet gone unnoticed.

Never did the most populous ancient societies, or even the Roman Empire, have as many men in the state as do our great monarchies in Europe. The slaves, then such a great part of the total population, were governed despotically by their masters and therefore belonged entirely to the family and were neither considered nor counted as subjects of the state. Moreover, because of the stronger constitution of the family and the weaker one of the public powers, women and children were much less in the state than they are today, as were the domestic servants who replaced the slaves. Christianity has called all men to the liberty of the children of God, has restored to man his primitive and natural dignity, even those weakest in age, sex, or condition, has restored to human nature its just rights, and, without weakening the legitimate subordination of the members of the family to the domestic power, has made the family with all its members pass into the state.

On the other hand, Christianity has initiated children into the highest moral truths. The knowledge of them has spread even to the lowest classes of society. Their minds elevated and their ignorance dissipated, they have become more able to seize the truth, and, by this, also more disposed to fall into errors, which are never other than incomplete truths. There are, therefore, in our public society, that is to say in our state, more minds and more bodies, and, consequently, our administrations require more moral force for the direction of minds and more physical force to contain the bodies. Moral force is all in religion and cannot be elsewhere: thus, when political authority is strong, religious authority must not be weak. Truly it would be a sad compensation to offer people weak religion in return for strong government, for society suffers equally when the government is stronger than religion and when it is weaker. In the former case morals are not strong enough to support the police, and in the latter case there are not enough police to support morals.

Thus, if in this way the Christian religion has multiplied the cares of administration for governments by spreading enlightenment and by making members of the state those who were previously only members of the family, in another way it has made the action of governments easier and milder, by teaching men principles of obedience towards those who govern and, above all, sentiments of love and fidelity that were unknown to the ancients. Power has become paternity, ministry service, and public station filial dependence. This change in the state of nations has even extended to the relations of peace and good neighborliness among peoples, even to the waging of war. Our modern public law is, to follow Montesquieu, "a benefit of the Christian religion that human nature cannot adequately repay."

Thus, those of us who govern and those of us who are governed owe everything to religion, everything that has produced security in the former and a just liberty in the rest. We particularly owe it that reciprocal confidence, that mutual indulgence that allows governments to pardon the faults of the ignorance or inconstancy of the people without endangering their stability, and that allows the people, without endangering their liberty, to pardon their government for the inevitable and involuntary errors of administration. It is as easy to govern with religion as it is difficult or impossible to govern without it. We owe it everything: force, reason, virtue, enlightenment, personal and public liberty. When we prefer to it a philosophy that by the laxity of its opinions and the softness of its maxims has incited men to revolt and has forced governments into despotism, we are ingrates and fools who have abandoned a spouse who made our fortune to run off with a courtesan who ruins us.

In Bossuet's time, philosophy was the science of moral beings, of God and man. In our days, God has been restricted to theology, physiology has taken up the charge of explaining the soul, and philosophy has seen itself reduced almost exclusively to the knowledge of material things. Thus we have seen chemical philosophy, zoological philosophy, botanical philosophy, and so on.

It is, however, difficult to discover what these kinds of knowledge can have in common with the love and study of wisdom. They are, if you will, accessories to the science of man, inasmuch as they serve his needs and extend his enjoyments. They can be counted for something in the study of the first cause, whose omnipotence and goodness they make manifest to us. Yet they cannot constitute philosophy by themselves, and, separated from moral science, they are but a dead letter, a vain spectacle for curiosity, and even food for luxury and the passions.

I even believe that a people exclusively devoted to the study of material things—which improve no other faculty than the student's memory—will eventually become inferior to other peoples with respect to the mind, reason, and other social qualities. They will lose in the moral sciences what they gain in physical knowledge. They may be able to conduct their own proper affairs, but they will more and more trouble those of their neighbors. There will be more calculation in their heads than there will be order in their minds and sentiments of justice in their hearts. They will *make* better than they will *compose*. Their mercantile commerce will be able to flourish, but their social commerce will be little agreeable.

Bossuet wrote the *Knowledge of God and of Oneself*, yet this work, undertaken for the education of the dauphin, was only printed posthumously. This late publicity, the theological title of the work, and even the name Bossuet, which is more famous as a theologian than as a philosopher, have misled many about the classic utility of this treatise, and it is not as well known in the schools as it deserves to be. Bossuet had first given it the title *Introduction to Philosophy*, but regrettably he did not keep this title, which would have suited it much better, and under which it would have been earlier and more widely known. Authorship of the *Treatise on the Knowledge of God and Oneself* was first attributed to Fénelon. That great cleric left among his papers a copy given to him by Bossuet for the instruction of the duke of Burgundy. It would be difficult to find, either in the name of the masters or in the quality of the students, a more sure and authentic guarantee of the merits of the work. Monsieur de Bausset has written approvingly about the *Treatise on the Knowledge of God and Oneself,* and he thus begins the important task of recommending those charged with philosophical education the work of the *Grand Siècle* that contains the most useful and practical notions of true philosophy.

In his letter to Innocent XI, Bossuet set out his ideas of and principles for moral instruction, and about the education of mind and heart that is fitting for a prince. "Logic and morals," he said,

> serve to cultivate the two principal operations of the human mind: the faculties of understanding and willing. For logic, we have drawn from Plato and Aristotle, not so as to serve vain disputes about words, but to form the judgment by solid reasoning, and we have restricted ourselves primarily to that part of logic that is used to find probable arguments, because these are the ones used in affairs of state.
>
> For the teaching of morals, we have mined the proper source: Scripture and the maxims of the Gospel. We have not, however, neglected to explain the morals of Aristotle, and that admirable doctrine of Socrates, truly sublime for his time, which may serve to give faith to the incredulous, and to make corrupt men blush.
>
> Yet we have at the same time noted what the Christian philosophy condemns in it, and what she adds to it, what she approves, and with what authority she confirms the sane maxims of Socrates, and how she is superior to them, in such a way that the philosophy of Socrates, as grave as it appears, compared to the wisdom of the Gospel is but the infancy of morals.
>
> As to philosophy, we have cleaved to those maxims

that carry with them the certain character of truth, and which might be useful for the conduct of human life. As to the systems and philosophical opinions that are subjects for the vain disputes of men, we have limited ourselves to reporting them under the form of an historical recital, for we have thought that it was fitting to the dignity of a young prince to know the diverse and opposed opinions that have much occupied the great minds, while equally protecting the parties and refusing to share their enthusiasm or their prejudice. The one who is called to command should learn to judge and not to dispute.

Yet after having considered that philosophy consists above all in recalling the mind to itself in order then to raise one's thoughts to God, we have first sought self-knowledge. This preliminary study, by presenting us with fewer difficulties, at the same time offers our researches the most useful and most noble end: for, to become a true philosopher, man must study himself, and without losing himself in the useless and puerile attempt to learn what others have said and thought, he need but seek into and ask questions of himself, and he will thus find the one who has given him the ability to be, to know, and to will.

Here is Monsieur de Bausset's account of Bossuet's inspiration for his admirable *Treatise on the Knowledge of God and Oneself*:

This work, whose only fault may be that it exceeded the limits of the intelligence of a child to whom nature neither gave a great liveliness of imagination nor a desire to learn that would complete an otherwise happy disposition, is one of those most worthy for the meditation of men conscious of their reason and aware of their dignity.

Never has any ancient or modern philosopher worthy of the thoughts of men professed a doctrine more simple in its exposition, better demonstrated in its proofs, more satisfying in its results, and more consoling in its hopes. What a remarkable thing! Bossuet, always so eloquent and so magnificent when he wishes to speak to the soul and the imagination, employs only the simplest and most accessible expressions when he wished to speak to the reason. He knows that clarity depends not only on the order of the ideas, but above all upon their expression.

Malebranche seduced the imagination with his brilliantly colorful style because he was creating a system. Bossuet simply expressed himself with clarity, because he desired only to show forth the truth.

It seems to me that there is something in this last phrase worth taking up again, and that the opposition between Bossuet and Malebranche is not an exact one. In upholding the truth Bossuet certainly did not wish and did not believe himself to be making a system, but Malebranche, in making what we call a system, wished and believed himself to be upholding the truth. Bossuet kept himself to known facts; Malebranche struck out into the realm of hypotheses. Bossuet only made use of the faculty of mind that describes; Malebranche had need of the one that discovers, and, as he presented new ideas or made new connections, he colored his designs so that we might take note of his objects and recognize them. Bossuet, particularly suspicious of the system of Malebranche, was not opposed to systems in general, inasmuch as we have seen that he thought it the duty of a prince to protect the defenders of them. At bottom, Bossuet himself, in his *Treatise on the Knowledge of God and Oneself,* only explains and unfolds an already existing system, the system of man. Malebranche wanted to make a new one, the one of human intelligence, and of its cooperation with the supreme intelligence, the source and light of all others. A system is a voyage to the land of truth; but all voyagers, even those who become lost, discover some new point of view, and their errors warn those who come after them to take another route. "This curiosity," said Fénelon,

> is inseparable from human reason, and it is because human reason is limited, while the divine reason is not. This curiosity in itself is not evil, for it comes from what is most excellent in our nature. For if to know everything is only proper to the one who has made everything, man approaches Him as much as he can by desiring to know everything. We know that this great and beautiful desire has been, in the wise men of all ages, the sentiment of their nobility and the presentiment of their immortality.

Bossuet did not depart from these sentiments of Fénelon, inasmuch as he recognized that systems had occupied many great minds. They did not, however, occupy his own, and this celebrated man had no more of that spirit of system that seeks when there is still more to discover than he had of that systematic spirit that seeks even after one has already found—the particular malady of our age, which is only the restlessness of weakness. Three kinds of minds are necessary in the world of human knowledge: the mind that discovers, the mind that cultivates, and the mind that fights and defends. Bossuet had to the highest degree, and to a degree that perhaps no one else has equaled, that third kind of mind, and all his life, the sword and the buckler of the moral world, he was occupied with ridding society of those opinions which after his death and under other standards have invaded our frontiers and even penetrated to the heart of our state. Amidst this hard-fought battle, Bossuet could not have dreamed of new conquests. One must defend one's land before pushing back the frontiers. Moreover, in the moral world as in the physical, discoveries are only to be made at the poles, the metaphysical poles, that is. The morals that are busy in the interior, and, so to speak, in the inhabited world, are completely known, and supposed discoveries in morals can only be dangerous illusions or deadly innovations.

This last reflection brings us back to Bossuet the historian. Monsieur de Bausset tells us that while reading the *Treatise on the Knowledge of God and Oneself,*

> with all the attention that was required by our role as historian of the life and works of Bossuet, a distressing reflection came upon us. The eighteenth century has seen England, France, and Germany produce numerous writers who showed the most deplorable determination to raze all the foundations of the natural, moral, religious, and political order, and we may confidently affirm that none of them ever read or reflected upon this work of Bossuet. We cannot, in truth, explain without this supposition how they could have presented so many extravagant systems already branded with the most just censure and the most profound disdain.

After having considered the soul, Bossuet considers the human body, and it is a remarkable singularity in the life of Bossuet to see him apply his mind, talent, and language to a science so novel to him and so strange to his habitual studies.

In this connection, Bossuet made a particular study of anatomy under the direction of the famous Duverney, who, according to Fénelon, put anatomy in fashion. "We have heard the most famous physicians," says Monsieur de Bausset, "declare that in spite of the profound inquiries that have taken the science of anatomy well beyond the place where it was a hundred and fifty years ago, there is no new discovery to contradict the different parts of Bossuet's exposition."

After having treated man, Bossuet treats God, and by a series of arguments drawn only from philosophy, and whose principles and their consequences hold together with the order and force befitting philosophical truths, he finishes by leading man to the very limits of human intelligence. There, he turns to revelation and leaves one in the arms of religion.

Bossuet did not believe that he should end his treatise on philosophy with the distinction between man and the beasts. We will limit ourselves, however, to citing this solitary and most just reflection:

> All the arguments that are made in favor of the animals reduce to two: animals do all things properly, just as man does, therefore they reason just as man does. Animals are similar to men on the exterior, both in their organs and in their actions, therefore they act by the same exterior principle and are capable of reasoning.
>
> Yet a simple observation suffices to show the failure of the first argument.
>
> It is one thing to do all things properly, it is another to sense fittingness. The first is true not only of animals, but of all things in the universe; the other is the true effect of reasoning and intelligence.
>
> Since the world is made by reason, everything must happen fittingly, for it is proper to an intelligent cause to order things and to place conduciveness to an end in all of its works.
>
> We love to praise the work of the swallow, who makes such a proper nest, and the bees, who construct their little hives with so much symmetry; the seeds of a seed-pod are no less well constructed, and yet we do not say that seed-pods have reason. One says that all is done fittingly by the animals, but this is still more true of plants. All of nature shows forth the truth that everything is done by intelligence, but not that everything is intelligent.

Such is this work, abounding in useful positive notions about the greatest objects that can occupy man in society. It should be placed in the hands of the young as the complement to their moral and literary studies, and a provision of reason and good sense for the conduct of their whole lives. The greatest number will go no further and will be happier and no doubt wiser for having read it. Others, spurred on by an active mind, will surpass it; they will wish to pass beyond the limits that Bossuet set for himself and his student, but which he nevertheless did not pose as the insurmountable limits of the human mind. They may stray a bit in those borderless regions that touch upon the limits of the world of sense and the world of intelligence, but their errors will not be dangerous so long as they retain the principles of all reasoning that Bossuet has traced with his firm hand, and which should be the result of any system, just as they are the beginning of every science. Thus the voyager, after having traversed faraway lands, fatigued by his often fruitless treks, will return with delight to repose in the shade of the paternal roof and in the places that were his childhood home.

Everything has long since been said about Bossuet and Fénelon as writers and orators; rhetoric has used up all its flowers in decorating the parallel between the Eagle of Meaux and the Swan of Cambrai. It would be more interesting and more novel to compare their political opinions and their personal characters. Modern philosophy has taken the lead; without knowing their lives or even their works it has hastened to judge them, and not daring to contest with Bossuet for the palm of genius, it has attributed to his rival every amiable quality and social virtue. It is easier to divine the motives for this partiality than to justify it. Those who for the past century have bribed all the writers and made all the reputations dread Bossuet's victorious eloquence and, one might say, his infallible reason. It is not that Fénelon had different sentiments on these matters, but that his mind was less firm and less protected against illusions because his imagination dominated it. He was mistaken in an important question, of which the most able of the two parties had already foreseen the final consequences. And some have so willingly seen Fénelon defend these dangerous opinions that they have conceived a hatred against Bossuet for having struck them down. Thus, while women applaud the lively portrayal of the love of Telemachus and Eucharis, and the makers of political theories admire the utopias from Mentor to Salente, and even Fénelon's most sentimental rubbish and ridiculous stories have found their credulous partisans thanks to his sensibility, Bossuet, on the other hand, who offers in his life and work no error of imagination, no romantic episode, and no philanthropic trait to put in the newspapers, has been regarded as a hard, prideful, and inflexible man.

Fénelon's politics were dreary. Although a witness to the disasters of Louis XIV's last years, he understood neither their causes nor their remedies. Impatient for peace, he would not wait for that peace which must succeed the long agitation of Europe (which for strong states is like the repose of sleep after great bodily labors); rather, he sought it in constitutional change and even proposed a revolution as the proper response to a passing calamity. He wanted the Estates General to meet every three years. He promised that they would be peaceable and affectionate, and, on this guarantee, he permitted them to prolong their deliberations as long as they judged necessary. By this same project, put in execution eighty years later, France was lost. And, setting aside Fénelon's theological illusions, this great political error would suffice to justify the hard words of Louis XIV. For the rest, there are in these political memoirs some excellent ideas on administration, amongst others that are impractical.

Bossuet's politics were realist, absolute, and less liberal. Fénelon saw men as he wished them to be. Bossuet saw society as it was and always will be. Fénelon's politics were the product of the imagination and desires of a virtuous soul. Bossuet's politics were the product of reason and experience.

As to Bossuet's personal character, Monsieur de Bausset has thoroughly refuted the calumnious accusations that have been so long and so stubbornly made against him about his part in the measures of Louis XIV against religious dissidents. The Protestants of his day, more equitable than the philosophers of our own, openly did justice to his moderation and declared that he had only employed evangelical means to persuade them of his religion.

Bossuet was mild in the commerce of life, while Fénelon was grave. Neither had more unction than the other, and, while Fénelon was a metaphysician, Bossuet was more often an orator, so the latter more frequently had occasion to put sentiment and unction in his writings.

For the rest, the philosophic party has equally disfigured the character of both: it has made Bossuet firm to the point of harshness, Fénelon mild to the point of weakness. Bossuet had his mildness and Fénelon his strength, but weak souls, who, for being weak, are no less unjust, no less prejudiced, and no less full of hatred, understand the mildness of a strong soul no better than they do the strength of a mild one.

THOUGHTS ON
VARIOUS SUBJECTS (1817)

Just as society is first a family and then a state, so the instruction of men had to begin with proverbs and end with thoughts. The proverb is a maxim of conduct applied to the moral or material government of a family, and the moral tale or fable is nothing other than a maxim or sometimes even a proverb dressed in a familiar image. Thoughts have a more general object, and should offer rules of opinion or conduct for men united in the society of a state, that is, a public society; they are at once fitting for men who are busier and minds that are more reflective. They are in teaching what analysis is in geometry and what bank notes are for the circulation of money. On the one hand, they reduce a great number of ideas to a briefer expression, and on the other, they offer general formulas that may be applied to a large number of circumstances. This is what moral and political thoughts should be, and I think that it is easier to define than to create them.

Even after the example of France, Europe lacks one last lesson. Woe to the people destined to give it to her!

Religion put the monarchy in our hearts. Philosophy pulled it out and put it in our heads. It had been sentiment; now it is a system, and society has gained nothing.

A government should do little for the pleasures of the people, enough for their needs, and everything for their virtues.

The agricultural state, the first condition of man, is essentially monarchical. The territorial property is a little kingdom, governed by the will of the head and the service of the subordinates. Thus the Gospel, which is the code of societies, often compares the kingdom to the agrarian family. The good sense or habits of an agrarian people are much closer to the best and most sane political ideas than are any of the idle minds in our cities, whatever be their knowledge in the arts and physical sciences.

Farmers live in peace, and can have neither rivalry nor competition among one another. Merchants are in a necessary conflict of interests with one another. We might say that the farmer, who leaves each to his own land, unites men without bringing them together, and that commerce, which shuts men up in cities and puts them in continual relations, brings them together without uniting them.

When the state is monarchical, the cities are and must be popular states. The monarchical authority would be too much felt there, because there the subject is too close to the political power. Thus formerly in France we mocked mayors, judges, and even regional governors, yet business did not suffer for it. But when modern politics wished to bring the popular regime into the state, it had to give mayors and prefects despotic authority.

For the inferior classes, the corporations of arts and trades were a sort of hereditary municipal nobility that gave importance and dignity to the most obscure individuals and the least exalted professions. These corporations were at the same time confraternities, and this is what excited the hatred of the *philosophes* who hunted down religion even in its most modest manifestations. This monarchical institution brought great benefits to administration. The power of the masters restrained youths who lacked education, who had been taken away from paternal authority at an early age by the necessity to learn a trade and win their bread, and whose obscurity hid from the public power. Finally, the inheritance of the mechanical professions also served public morals by posing a check to ruinous and ridiculous changes of fashion.

Happy England, she has preserved her old sentiments alongside, or rather in spite of, her institutions. In France, we labored to remove our sentiments before changing our institutions. The English Revolution was an accident; ours was a system.

Wherever there are many machines to take the place of men, many men will be mere machines. The effect of machines, in sparing men, must be to diminish the population.

Religion must be considered in the statesman, and politics in the religious man: Suger, Ximenes, Richelieu never considered them separately.

What an exalted idea of royalty our fathers must have had, for they respected kings who walked among them lacking all the splendor that surrounds them today!

The English dismiss their women at dessert, and put them on the throne. In France, women are everything in the family and nothing in the state. In all things we were closer to nature, which, in making man for public concerns, made woman for domestic ones. This difference in fundamental principles explains the different destinies of the two peoples.

I believe that Aristotle's *Politics* is his worst work, and that attempts to explain the sense of it are doomed to fail. How could he have written well about politics when the whole world was divided into tyrants and slaves? His last translator said that we must be cautious in judging a man who studied 158 different constitutions, as if there were in fact more than two, one good and in conformity with the nature of man and society, one bad and against their natures, the former with unity of power, and the latter with a plurality of powers. Yet Aristotle and his translator take cities to be states, and police regulations to be constitutions.

The heredity of the throne is the guarantee of all heredity and the safeguard of all inheritances.

With his hand full of bank notes, a child may control the destiny of a whole kingdom. A wise policy, one more attentive to general interests than to private ones, would seek to render the circulation of money less rapid: in Sparta, by using iron money, in modern states, by the prohibition of lending at usury.

In olden days in France, our manners were lighthearted and our minds were serious. The Revolution changed all that. It made our minds superficial and our manners grave. Today we have neither reason nor joy.

Revolutions have proximate and material causes that capture the attention of the less attentive. These causes are really only occasions. The true causes, the profound and efficacious causes, are moral ones, which small minds and corrupt men fail to see. A shock, they say, a sudden storm has toppled the edifice: doubtless true. Yet the walls had long since lost their stability. You believe that a financial deficit was the cause of the Revolution. Dig deeper and you will find a deficit in the very principles of the social order.

The factories and workshops that pile up children of both sexes in hot and humid places alter the form of their bodies and corrupt their souls. From this, the family gains a little money, ill health, and vices, and the state a population that lives in the cabarets and dies in the hospitals.

Our tone of voice in conversation has become lower and our expression less frank and more studied to the point that we now have less good faith in our opinions and less strength of character. One might say that we not only fear to be understood, but even to be heard.

The monied men who display such a furious prejudice against the nobility must not realize that to the lower classes nobility is only wealth.

Nobility in France was, for the family, a hereditary devotion to public service, and for the individual, the exclusion from all mercantile professions.

Why is it contrary to civility to fix one's gaze upon someone without saying anything to him? It is to interrogate him without his being able to respond. Therefore the first thing done by one thus looked at is to ask what one wants of him. The eyes interrogate as well as respond: they test the soul, whose reflection they are.

Wise government should constitute the administration in such a way that individuals have the fewest possible occasions to ask favors, and the administration the fewest possible occasions to bestow them. When advancement is an effect of favor, men intrigue and become ignoble. The government chooses, it errs, and it is almost always the case that the malcontent is more dangerous than the favorite is useful. Thus one makes the different ranks in society a battle of ambition, instead of making them a career in which, as in life itself, the oldest walk in front. If society has need of young talents, nature will give birth to them and will know how to place them.

In a time when only graceful manners and charm are praised, one only finds strong characters, manly virtues, and solid minds by chance.

In the newspapers, immediately after the story of a battle that cost the lives of thirty or forty thousand men, or of a fire that consumed two-thirds of a town, or of an epidemic that carried away half the population, we read that Mademoiselle N., the celebrated diva, danced a delightful waltz with Monsieur N., the famous dancer, or that Madame M., the celebrated singer, is engaged at twelve thousand francs per concert in London, or that there was a ball or a gala at the house of such-and-such a prince. This juxtaposition of disasters and pleasures is harmful to the charity of a Christian people, and even to the philanthropy of the *philosophes*. We must tell of the miseries common to all men in order to call upon charity and make men remember their condition, but we should keep silent our pleasures, so as not to awaken envy and afflict the miserable.

A republic is a society of private individuals who want to obtain power, just as a commercial society is an association of private individuals who want to make money. This identity of principles makes republics commercial and commerce republican.

Nothing is useful in the constitution of a state other than what is necessary to it. In olden days, one said the lord of Joinville, the lord Bertrand du Guesclin. The nobles often took no name other than the one that religion had given them at baptism, and no other decoration than their coat of arms. They were, nevertheless, of good families. One spoke collectively of the barons, or the baronage, when speaking of the nobles assembled before the king for counsel or judgment. Yet not one of them wore the trappings of a baron in his private life: the order was more and the individual less. If, later, one called kings "Majesty," it was only in the Latin idiom, in which this title, borrowed from the laws of the Roman emperors, was without consequence, and to Christians it seemed reserved to God alone. One called ministers neither "Milord" nor "Excellency." In sum, there was greater modesty in our customs, and consequently more equality among men. The accumulation and exaggeration of titles in states has always been a necessary accompaniment of despotism and an infallible sign of decadence. We have the proof of both in the Greek superlative *archi*, with which Bonaparte burdened the titles of the simplest of our ancient dignities. This and many other vanities were taken to the highest degree with the Greeks of the late empire, and modern people should have prohibited them.

Absolute liberty of the press is a tax upon those who read. It is demanded only by those who write.

A people shines in war, the arts, and its laws. Yet in a people who have arrived at a high degree of civilization or moral goodness, war, to be honorable, must be defensive; the arts, to be useful, must be chaste; the laws, to be good, must be perfect.

The cry "Liberty, equality, fraternity or death!" was much in vogue during the Revolution. Liberty ended by covering France with prisons, equality by multiplying titles and decorations, and fraternity by dividing us. Death alone prevailed.

Fashions change ceaselessly in a people that no longer has morals, in the broadest sense of the term.

Lofty sentiments, lively affections, and simple tastes make a man.

All things beautiful are severe.

The use of common things, temples, waters, woods, and pastures, constitutes the property of the community. Indeed, there is no more community where there is no longer a community of use. It may be true that the commons were poorly administered. I would even believe that their division, in some places, has produced a little more wheat. Yet in some lands this division hems in the movement of flocks and restricts them to spaces that are too small for them and thus ruins an important branch of agriculture. But more importantly, there is no more common property among the inhabitants of the same place, and, consequently, no more community of interests, no more occasions for deliberation and agreement. An example will allow my thoughts to be better understood. If there were only one public fountain in a village from which water was distributed to all the households, to take away the fountain would be to deny the inhabitants a continual occasion to see, speak, and hear one another. When opinions divide men, they should not be brought together. When need unites them, they should not be isolated.

In olden days in France, the clergy was the first body of the constitution, and the judiciary the first body of the administration. What a great and noble idea to have put religion and justice at the head of society!

The most beautiful monuments executed in Paris under Bonaparte's orders are the rue de Rivoli, the rue de la Paix, and la Place du Carrousel. For these, he had only to demolish, and he was in his element. This man decorated many things and even built many things, but he built neither palace nor church. This is an image of his fortune, by which he was denied to found anything either in politics or religion.

A mind employed to corrupt is nothing other than force employed to destroy.

It is difficult for the father of a family not to regard as a personal enemy the author of a bad book that brings corruption into the heart of his children.

Today every passion that is not for money, honor, or pleasure is called unreasonable and fanatical.

In every society there are more domestic sorrows to the extent that there are more public pleasures. In olden times, there was less pleasure and more happiness.

A man must read many books to furnish his memory, but when he wants to form solid taste and good style, he should read few of them, and they must all be the genre of his talent. The immense quantity of books makes us read more, and, among the society of the dead as among that of the living, an overextended acquaintance does not leave enough time for good friendships to form.

OBSERVATIONS UPON MADAME DE STAËL'S "CONSIDERATIONS" (1818)

ON THE REVOLUTION

From the first page of her *Considerations*, Madame de Staël[1] regards the French Revolution as having been inevitable. For my part, I believe that a revolution was no more inevitable in France in 1789 than it is in Austria today. But I prefer to let Madame de Staël refute herself: "One popular philosophy believes that everything that happens is inevitable; but what then would man's reason and liberty be for, if his will could not prevent what his will so visibly carries out?"

It is, however, true that the Revolution was inevitable once the three orders of the state were combined in one assembly with only one vote, for the excellent reason that the Revolution had already been accomplished and the old constitution already overturned. Like all the writers of her school, Madame de Staël makes much of the variations in the number of deputies at the meetings of the Estates General held at different times under

[1] Germaine de Staël (1766–1817) was one of the leading political figures in France under the Directory (1795–99). She was also an important literary figure, best known for her 1813 *On Germany*, a seminal work in the Romantic movement. Madame de Staël was the daughter of Jacques Necker (1732–1804), the Swiss banker who was Louis XVI's minister of finance from 1776 to 1781 and then prime minister from 1788 to 1790.

our monarchy. Yet the number of deputies did not and should not matter in the least. The constitution considered the orders of the state from a moral point of view and not in their physical quantity. In this way, when the third order was represented, even by only ten members, it became a person, deliberating equally with the other orders, even if they had a thousand representatives. These three public persons had each the same weight and the same veto in the deliberations. This seems very moral to me, and even very liberal; and the division into orders may even have fewer disadvantages than the division into parties. The variation of the number of deputies of the different orders was of no importance, and was therefore never even noticed in the past. And to this we should add that because the Estates General were most often convoked when the English were occupying our most beautiful provinces, their convocation was not even complete.

Madame de Staël forgets none of her emotions, and she willingly speaks of those brought to her by the convocation of the Estates General. She treats of the personages and their costumes, the unmannerly behavior of the recently ennobled, and the self-assured and imposing attitude of the Third Estate. Elsewhere she recalls what everyone, even then, had forgotten: the old custom, which had been the practice of the Third Estate, of kneeling while presenting petitions to the king. In truth, she should have said that the king of England is still approached with genuflection today. In Spain, the grandees put on their hats before the king. Will the liberals take more pride in the English custom than the Castilian one? Yet on that day, when Madame de Staël cried for joy at the prospect of so much felicity for France, Madame de Montmorin—not a bright woman—said to her in a decided tone: "You are wrong to rejoice. Great calamities for France and us will come from all this." In this, Madame de Staël saw a premonition. For those of us who are not so quick to believe in miracles, we might see how in political affairs it is better to have good sense than a quick wit.

Madame de Staël saw the Revolution as inevitable. This is to absolve Necker for the role he is said to have played in it. The

Revolution was inevitable, she says, because the French people were the most miserable and oppressed in the world. Such a claim also justifies the Revolution.

She takes this justification for the Revolution and Necker directly from Necker's own writings, from which she naively, and perhaps imprudently, quotes in her own. In his 1791 pamphlet *On Monsieur Necker's Administration*, he wrote: "Ah! If they were not so miserable and oppressed, how I would have to reproach myself!" The word "if" brings a measure of doubt into this exclamation, and by it Necker gives us a glimpse of his own regrets. But Madame de Staël does not include it in her quotation, so that Necker might not be left open to critique. Rather, she affirms boldly that the French were the most miserable and oppressed of any people.

I do not refute this assertion in order to denigrate our own times, but instead to render our kings and our nation the justice they are due and to show that our kings were good and humane, and that the nation was happy and grateful until, having been fed lies about its past misfortunes and illusions about its future happiness, it was cast into an abyss of suffering and crime.

Do we know what we mean when we speak of the misery and oppression of an entire people? The physical evils that can harm a people are plague, war, and famine. The last two of these scourges we have only known since the Revolution. Our old wars were between monarchs, not peoples; they were fought on the extreme frontiers, and more with the force of art and science than the force of men. These wars left things more or less as they were, the provinces with their capitals, the kings with the people's affection. For the nation they were but the exercise of its powers and not a cause of disaster or ruin. Moral evil is error. I do not believe that anyone would dare uphold the thesis that the French people, among whom were found the most brilliant models in all modes of thought, were less enlightened and more given to error than every other people in Europe. Yes, the French were miserable and oppressed, and from the most deadly and cruel oppression, the oppression of false doctrines and impious and seditious writings.

And for this, it is certain, the government has been punished enough that we may abstain from reproaching its memory. This oppression was the true cause of the Revolution and all of the crimes that have so appalled the world. If this is what Madame de Staël means to say, then I am entirely of her opinion. Yet she seeks oppression in different quarters, and her reasonings did not cost her a great deal of mental exercise. According to Madame de Staël, every people is miserable and oppressed when it is not free, and a people is not free except when it has a constitution like the English. Nor is a people virtuous except when it is free, and all the excesses of the French people are thus to be blamed upon the oppression under which they groaned. Thus, the French people were not miserable because they lacked a constitution, for this they certainly had, just as the states of Austria and Germany had one and were not accounted oppressed. No, the French were miserable because they did not have an English constitution. For her this proves that the English constitution is the best of all. Her argument ends where it should have begun.

Yet, in the end, we wish to know how the French people were so miserable and sorely oppressed. They paid taxes, it is true. But they still pay taxes, and some provinces now pay taxes from which they were previously exempt. Moreover, every people pays taxes, and, according to Montesquieu, taxes are higher in republics than they are in monarchies. The English pay higher taxes than any other people. Finally, now that the costs of royalty and the Church are to be borne entirely by the treasury, thanks to the sale of the public lands, we will pay taxes forever.

Again, we were liable for service in the militia. Yet in England they have impress gangs to round up unwilling sailors. How can we complain of the militia when they have thought it necessary to reestablish conscription?

Did we lack civil tribunals to judge our differences? Are not legal costs as high or higher than they were in the past? It is true that we did not have trial by jury in criminal affairs—which the liberals see as intolerable oppression. Yet to judge crimes by legal and positive proof is at least as philanthropic as to judge them by the mere conviction of the jury. If the juries have occasionally absolved those whom the judges would have condemned, I can assure you that the judges would have absolved some of those condemned by the juries. And certainly the elements that make up personal conviction are vague, arbitrary, and uncertain compared to the positive determination of legal proofs. Moreover, society is only oppressed with respect to criminal justice when the public prosecution is either too weak, too slow, or too few in number to punish crime. If one were to reproach our former judiciary, it would not be for their lack of vigilance and severity. Another alleged oppression is that criminal procedure was secret. Yet publicity given to trials, or rather to the pleas of the criminals, permits a lawyer to employ all his eloquence to attenuate a crime, and allows the public to listen to and to take long droughts of scandals for which, in their hearts, they too often find the secret motives. Is this publicity, so useful to save the accused in a bad affair, equally advantageous to public morals? Does it not too often degrade the noble profession of lawyer? Besides, no honest men have ever thought themselves oppressed by the form of criminal judgments employed in their country. This fear has never troubled the sleep of good men. If the French suffered for this reason, they were certainly unaware of it. Was respect for property anywhere carried further than in France? Was not everyone free to come and go as he pleased, even without a passport? And to devote himself to any kind of work, and to sleep in peace beneath the shadow of his vine and his fig tree?

Yet not all citizens were admissible to all offices. It is something to be admissible, but it is everything to be admitted. No more today than before are all citizens admitted to all offices. We will discuss this question further below, and we shall see that, even under this heading, there was more political liberty and equality in France than in any other state in Europe, even England.

But what about the tithe and feudal dues! These exist in England, but Madame de Staël does not mention it. I will not give the political reasons for them, which are understood in England, but no longer in our own country. To give only arguments taken from civil law, which our liberals understand better, I should say that if the tithe and feudal dues are bad for agriculture, they were no injustice or oppression for the landowners. All landowners in France since Charlemagne purchased their landed properties at a price that reflected the deduction of the cost of the tithe and feudal dues. Thus, the owner of a house subject to service should not have complained if this service had been disclosed by the seller and taken account of in the price. I shall speak elsewhere of pecuniary privileges.

When a longer experience allows us to make the comparison, we shall have an infallible method by which to judge which form of government provides the greatest happiness. Will there be fewer abandoned children, crimes, and lawsuits? Will the houses of detention and the places of deportation be less heavily populated? Will there be more respect for religion, more fidelity to political power, more deference towards fathers and mothers, more good faith in commerce, more independence and integrity in the administration of justice, and so on? By these traits we recognize the progress of a people towards happiness and liberty. A virtuous people is always happy and free, and it is happy and free only by its virtues. In this way we might even compare the France of yesteryear with England today. If one consents to the parallel, the matter is soon decided. While we await such a comparison, we may note how slippery and equivocal are those things generally viewed as signs of happiness and contentment in a nation. The beneficent constitution of England has made the English people morose, grumbling, discontented, and selfish, even according to Madame de Staël. The oppressive laws of France made the French people amiable, loving, lighthearted, and communicative, and more so in the south of France, which was more subject to feudal laws than was the north. The miserable Frenchman always pined after his country and did not call it life to live away from her. The happy Englishman, and the people of the north generally, are in a continual state of emigration. It was in miserable and oppressed France that the English, even the wealthiest of them, came to seek pleasure and health, and to enjoy the salubriousness of the climate, the surveillance of the police, and the protection of the laws.

Did not Madame de Staël herself always prefer a stay in France to one in her happy and liberal fatherland, and even to one in England? Why had she such lively regrets when she was exiled, and moreover when she was exiled to her own fatherland, her own property, with all her fortune and amidst her family? How could such a beneficent and sensible soul find it agreeable to remain amidst an oppressed people whose sufferings she could not relieve? With a bit more knowledge of men and things, and a bit less prejudice, she would have seen farther. She would have known that under pagan laws and morals there were peoples who suffered from and were oppressed by the excesses of war, the abuses of conquest, the instability of governments, and the cruel extravagances of religion. But the reign of Christianity has brought unction and charity to the relations of men, has made governments more solid, and has even lightened the burdens of war. Under Christianity, only families could be miserable, and this too often by their own fault. Usury, drunkenness, debauchery, feuds, lawsuits, and idleness make for more suffering than governments either create or are able to relieve. And finally, she would have known that the only period of our history when the French people were miserable and oppressed was when the Revolution—which she would have us praise—caused the worst of tyrannies to be reborn amongst us, with all the excesses, extravagances, and corruptions of an idolatrous land. With more knowledge of men and affairs and less prejudice, she would have known that no country in which it is so sweet to live, even for foreigners, and where dealings with one's fellows are so agreeable and the general disposition so benevolent, could really be miserable. She would have known that oppression, which is but the action of the superior class upon the inferior, makes the former hard and gives the latter an air of discontent and bitterness incompatible with the qualities that make men sociable and easy to get along with. To adopt her own style, it might even be said that in France, agreeableness, sweetness, benevolence, and sociability were like the perfume of general well-being.

It is said that the misery and oppression that weighed upon the French people led to the Revolution. Yet it is not known how much violence, deceit, intrigue, and money was required to push the people to innovations or disorders repellant to their habits, affections, and virtues. Madame de Staël may be ignorant of this, for she lived only with those who advocated the changes, and saw only the population of the capital, that is, the most ignorant and corrupt of France. Yet those who know the mind and morals of the provinces, and especially those who, like this author, were at the head of the provincial administration in those days, can attest that the country people opposed the Revolution for a long time with the only force that the government allowed them to employ: the force of inertia. Indeed, it would have cost the government much less effort to prevent the Revolution than the Revolutionaries needed to effect it. Was the Vendée, with its heroic and active resistance to the Revolution, happier than other parts of the kingdom? Did she pay less in tithes and feudal dues than the other provinces? Was she not the most feudal of our provinces? Why did Spain, which, as our liberals would have it, was groaning under the cruelest oppression from the Inquisition and the most absolute government in Europe, and having neither jury nor freedom of the press, why did she refuse the assistance of the Revolution? Why did Spain prefer the foreigners who came to fight against the Revolution to the foreigners who brought it?

Madame de Staël attributes all the crimes of the Revolution to the oppression to which the French people were subject. But the errors and crimes of the Constituent Assembly preceded and commanded those of the people. And when she says that no other people has committed similar excesses, she forgets that in Geneva, home to those happy and liberal people with their constitutional government, the people slaughtered a great number of the most respectable citizens when, in imitation of France, they made their own revolution.

Raised in the opulence and purple of the ministry and accustomed to all the attractions that the great world has for an intelligent woman, Madame de Staël was far too disposed to see only the flashy side of men and things, and to attribute happiness only to brilliance, life to agitation, and reason to the successes of a quick wit. All her philosophy abandons her when she gives in to these habits. "Never," she wrote, "was society as brilliant and serious as during the three or four initial years of the Revolution, from 1788 to the end of 1791." Alas! All the brilliance that came before and after such sad and cloudy days was but a flash of sunlight shining between two storms. If we recall all that took place during that interval, we may believe that society was serious, but we are at a loss to see how Madame de Staël could call it brilliant. But she explained herself: "In no other country and at no other time was the art of speaking as remarkable as during the first years of the Revolution."

Thus it is the art of speaking that Madame de Staël admired. Sensible of the famous successes in this art in which she was herself only too accomplished, she saw a constitution and a government only in the noisy speeches made from the rostrum. She forgot that while a childlike people can be managed with words and mere sounds arranged in an artful manner, an advanced society, that is, a Christian and reasonable society of adults, cannot be governed with thoughts that come to the mind as quickly as words from memory, and that at the rostrum, or even in private discussion, our words are not to be improvised.

Mirabeau,[2] the most brilliant and damaging orator of the Constituent Assembly, won approval in the eyes of Madame de

[2] Honoré-Gabriel Riquetti, comte de Mirabeau (1749–91) an ambitious member of the Third Estate, played a double game: publicly he was a radical leader in the Assembly; privately he was a consultant to Louis XVI.

Staël. She sacrificed all the other orators in order to show him in a favorable light. It is only by contradicting herself that she utters a self-reproach for mourning the death of a character so unworthy of our esteem, whose only talent was to lead people astray, and whose only ability was the ability to destroy. A bad son and a bad spouse, a disloyal lover and a rebellious citizen, dominated by the love of money even more than the love of power, he was not even faithful to the party he founded. Madame de Staël sees it as an evil that over the course of her life she never met his equal for eloquence because she takes eloquence to be the art of speaking, and she takes the burning fever of the passions for depth of soul and ardent genius. She should not mourn him. Meteors such as these are seen only during storms, and it cost us far too much to give such a spectacle to foreigners.

DID FRANCE HAVE A CONSTITUTION?

After fourteen centuries of existence, thirty years of revolution, and ten different constitutions, and after a hundred solid and well-reasoned works have demonstrated that France did have a constitution, Madame de Staël asked whether France had a constitution and decided in the negative.

She always reasoned in the same way. "The French people were miserable because they did not have a constitution, and they did not have a constitution because they did not have the English constitution."

Madame de Staël did not foresee the risk to which she exposed herself. In one part of her work she asked whether the English might one day lose their liberty. By allowing for such a possibility, she runs the risk, if they ever do fall into a revolution, that what is said of us will be said of them, namely, that they never had a constitution.

At bottom, the question is absurd. The constitution of a people is its mode of existence, and to ask whether a people that has lived for fourteen centuries and still exists has a constitution is to ask whether that people has what it requires to exist. This is like asking an eighty-year-old man whether he was made with what is required to live.

In France, royalty was constituted, and so well constituted that the king never died. Royalty was masculine, hereditary in order of primogeniture, and independent. It was to this strong constitution of royalty that France owed her powers of resistance and expansion.

The nation was constituted, and so well constituted that it never asked a neighboring nation to guarantee its constitution. It was constituted in three orders, each one forming an independent person no matter the number of its members. These orders represented all that there is to be represented in the nation and everything that makes up a nation: religion, the state, and the family.

Religion was constituted, and so well constituted that it resisted, still resists, and will always resist every attack against it. The French clergy held the first rank in Christian Europe by its doctors and orators. The king himself merited the title of Most Christian King.

Justice was constituted, and so well constituted that the constitution of the judiciary in France was, in the eyes of all politicians, the most perfect of its kind in the world. Every country has judges, but only in France did the judges have the duty to give political counsel.

The limits to the independent power of the king were constituted, and so well constituted that it is not possible to cite a single necessary law that was rejected, nor a false law that was upheld. I speak not of fiscal laws, for these do not merit the name of law. The right of remonstrance before the supreme tribunals was an admirable institution, and the source of all that was highest in the French character of noble obedience. It was the king's justice that remonstrated with the king's power, and what counselor or moderator could power have other than justice?

Religion, royalty, and justice were independent within the sphere of their activities, as independent as the owners of goods or offices. The nation also was the most independent of all nations.

France, therefore, had a constitution. For it is neither commerce nor academies, neither arts nor administration that constitute a state, but royalty, religion, and justice.

Moreover, because France had a constitution, and a strong one, she grew from reign to reign, even under the weakest kings. She was always envied, but never undermined, often troubled, but never defeated. She emerged victorious from the most unexpected reverses through means unhoped for, and she could never perish except by losing faith in her destiny.

It is certain that he who never ceased to praise the old constitution of France under the constitutions of the Empire has the right to speak of it under the king of France. And if he needed a justification, there it is.

We should now return to the work of Madame de Staël. I would be taking unfair advantages were I to discuss all of her claims in detail. Suffice it to say that she always takes the accidents for the substance by considering administrative disputes to be holes in the constitution. One is shocked by her ignorance of our old constitution. A complete constitution is not one that terminates in advance all the difficulties to which the passions of men and chance events can give rise, but one that includes the ability to terminate them when they present themselves. It is the same with health: a good temperament is not one that prevents illness, but one that gives the body the ability to resist it and quickly to repair its ravages. No doubt there were many disputes in France, but there were still more in England. And without the disputes that exercise our minds and uncover the truth, what would become of the art of speaking so dear to Madame de Staël?

There are those who wish to see in moral things the precision of movement, measure, extension, power, and resistance that is found only in bodies or material things. They wish for the impossible. To them, I respond that it is a great error to wish to trace precise lines of demarcation between authority and obedience and to pose in advance, in the constitution of societies, fixed limits to the power of the head, the cooperation of his agents, and the duties of his subjects. If the limits are marked out, each one, in a time of war, will carry himself to his farthest frontier. The parties having arrived, combat will commence, and, instead of disputing to determine the limits, each will attempt to roll them back. If, however, a cloud remains over delicate matters, one passes beside the others without running into them. Sometimes one side goes too far, sometimes the other does. Yet after a few excursions, each side returns to its own terrain. God Himself wished to leave us ignorant of how He influences our liberty and triumphs over our resistance. And there have been many more disputes about the power of God and the free will of man than about the power of kings and political liberty. Yet these have not kept God from being omnipotent nor our souls from being free.

ON THE NOBILITY IN FRANCE AND ENGLAND

On the subject of the nobility, Madame de Staël has shown her greatest ignorance of institutions and strongest prejudices and injustices with respect to persons. She protested against the metaphysical analysis of the constitution. Nevertheless, politics is the concern of reason and not, as she would have it, of the affections and emotions.

In an independent monarchy, where the legislative power is found whole and entire in the hands of the king, the function and purpose of the nobility is only to exercise public functions at the king's command. Thus, in France the nobility was a body of families with a hereditary devotion to the service of the state in the only two professions that are public or political: justice and military force. This destination was actual for the family and potential for individuals. It was less an obligation imposed upon all the members than a disposition of the family as a whole.

The nobility in France, and in every state with a natural constitution, is properly the action of political power. It therefore conforms to the successive phases of political power in every age: in the early times, transitory and temporary, and in later times, hereditary. From this stem the disputes about the status and existence of the nobility in France, which several writers do not admit to have existed in the early years of the monarchy because it was not constituted as it was in more recent times.

As the nobility is consecrated to public service, in both body and wealth, it cannot attend to any commerce or private service. It is true that modern laws have permitted large-scale commerce to nobles. Yet our old customs were wiser, and they were correct to prohibit it, because commerce, even at its largest extent, is the service of individuals. The merchant who arranges for a whole fleet of sugar and coffee serves individuals no less than the shopkeeper who sells them to me.

For the same reason, that is, the perpetual availability for service, the noble is not permitted to enter into contracts secured by his own freedom. The impossibility for the nobility to enlarge its fortunes through the lucrative professions led to the wise custom of entailment, so imprudently abolished and to which we have recently returned under another name.

❊ ❊ ❊

By the nature of its institution, the nobility diminishes more rapidly than other families. It has been reduced by almost half since Louis XIII. At the beginning of the Revolution, there were barely more than fifteen thousand families. This number was far too small compared with the size of the nation and was clearly a cause of the Revolution, that is to say, of the conversion of the monarchy into a democracy (for a revolution is nothing else), because the monarchical power lacked its necessary and constitutional action.

The nobility was, therefore, a political militia, of which the king, in his quality of supreme head of justice and military force, was the head. Just as the general of an army has an authority of jurisdiction over his subalterns that he does not have over civilians, so the king had a jurisdiction over nobles that he did not have over his other subjects. In the case of his common subjects, the king had to defer to the tribunals, but in the case of the nobles, he could arrest them or exile them from the court for faults that did not fall within the purview of criminal law. Thus, I think that every citizen in France except the nobles had the right to complain about the *lettres de cachet*.[3] Terrasson spoke truly when he said that "subordination is more marked in the first ranks than in the last."

There are two ways to increase the number of nobles. The first is the ordinary way, through the will of private families. The second is extraordinary, by the choice of the sovereign.

Madame de Staël prefers the extraordinary in all things and thus wanted the creation of nobles only to be by royal choice. She rejected with unphilosophic disdain what in France was commonly called ennobling.

As a regular means of recruiting to the institution of the nobility, the sovereign's choice of a certain number of individuals from a nation, and especially from a rich and literate nation, is troublesome for the head of state. It surrounds him with intrigues and exposes him to the errors, injustices, and discontent of those who believe they have a claim upon his favor. It is not to be doubted that the sovereign should elevate those who have done great services, and that the voice of the public will point them out to him. Yet these great men generally appear only in times of war or other great calamities, and we may be sure that society pays a high cost to have them. This means of recruitment is therefore insufficient for ordinary occasions. The French constitution, while not excluding the spontaneous choice of the sovereign (too often the choice of his courtiers) wisely established a common and regular method of advancement. This, I dare say, is the most moral and most political part of our laws, and I would even say the most rational, because it was established by the reason of society and not by the reasonings of men.

[3] Royal arrest warrants by which a person could be indefinitely incarcerated.

The natural tendency of every man and every family and the principle of all imitation and diligence is to rise in rank, that is, to leave one state for a better one, and to exchange a trade that employs the body for a profession that exerts the mind. In the language of the passions, to rise in rank signifies the acquisition of riches and the means of dominating others. In the moral language of politics, to rise in rank signifies service, service to the public in the public professions of justice and military force. And this sublime understanding of the word service, the accepted meaning in all the Christian languages of Europe, comes from this passage of the Gospel: "Let he who wishes to be above others serve them." Thus, the constitution said to every private family: "When you have fulfilled your destination in domestic society, which is to acquire an independent property through legitimate work, order, and thrift, when, that is, you have acquired enough that you have no need of others and are able to serve the state at your own expense, from your own income, and, if necessary, with your capital, the greatest honor to which you can aspire will be to pass into the order particularly devoted to the service of the state. From then on you will be capable of every public function."

A family that had made a sufficient fortune purchased a public office, generally in the judiciary and sometimes in the administration. In this way, the most grave and serious professions were the prelude to a public career. The essence of this order was its disinterestedness, for, once ennobled, the person was barred from any lucrative profession. The newly ennobled family acquired new morals in the first generation and new manners in the second. Madame de Staël put too much emphasis on these manners, which, in her view, were none too popular in France. In the eyes of the philosopher, however, these manners were the necessary consequence and exterior expression of the noble order.

The ennobled family, therefore, was equally noble to the ancient ones. The most recently ennobled sat next to the duke or peer in the convocations of the nobility, and showed himself more noble than they to the extent that he was more faithful. From that point on he was admissible to all offices. It was not rare to see, in one and the same ennobled family, the eldest son become counselor in one of the sovereign courts, the second one a bishop, and the third a higher officer in the military.

Can we speak endlessly of equality and also argue against ennobling? It tended to raise every family equally and gave all the desire for an honorable destiny that was also useful for the state.

The constitution, therefore, admitted only one order of nobility. Opinion gave to the most ancient families, which can be seen as the elders of public society, the consideration that it also accords to elders in families. Nothing could be more reasonable than this, nor could anything be more natural. The court, however, went too far when it distinguished different degrees within the same order: *gens de qualité, gens présentés*. These recent distinctions tended to create an unconstitutional aristocracy lacking special functions. It is nevertheless true that the royal family, being the most ancient of our society, should have been surrounded by the most ancient families. Yet this distinction should have been left to customs and usages, and it should not have been established by positive laws and regulations. Everything that was accorded to the vanity of individuals was at the same time taken away from the unity and force of the institution. The great lords wanted to create an order within an order. The families of younger sons, humiliated by their elders, exacted their revenge upon their own younger siblings, who in turn did the same to others beneath them. All this could have been corrected without a revolution, and I even believe that certain *cahiers*[4] of the nobility made this very point.

The ennobled family, like the ancient ones, renounced every lucrative profession. At times this even happened too quickly, before the family's independent fortune had been assured. I do not know

---

[4] The *cahiers de doléances*, or notebooks of complaints, were drawn up by regional assemblies for presentation to the Estates General. Each of the three estates had its own collection of *cahiers*.

whether this renunciation may be thought liberal, but it was philosophical, moral, and, above all, wise politically. There could be no more moral an institution than one which, by the most honorable motives, gave an example of disinterestedness to men devoured by the thirst for money in a society in which this passion was a fertile source of injustice and crime. There could be no better policy than to stop, by a powerful yet voluntary means, and by the motive of honor, the immoderate accumulation of wealth in the same hands. It is precisely this that Madame de Staël, good citizen of Geneva, found wanting in our custom of ennobling. She thus agrees with the contradictory views of her age: the same men who stridently demanded the indefinite division of landed property also favored with all their might the indefinite accumulation of movable property and capital. The accumulation of land has a natural limit, but that of movable wealth does not, for a single merchant can do business with each of the four corners of the globe. But luxury follows wealth, and the rich merchant, who no longer needs to sell, will raise his prices and thus force the consumer to support his luxurious life. This is one of the causes of inflation in England, Holland, and even in France, and wherever commerce has no end but commerce, and where millions only produce more millions. Great landed fortunes incline a state towards aristocracy, but great movable fortunes lead it towards democracy. The monied men, now masters of the state, purchase power cheaply from those to whom they sell sugar and coffee dearly. Holland has the wealthiest merchants in the world. The little cantons of Switzerland have only shepherds and Capuchins. Which of the two has better defended its independence and lived most honorably? This is the question that should be brought before our politicians.

Madame de Staël, who already read her name in the history books and whose family flew straight from the sales desk to the ministry, treats ennobling with great disdain. She wants only the great historic families. Yet Catilina[5] was as historic as Caesar, and

---

[5] Lucius Sergius Catilina (died 62 B.C.), the leader of a conspiracy against the Roman Republic. He was denounced in some of Cicero's most celebrated orations.

Mirabeau as Necker. Madame de Staël herself admits that there are great men who do not wish to be historic figures. These virtuous men, and not the famous ones, are the strength and salvation of an empire.

Because she sees only great things, Madame de Staël only considers universal history to be history. Yet each province has its history. And if these local histories do not report brilliant actions and shocking crimes, they may nevertheless recall virtue and goodness. In defending the cause of the provincial nobles, who lack historic names and are therefore disdained by Madame de Staël, I believe that I am more truly philosophical than she was.

It is true that the provincial nobility is less elegant in manners and less skilled in the art of speaking than the court nobility. Yet at the meeting of the Estates General that preceded the Revolution, did they show themselves to be less faithful or less devout? Did not the ennobled protect the monarchical principles better than the ancient nobility? I leave it to the historians to decide the question. Yet if the provincial nobles were no more faithful, they were more unfortunate, for the Revolution and its terrible decrees weighed much heavier upon those who had the least to lose and therefore fewer means of regaining what they had lost.

I trust that my account of the nobility shall not be countered by an argument drawn from the vices and crimes of a few individuals. Such an argument would be like one that denied the incontestable benefits of commerce on the basis of the few merchants who suffer bankruptcy.

Madame de Staël reduces the number of great families to about two hundred in number. These families were recruited to the nobility only through great talents, great services, and great genius: in a word, by great men. But since these men appear only during times of great danger and great need, on her view we will always be requiring great events in order to have our great men. We should no longer hope for tranquility.

Two hundred families do not suffice to make a military or judicial institution for a nation of 25 million. Therefore Madame de Staël makes them into a legislative institution. Not being able to make them nobles, she makes them kings, and hereditary ones at that. That is, she turns the nobility into a senate. She wants this office to be hereditary, but not belonging to a particular line. These desires seem difficult to keep together. For if the senate does not belong to a particular line for those who commence it, it does for their heirs.

This brings us to the example of England, where there is no body of nobles destined to serve political power, but a senate destined to exercise it. This institution is found in all republics. Rousseau rightly noted that the bourgeois senate in Geneva was no different from the noble one in Venice. Nor does it differ essentially from democracy. Aristocracy is but democracy within narrow limits, while democracy is a more extended aristocracy.

I do not consider this institution from a political point of view, relative to the stability and force of the state. Rather, I consider it as Madame de Staël does, that is, with respect to liberty and equality. It is from this point of view that I prefer the old institutions of the French monarchy to it.

We must first note an essential and characteristic difference between all republics and the French monarchy. Republics, particularly the English one, only count individuals. The French monarchy saw only families. The result is that there is more movement and agitation in republics, and more stability and repose in our monarchy. The Roman Republic was the only one to consider the family in its political institutions, and this is why it enjoyed such a long duration and such a great superiority over other peoples.

For an individual, physical liberty consists in the power to go and come as he pleases. For the family, domestic liberty consists in the power to exercise all manner of legitimate industry in conformity with its tastes, habits, fortune, and political liberty. That is, this liberty consists in the power of following the natural tendency of all families and thus to pass from domestic obligation to the service of society, or to raise itself.

Now, in France a family needed only to make a legitimate fortune in order to gain an office that would make it pass into the political order. The payment that it gave to the state was a proof of its fortune and independence.

In England, the individual, even in rising to the nobility, never leaves the private state. The peer who makes laws for three months of the year sells linens the other nine. His younger children and his brothers can exercise the mechanical or mercantile professions, and these even to the disadvantage of ordinary families, from whom this competition in high places is not without its drawbacks.

Thus, in France a family once ennobled ennobles all its members. The father works for all his children. This led to a greater family spirit and a more unanimous concert of efforts and work. In England, only the eldest passes into the political order; the others remain in the private state. Thus, Madame de Staël remarks that "domestic bonds that are so intimate in marriage are otherwise less so in England, because the interest of the younger brothers is very different from that of their elders." Her discussion of this is most curious. In it can be found the correction to all she has said elsewhere in praise of England and the English.

In England, every elevation, even to the highest dignity, that is, to the peerage, comes only from the favor of the sovereign king or the sovereign people. To be a member of the House of Commons one must pay assiduous court to the people. It seems to me, therefore, that there is less liberty there than in France, for political liberty consists in the family's ability to raise itself through its own forces and industry.

Was there more equality in England? According to the law, there was much less. The nation was divided into two classes, one with the privilege to make the laws and the other to receive. Politically speaking, there is an infinite gulf between the two conditions. It is true that their customs corrected the inequalities of the law to some extent. Dignity made itself popular there, even populist. The servants were permitted to be familiar, and at times even insolent. This did not, however, prevent dignity from taking up its rights again in the habits of private life, where, through harsh etiquette, distinctions were made between men and women of different ranks that we would not have stood for in France.

In France, both in the state and the family, there were eldest sons and younger ones, and also the children who, growing older, in their turn became the eldest. In England, there were, politically speaking, only the great and the small. The small did not grow by their own power and could not leave their rank except by some special favor. There was really no distinction there except between fortunes, which are as unequal as political ranks. For if there are millionaires in England, there is also the tenth of the population that lives on the dole. Poverty and even mediocrity are more shameful there than in France. We need not return as far as the maxims of Epictetus to discover that distinctions based on money are not the most moral ones that can be made among men. There was indeed a certain wisdom in that saying of French peasant families that they would not trade their poverty for the rich office of a tax collector.

In France, everyone had his class, and thanks to the trade corporations, everyone had his specific weight. The Third Estate had its voice and its veto just as the other two did, and the corporation of tailors would have been admitted to a royal audience just as if it were a regional deputation.

I do not condemn English institutions. I merely make the comparison in order to defend our old customs against the bitter and unjust reproaches leveled against them by Madame de Staël. Life and movement she saw only in agitation, and it must be admitted that English institutions have preserved that country from the monotony of uniformity and repose.

Upon reading Madame de Staël, one would be tempted to say that one must be noble for four generations in order to be worth a nickel. But in France, every family was able, through its own industry, to raise itself to the nobility, that nursery of all public functions. No individual was excluded from rising through his own merits to the highest offices. There is but one difference between England and France, and it is the difference between democracies and monarchies in general. The difference is that in France, once a family had raised itself, it could only be deprived of its status through legal judgment, while in England, the elevation of the individual had no legal effect upon the family. I say legal because the law was so imperfect and so unnatural that morals were obliged to correct it; I doubt not that in England, as elsewhere, there are families that are distinguished because of the offices they have filled.

In France, whether the family ennobled the individual or the individual the family, the sword, the Church, and especially the judiciary (which, as a body, belongs to the Third Estate) witnessed examples of these extraordinary elevations in every age. If they were not more frequent, this is because extraordinary talents are rare. Every society that conforms to its nature produces extraordinary men only in times of need, when it always produces them. In France, therefore, the fortune of a man of genius was limited only by the existence of those trials that prod genius into action and which genius is always sure to conquer. Open the door wide and the mob will pass through it. The mob is mediocre, and so there are always enough mediocre men to occupy positions, and there are so many of these mediocre men that they will always find a way to elevate themselves. I will even say that it is not possible to find a single man of genius in France, in any condition of birth, who failed to raise himself. After all, how would we know that he was suited for such and such an office if he did not exercise it? What if it be said that Montesquieu should have been chancellor of France? I respond that he was president of the parlement, then a high dignity, and that as such this great writer, able publicist, and ingenious observer proved himself to be a mediocre judge. He understood the theory of the laws far better than he did their application. Domat, far more skilled than Montesquieu in that regard, became the king's advocate, and, in a time when the judiciary was so highly honored and when men's desires were moderate, he was content with his lot and satisfied in his ambition. The same might be said of many other men in the provinces, who would not have left offices, families, homes, and fortunes to go running to Paris in search of honors. It was this disposition, good in itself and happy though it be, that slowly gave the capital the exclusive privilege of all the administrative offices.

It will be said that the Revolution resulted in a profusion of talented men that never would have otherwise seen the light of day. And we would not have been unhappy had they not. They themselves more than once regretted their loss of obscurity. I will even admit that, like Madame de Staël, I regret having been excited by the talents of the Girondins.[6] The most brilliant fortunes were the military ones, and here we must note with Madame de Staël that military talents are not always the proof of a superior mind. Yet I would argue that, at any time in our history, a war that was as long and as deadly as the one the Revolution brought to Europe would have led to the same examples of sudden elevations thanks to the very constitution of the military. If, in a ship of the line, there are but ten sailors left after the battle, the eldest of them takes command. And, in the Thirty Years War, the greater part of the German generals originated in the ranks. Moreover, the military state is perhaps the most natural to man; Voltaire himself said it. It is also the state which has at all times witnessed the greatest number of unexpected fortunes. Today, all that is seen is the ambition that has seized us since the Revolution changed everything. In the past there was little ambition, perhaps not enough. The majority of military men aspired only to win the Cross of St. Louis and then retire to make way for others. Ambition for civilian offices existed only in Paris. Today, this ambition for civilian offices is everywhere, and military ambition, the most excusable of all ambitions because it most

---

[6] The Girondins were a loose collection of renowned orators in the Legislative Assembly who pushed for war with Austria in 1791–92.

exposes one to sacrifice and danger, is extinguished, and far more than we realize, thanks to the secret influence of the republican spirit. In some republics, the state is obliged to confide its defenses to foreigners, and in others, to temporary militias. In all of them, the civil administration, more tranquil and better paid, carries the day over the military profession. The government should foresee the ultimate effects that this tendency, once become general, will have upon a powerful state surrounded by neighbors who preserve another spirit.

In general, we may conclude, in all the complaints that are lodged against those governments accused of not seeking to recompense merit, we do not hear "the government is unjust because so and so was not preferred." Rather each one says for himself "because I was not preferred." But men who dispose of official duties cannot make the amount of self-love the rule of their duty nor the measure of their favors.

ON THE AGRICULTURAL FAMILY, THE INDUSTRIAL FAMILY, AND THE RIGHT OF PRIMOGENITURE (1826)

When we see our liberal philosophers so exclusively preoccupied with commerce, industry, the progress of manufacturing, and the discoveries of the mechanical arts, we are led to admire the mutable nature of philosophical opinion. There is no lack of material for a new Bossuet to write a *History of Its Variations*.

Thus Rousseau admires nature, and that only in its wild state. He would willingly take us back to eating our meat raw, wearing the skins of beasts, and sleeping in the shelter of trees or in a lair. In society he saw naught but servitude, weakness, crime, and misery. His complaints against it were all drawn from wild nature: the savage's independence from men and human needs, his natural goodness, his bodily rigor.

But our hard Spartans have become effeminate Sybarites. The other philosophers speak only of the arts and industries that multiply our needs and pleasures, and they should like to see us all floating through life in palaces of gold and silk. Of frugality, temperance, and moderation of desires they no longer speak. For man in society, life is reduced to producing for consumption and consuming to produce. To them, society as a whole is divided into two classes: producers and consumers. The philosophers of recent centuries also bitterly and arrogantly denounce conquerors and their wars of conquest. Yet when they found these conquests profitable to their doctrines, they sounded trumpets to honor the conqueror, and in their philanthropy, benevolence, and humanity, they pardoned him for these appalling wars, whose success was secured by a profound disregard for a mankind pitilessly sacrificed to the extravagant dreams of ambition.

Today these philosophers demand the independence of industry, the most dependent of all professions. They see commerce as the bond of peoples and the guarantee of peace in the world, even though the jealousies of commerce have been the subject of all our wars for some time, as they shall be for all those waged in the future. To commerce they attribute the spirit of liberty that has spread over Europe, although all the merchants, even the wealthiest of them, daily or even hourly shackle their personal liberty by pledging themselves as security for loans both large and small.

Today some would confuse industry and agriculture and even place them in the same rank in society. Let us, however, distinguish them in their character and effects, and by their varying influences upon the mind and habits of men and the constitutions of states. This question is not foreign to the measure on primogeniture that has been submitted to the chambers, inasmuch as those who would establish or permit it for the land-owning family have never intended to extend it to the industrial family.

※ ※ ※

Agriculture feeds her children, but industry gives birth to children she cannot always feed.

The child who comes into the world in an agricultural family finds his sustenance already assured, for the earth that his parents cultivate and that he will cultivate in his turn awaits him to give him his bread.

The child born into an industrial family expects his sustenance from the salary he will earn if a master employs him, and if his industry is not stricken by events that could make it falter, or shut down, or prevent the sale of its products.

The farmer lives from his produce even when he does not sell it. The industrial worker cannot live unless he sells what he produces.

Thus, the agricultural family enjoys an existence independent of men and events, while the industrial family is dependent upon them both.

A farm is indeed a family whose head is the father. Whether he owns or rents the farm, he busies himself with the same labors as his servants and eats the same bread, often at the same table. The farm nourishes all its offspring. It has occupations for those of all ages and both sexes. Even the elderly, who cannot perform heavy labor, finish their careers as they began it and stay around the house watching the children and animals.

There is nothing similar to this in the industrial family, whose members work in isolation and often in different industries, and who do not know their master apart from the exigencies of his commands. Industry does not nourish all ages and both sexes. It does employ the child, and often so young that his health and strength are ruined. The child may receive some instruction, but he is abandoned in his advanced years when he can no longer work. Then the industrial worker has no bread except what he takes from his children's salary or what he receives from public charity.

The farmer toils from the rising to the setting of the sun but never at night. He rests on Sunday and takes up his work again on Monday. The industrial worker works even at night in order to gain a higher salary, especially when he works at home by the piece. Whether he rests on Sunday or not, overheated by his forced labor, on Monday he debauches.

The farmer works outside and standing up. He strengthens his body by the hard and painful labor of the fields and exerts his intelligence upon the numerous details and variations in the culture of the earth, trees, and beasts. He tames the animals and forces rebellious nature to submit to his care. The industrial worker works hunched over and sedentary, turns a crank, makes the shuttle go to and fro, and pulls together the threads. He spends his life in cellars or attics and, becoming a machine himself, he exerts his fingers, but never his mind. It can thus be said that there is nothing less industrious than the industrial worker.

Everything improves the intelligence of the farmer and lifts his thoughts towards Him who gives fruitfulness to the earth, dispenses the seasons, and makes the fruit ripen. Everything debases the intelligence of the worker. He sees nothing above the master who employs him, or at best the inventor of the machine to which he is attached.

We can thus say that the former waits for everything from God, and that the latter receives everything from man.

The farmer tells his neighbors of his discoveries and the new processes that he invents to improve his cultivation. The industrialist and the merchant keep their speculations secret. We can thus say that the agriculture that disperses men about the countryside unites them without bringing them together, while the commerce that crowds them into cities brings them together without uniting them.

The agricultural population is strong and vigorous, the industrial population frail and sickly. Not long ago a judge in a small canton in Switzerland bitterly deplored the degeneration of the beautiful people of his country since workshops and factories had been established in it.

Nor am I afraid to advance that there are nowhere more beggars than in manufacturing cities and industrial countries. England is the proof of this, for in spite of its immense fortune and widely extended industry, a large part of its inhabitants falls under the charge of the landholders. Their poor-laws are an oppressive tax. What does it matter that their poor are better clothed and better nourished than ours, if they are clothed and nourished only by public charity and parish offices?

If we are not careful, these poor-laws will come to France under other forms and will spread and worsen in proportion to the progress of industry. Is this not a tax on the poor? The upkeep of the ever-increasing number of foundlings and orphans, detainees and convicts is paid by taxes and consequently by individuals. Those who study statistics could be easily convinced that these public poor, these poor of the state, some of whom require to be fed and all of whom need to be supported, kept, and watched, come in greater numbers from the workshops of industry than from the farms.

I do not speak of that local industry, or, if you will, the national industry, which is the companion of agriculture and puts the produce of the soil to work for the needs of those who cultivate it. This exists always and everywhere, for men have always built houses, spun flax and wool, forged arms and tools, and exercised all the arts necessary to human existence. I speak, rather, of that cosmopolitan industry that would furnish the entire world with products whose primary materials it has scoured from the four corners of the earth. This furious industry causes our political leaders to consider foreign nations not as friends or allies, but only as customers.

Local industry serves agriculture, which demands its products by furnishing it the material and paying for them in the same fashion. The larger industry serves the whole earth, and the nation that produces the most for the foreigner is the one that most serves the nations who consume these products, and, consequently, it is the most dependent upon their needs or caprices.

Yet almost every country has the primary materials for those industries and arts necessary for human existence, while the taste for these arts is widespread, the workers easy to move, and a machine spins or makes its products just as well in Russia as it does in France or England. Therefore it does not seem to be a wise or farsighted policy to depend overmuch upon foreign consumption for the prosperity of our country.

Necessities can be found and made everywhere, but superfluities can be kept out by governments.

Thus, by a singular contradiction, while all governments favor the progress of industries that provide for other states and try to extend their commercial relations beyond all bounds, these same states, through protective laws and armies of toll collectors, seek to limit the competition of foreign products with domestic ones. Everyone would sell and no one would buy. One may at least hope that the now-popular republican principles and sentiments will one day inspire us with the spirit of frugality, temperance, moderation, and economy, those virtues so strongly honored by the ancient republics. For they would be strange republics, and would doubtless soon submit to the yoke of a master, if they wished to begin as our monarchies ended, that is, in luxury. And another thing: in our monarchies, luxury was good morals and almost a duty of rank, whereas in our republics it will be only private and personal taste.

It is amply proven that great profits are to be made by culling primary materials from the four corners of the earth, submitting them to labor at home, and then exporting the products to the whole world. The worker earns his keep, the captain his freight, the banker his commission, the state its entry and exit tolls, and so on. But let the state consider that large industry brings great expenses that are more political than fiscal: laziness, missed work, the sick and the aged left to the charge of public and private charity, the lack of instruction for the children of both sexes crowded into workshops, their libertinism—about which we have read such horrifying accounts by several English writers—and intemperance that necessitate prisons and houses of detention and correction, the need to watch and police the armies of rustics who flood into the manufacturing cities, and the need to prevent or punish those workshop revolts so alarmingly common in England and recently spreading to France. Then the state may discover that there is not so much profit after all in this large industry that makes the population grow boundlessly, and for which a precarious subsistence can only be procured by constantly extending the industry, and consequently further increasing the population. The agricultural population is limited by the extent and fertility of the soil it cultivates, but the industrial population is not. It produces without end, until the failure of primary materials or the consumption of its products forces it to withdraw into itself and to close the workshops.

I return to the proposition with which I began this essay: agriculture feeds her children, but industry gives birth to children she cannot always feed.

In an agricultural region (or an entire kingdom) with only the industry required to make use of the products of the soil and the primary materials furnished by it, local industry would employ the agricultural population in excess of that needed for the cultivation of the earth. All those able to work would find work either in the fields or in industry. There would be a natural proportion between the two parts of the population occupied with one or the other set of tasks. There would be neither too much nor too little work, neither too few nor too many hands, and no one would suffer.

Yet should one suppose that large industrial establishments destined to produce for foreign lands were suddenly to arise, the population that furnished labor to the agriculture of the land and to local industry would no longer suffice. New modes of labor will demand a new population. It will form rapidly. A loom to make wool or linen cloth will be a dowry and tools a patrimony. The people will marry, build houses, and bear children. A village will become a town, a town a city. And to see such examples of rapid growth we need not leave France.

Thus, if the manufacture of cotton fabric formerly prohibited in France (when the government judged that the native materials of wool, linen, and silk sufficed to clothe us) today employs several thousand men, it is almost as if, when the time of prohibition was lifted, we had imported several thousand Indians into France. As these industries prosper, they create great private fortunes. This is what is today called the national wealth, although it is difficult to understand why we call wealthy a nation where alongside a few millionaires there are several million paupers who labor much, earn little, save nothing, live in the cabarets, and die in the hospitals. Such is the internal condition of the nations we call rich, while in those thought to be poor because they have few large fortunes, as for example Sweden and Norway, there are, in proportion, fewer paupers than in France and in England.

Yet these large industrial establishments can come to ruin, either through the loss of primary materials taken from far and wide, the importation of which can be thwarted by political circumstance or bad weather, or through the caprice of fashion, the tariff barriers of foreign states, the establishment elsewhere of a more advanced or successful industry of the same kind, or, finally, from the retirement or death of the rich and industrious founder of the establishment. When this ruin comes, a flourishing city loses its population, men lose their jobs, and homes lose their inhabitants. We see many examples of this throughout Europe.

Let me not be accused of calling into question the utility, or rather the necessity, of industry. For it is to industry that we owe the use and enjoyment of all the goods that the Creator has put within man's reach in order to support, to preserve, even to embellish his fleeting existence. Yet I warn governments of the danger an overextended industry poses to their tranquility when, in order to serve all its neighbors and even the most distant people, it gives birth to a larger population than religion can instruct or authority restrain, and sometimes even larger than industry can feed. These considerations are unnecessary in times of prosperity, when governments have nothing to do and sleep like a captain whose sails are filled with a favorable wind. They are for the reverses and the times of misery to which industry can be exposed when the hungry multitude demands tomorrow's bread from a government whose supply ran out the day before.

Agriculture waits for everything from God and does not rebel against the author of nature if hail or frost ravages the crop. But industry, which waits for everything from man, blames everyone for its miseries: the masters, the rich, and the government. The government is forced to use stern measures to maintain public tranquility against these desperate men whose need carries them to every excess, and whose discontent is all too often heated up and set alight by malice. It is a deplorable situation when authority is forced to respond with rifle shots to the complaints of those miserable men who ask only to keep the career the government has forced upon them. In truth, a century of industrial prosperity does not make up for an hour of this terrible but necessary use of force.

This is, however, what has frequently been seen in England, and at this moment Liverpool and other manufacturing cities are soliciting loans from the government in order to feed one hundred fifty thousand unemployed and hungry workers. Here is a new danger for government: to accustom an idle population to live at the public expense.

Yet even in this respect the situation of France is more dangerous than that of England. The English remain a nomadic people, and the government can send its excess population to the colonies, foreign bureaus, mines, and enterprises that have made the whole globe a veritable tributary of England. Thus, in an astute policy, England favors the emigration of the rich, who disseminate the tastes and habits of their land without ever picking up the tastes and habits of other peoples. France does not have this resource, for she has no more colonies. And the Frenchman is more attached to his land. The government is unable to rid itself of an idle and disquieted population, and a boiling pot breaks if it cannot spill over.

Let it not be doubted that it is in hopes of one day taking this superabundant population into its pay that one party in Europe promotes the exaggerated growth of industry and never finds enough of it, certain that it can give work to these idle arms, no matter how many, in the immense workshop of the revolutionary industry.

In this comparison of agriculture and industry, I have had to reserve until the end the final and most characteristic of their differences.

The farmer, forced to be moderate in his tastes, economizes in his purchases, and as all that he has is under the sun, cannot compromise the future of his creditors, who, by consulting the table of probabilities and by estimating the goods that they can see before their eyes, can judge with certitude to what point it is prudent to engage their funds in agricultural investments. But the industrialist and the merchant, for whom the active and the passive are equally unknown, and who today compete with the highest nobility in purchases and luxuries, only present to their creditors as a pledge of their credit bold and exaggerated speculations, whose ill success ruins the creditor and does not always ruin the debtor, who, even on the most unfortunate hypothesis, acquits himself with respect to his creditors with a balance sheet and a suicide. And who can know how many families have been ruined by the numerous failures that have of late broken out in all the commercial centers of Europe?

✻ ✻ ✻

These reflections on agriculture and industry were suggested to me by an article in a journal of wide circulation that questions the practicality and utility of the measure—announced in the discourse of His Majesty at the opening of the session and since then proposed as a law—to reconstitute the landowning family and to forestall, if there is still time, the extreme division of landed property.

Since then, the same journal, in the number for February 25th, has favorably reviewed a treatise *On the Right of Primogeniture* by the celebrated advocate Monsieur Dupin, who opposes the proposed law.

I will hazard several observations upon what I have read in the journal.

I dare say that on such a grave question we must not consult either the policies of lawyers or bankers. These two professions, by habit, interest, and duty, are exclusively occupied with private interests. But on this matter private interests and personal affections must be sacrificed to the general interest of society and to public affection.

The profound motives behind the proposed law cannot be appreciated in Paris, where a man takes his street to be a fatherland, an apartment let for three, six, or nine years to be a paternal house, and rents tallied in an accountant's ledger to be a patrimony.

Monsieur Dupin's letter to his brothers, reported in the journal, is a masterpiece of fraternal tenderness and sensibility, and we are happy to find such touching expression in it during these miserable times when one hears only of domestic crimes, wives who poison their husbands, husbands who assassinate their wives, sons who destroy their fathers or brothers, and, a thing unknown and reserved for our day! mothers, legitimate mothers, who destroy the children to whom they have given the light of day.

No doubt it is respectable, this sensibility of fathers and mothers, brothers and sisters who complain of the lot of their younger brothers, who are treated by the law with less favor than their elders. Or who, at any rate, seem thus treated, for the eldest, attached to the soil by a larger share of the paternal inheritance, has the often heavy charge of family affairs. Yet there is a more manly sentiment, that of the statesman for the lot of families without permanence and without a future, where the brothers only await the death of the father to leave their homes and begin a division that will leave them nothing in common but a ruinous legal proceeding in which their affections and, all too often, their patrimony will disappear.

It is absurd to ask whether the right of primogeniture be of divine or natural right. The law was not made for the eldest. In the eyes of God or nature, he is no greater than his cadets, even in royal families. The law exists for the preservation and permanence of the landowning family. Now the families that cultivate the earth that the Father of mankind has given them for their dwelling assuredly are of divine and natural right. Thus it is that the law of male heredity by primogeniture exists for the permanence of states. So it is that nature has by the same means and for the same ends established it in domestic society, just as it has in that public society of which the family is the element and type.

Let us then say that the right of primogeniture is but an abridged saying to express the first and sole means of the permanence of families, and it is true both that the right of primogeniture is not a right of the eldest and that the father may transfer the right of the first-born to the youngest of his children.

In our age, individuals see nothing but individuals like themselves, particularly when everything in society has been individualized. The state does not and should not see man except in the family, because it only sees the family in the state. In the eyes of the state, there is no individual apart from a family.

Monsieur Dupin congratulates our new laws for having abolished free testaments and the right of primogeniture, the two great branches of our former legislation, because they were inexhaustible sources of long and expensive lawsuits. But I assure him that these two sources of lawsuits have been replaced, at least in agricultural lands, by a still more fertile and inexhaustible source of lawsuits: the equality of inheritance. I speak of suits for supplements to legitimate inheritance. There is a difference. Suits against testaments in general only took place in wealthy families, whereas suits for supplements to legitimate inheritance, a veritable gold mine for the lawyers and expert land brokers, ravage and ruin the smallest land-owning families. For the cadets, who stubbornly believe that their father has given their elder secret advantages, and who no longer respect either their father's will or their elder brother's (a respect and deference that the former laws inspired in them) will overturn the house ten times and even dig up the cinders in the hearth to discover the few pennies kept out of the common inheritance.

What are we to say of the example of the Hebrews and the Romans adduced by our celebrated jurist? The monarchy of the Hebrews was not our monarchy, nor the Roman Republic our republic. "The ancients," said Montesquieu, "did not have a tempered monarchy." Thus we can say that their monarchies were not as good as ours, while their democracies were perhaps better, at least they were better than the Convention, because nature wills that good institutions improve over time while bad ones become worse.

Yet the Hebrews had the right of primogeniture: the law of Moses gave two shares of all the father's wealth to the eldest. As Jacob lay dying, he called his eldest son Ruben his strength, the first of his gifts, the greatest in authority: *Rubens fortitudo mea, prior in donis, major in imperio.*[1]

If a man had two wives, one beloved and the other hated, Moses did not allow the son of the cherished wife to be preferred to that of the odious wife if the latter were the eldest, and gave him two shares of all the goods, the share of the firstborn.

While the Hebrews did not have the right of primogeniture as we understand it, they had something better for the preservation of family name and property, which is the only purpose of the right of primogeniture. In order to perpetuate the family name, the law commanded that the brother marry the widow of a brother who had died without issue, *ut suscitaret semen fratri suo,*[2] and, to preserve property, it commanded that in the Jubilee year—that is, every fifty years—alienated goods return to the original families: *Anno Jubiloei redient omnes ad possessiones suas.*[3]

These laws were effective in ways different from our own, nay, they were more able to preserve the family name and property. Monsieur Dupin thinks them harsh. Indeed, they were severe. These laws separated the Hebrews from foreigners in order to preserve them from contact with idolaters and to maintain their faith in the unity of God. Yet they were admirable for making a people of brothers, an indestructible people. They were, as Rousseau said, "proof against time, fortune, and conquerors."

---

[1] Genesis 49:3. In the Douay-Rheims translation of the Vulgate, this reads "Ruben . . . thou art my strength . . . excelling in gifts, greater in command."

[2] Deuteronomy 25:5, "and raise up seed for his brother."

[3] Leviticus 25:10, "In the Jubilee year . . . every man shall return to his possession."

Whether or not the Romans had the right of primogeniture and the prerogative of the firstborn before Augustus, they valued the permanence of the family and the preservation of its goods. Their laws prevented the father from naming his wife or only daughter as heir for fear that she would take the goods to another family. In their lessons and tales they spoke only of their ancestors. Their laws, customs, and manners were all based upon the ways of the fathers, whose images they preserved with great care and whose funeral rites they nobly decorated. Shall we say that this attachment to family was only seen in the patricians? Yet these were the only ones with names and properties to preserve. The people were clients of the great families and lived on the distributions of their government and the fruits of their conquests. Their tribunals only speak about the division of lands because they did not have any.

"When the Romans agree with me," said Montesquieu, "I am confident." Now then! these Romans, so great as a republic, so strong an aristocracy, our masters in legislation, gave immense power to the father of a family. To preserve the family property they needed neither the Twelve Tables nor any other law, for the father's power was already established. It was very conservative in another way, because he had absolute authority over his children, both during his life and after his death. This domestic monarchy was the corrective of political democracy during the republic's best centuries, and when it was destroyed by the introduction of democracy into both family and state, Augustus attempted to reestablish it and instituted the right of primogeniture in families at the same time as he established monarchy in the state.

When the father had the right of life and death over his children, can it be believed that he lacked the power to regulate his succession and thereby insure the permanence of his family? We must cite the full passage from Montesquieu to oppose his authority to all those so-called natural laws about the equality of inheritance. "Natural law," he says, "ordains that fathers feed their children, but it does not oblige him to make them his heirs. The division of wealth, laws about this division, and the procedure for inheritance can only be regulated by society, and, therefore, by political or civil laws."

It seems to me that after the example of the Hebrews and the Romans, our elders in religion and our masters in legislation, after the constitutions of the legislators of the late Empire, Monsieur Dupin need not resort to the invasions of the barbarians in order to explain the establishment of the right of primogeniture in Europe. Yet some would see it as the result of the feudal laws, an origin which, it is held, would brand it as infamous.

Yet Montesquieu was speaking of these barbarians when he said "they established the best form of government that men could imagine." So if it is true that representative government was the ancient government of France, we owe it to these barbarians. "This beautiful government," Montesquieu said, "was found in the woods." And we may find it again in our salons.

In Tacitus's sublime treatise on the customs of the Germans, we can see who were the true barbarians in the eyes of reason and a purely human philosophy: the refined and much-vaunted Greeks and Romans, or these people who spoke neither Greek nor Latin and had neither arts nor civilized luxuries, but who, in their native simplicity, retained the primitive conditions of the natural law that elsewhere had been disfigured by false policies. While it is true that Tacitus wished to satirize the customs of his day by opposing to them an embellished picture of the Germans, it only follows that this illustrious historian, better than any philosopher of his day, knew or divined the rules of laws and customs and the true principles of society. And Christianity, which had just arisen in the world, was not a stranger to this new direction of moral and political ideas.

I need not say that Monsieur Dupin disagrees with Montesquieu about feudal law. "But it was," continues the jurist, "during almost five centuries, in a time of darkest ignorance and lowest barbarism, a time of private wars, highway robbery, and violence of all kinds, amidst these shadows and violence that feudal law was established." He should have contented himself with saying the abuses of feudal rights, for it would be necessary to return to higher principles to find the origin and reason of the feudal bond, which takes its birth with the regulated monarchy in order to serve it feudally, that is, faithfully. Yet while Monsieur Dupin condemns the right of primogeniture by linking it to the feudal law and its deplorable origins, he does not fear that one may retort with his own argument used against him and say: "It was at the time of the Constituent Assembly and the Convention that the right of primogeniture was abolished together with so many other institutions, that is to say, in a time of the darkest ignorance of the principles of monarchical society, the most atrocious barbarism, the most outrageous impiety, not of private wars but of general wars bloodier than those seen by any Christian age, of thefts, not on the highways, but in homes, of the creation of forty or fifty thousand transitory laws, each more senseless than the last. It was in the time, finally, of the goddess Reason, the law of suspects, the code of émigrés, drownings, firing squads, exiles, deportations, the proscription of all talents, virtues, and fortunes, and when the only decoration of our public squares was an instrument of execution."

The ignorance of the barbarians was that of infancy, but ours is an ignorance that comes from the vain sciences of which we are so proud and which make man neither better nor happier. Their violence was that of passion and youthful lack of reflection; their crimes were unpremeditated.

Yet what expiations, what sacrifices attest to the remorse and repentance of the guilty! They left for the Holy Land, built pious foundations, and went far from the world and into the obscurity and silence of the cloisters to pour out tears for their faults and to edify the society they had scandalized. Our ignorance is that of a society grown old in corruption and led astray by false doctrines, and our violent actions were reflected upon and legalized by an execrable parody of all that is most holy and most sacred: justice. Repentance! God alone can see it. Men have seen less of it than regret, and for our expiation, we have thrown ourselves into the professions.

It is the enlightened jurist, the profound moralist, the sensible man, the orator accustomed to defending the sacred rights of misery and humanity and to invoke in their favor divine and human laws, it is Monsieur Dupin himself whom I ask whether, in considering the age and level of civilization to which our society has succeeded, the progress it has made in moral and legal science, the lessons it has received, the great examples of public and private virtue that have been given it, I ask him, I say, whether several years of the Convention were not a more shameful era for human reason than whole centuries of the barbarism of the Middle Ages. Consider the Hebrews, the Romans, the people of the North, that is to say, the people of God and the peoples of men, the peoples of art and of nature, the English, so often proposed for our admiration, the Germans, and the Spanish, who put even the tools of mechanical art into entail. I speak not of ourselves. Long ago we disavowed our own examples and repudiated our ancient wisdom. See how they agree on the great principle of the permanence of families and the preservation of their properties by institutions, by the right of primogeniture, entail, or other testaments. Let us examine at present this grave question with reference to fathers, children, property, and the state. One must lack all notion of the things of this world, of the ardent attachment that property inspires in the man who cultivates and nourishes it, and the habits to which it gives birth, in order to believe that the father of a family puts more interest in giving something more to his younger children than to preserving his house and transmitting to his descendants the property he received from his fathers and which he has spent his life cultivating, improving, and embellishing. It is not without a profound sadness and bitterness that he anticipates that the equality of inheritance will dissipate his work as soon as he dies and give his possessions into the hands of a stranger, a jealous neighbor, or even an enemy. A rich cultivator whom the author of this piece congratulated for the good state of his beautiful properties responded in a dolorous tone difficult to reproduce: "It is true, my property is beautiful and well cultivated. My fathers for several centuries and I for fifty years have worked to extend, to improve, and to embellish it. But you see my large family, and with *their laws* on inheritance, my children will one day be servants here where they were the masters." Yet the father has a still stronger interest than that of his affections and habits, and this is especially true of the small landowners in France who are an important body within the state, even though they are neither electors nor eligible for the Assembly.

If in a small agricultural holding, the father must divide his wealth equally among his children, then no one of them has a reason to stay beside his parents to work without pay to improve an inheritance that his brothers will profit from as much as he will when his father dies. Therefore, as soon as the children are of age to work, they leave the family house to seek high salaries on other farms or in the workshops of industry. The parents, however, grow older, and soon old age or infirmity prevents them from cultivating their land. Then they sell it off piecemeal as their needs dictate, or they let it go to waste, and as soon as they die, the children come to divide what remains, sometimes cursing their father for having let their patrimony slip away, or, too often, suing one another over the inheritance. Their hearts remain even more divided than the fractured properties.

The disposable share of the inheritance does not entirely remedy this misery, because one of the brothers, generally the eldest, who by vanity or some other motive wants to keep the farm buildings, acquires a share of unproductive value at the expense of more useful properties. His is a property of ruinous upkeep, and it is even in part useless because the buildings, usually contiguous and indivisible, were constructed for a more considerable farm than what remains after the division. Soon the buildings will fall into ruin, the soil cover itself with shanties, the brothers sell their portion to neighbors, and the family perish, not to return.

What becomes of the mother should she survive her spouse as the sole authority of the children? Widowed of her husband, widowed of her children, who, without a rallying point, each go to their own place, she watches them sell her marriage bed, the cradle in which she rocked her children, and the house for which she left her father's home and where she thought she would end her days. She is left alone, without honor or dignity, abandoned by both the family to whom she gave the light of day and the family that received her.

And the younger children? Do they have as much to congratulate themselves for from the equality of inheritance as is believed? No doubt in some rich but small families the initial shares are large. Yet each child wants to have a family, and the land, first divided into a small number, divides itself anew into a larger one, and sooner or later this fracturing proceeds geometrically. For small landowners, this evil is felt in the first generation. Each nevertheless stays attached to his small bit of property, tormenting and exhausting himself in order to eke out a wretched existence that he would have earned with less pain and more profit in another profession. He dies young, or, not being able to support himself and his children from his own property, he ravages his neighbor's. One must live in a land where all the people are property-holders in order to gain the correct idea of the inconveniences and misery of these infinite divisions of landed livings.

The equality of inheritance has had another effect, a political effect of great consequence. It has caused voluntary service to fall off and has forced the government to establish and generalize conscription, a deplorable necessity that weighs on everyone and most especially on the poorest and most miserable, who have neither wealth nor affection other than their children. The liberals see this forced service as the obligatory accompaniment to and support for liberty. Where domestic affections were strongest, landowning families, even the less well off, made enormous sacrifices to protect their children from recruitment, and by tenderness, some also by vanity, or in order not to appear more poor than their neighbors, more often than not they gave as a replacement for a younger son him who had the right of primogeniture, and this cause of ruin has increased still more the fracturing of properties in the agricultural provinces.

A youth who would be better clothed, better fed, and better lodged in our army than at home, dreads the military service that in the past he would have embraced with ardor and alacrity, and more and more of those who in the past set the example for the people by accepting its risks now develop a disliking for this noble profession. Since then, civil employments and dignities, by the renown and importance of their functions, have taken pride of place in France away from the profession of arms.

I do not think that, in a continental state, one can view indifferently a change of spirit and manners that comes from republican opinions. The military spirit is the seedbed of all the virtues that defend and preserve societies: the willingness to risk one's life that comes of courage, disinterestedness, generosity, and resignation to sacrifice. It was in the lands of agricultural and warlike people, like the Vendée, the small cantons of Switzerland, and Spain, that the Revolution found the most resistance. Never has an industrial and commercial people defended its land. Farmers beat ploughshares into arms. Workers will make wool and fabric even for the enemy.

The equality of inheritance strikes a mortal blow to property. Why should the landowner acquire and improve a property that gives him so much trouble during his life and that must at his death disappear into imperceptible fractions and increase the patrimony of another family? Why should he attempt risky improvements that he might not complete and that no one after him will continue? Who will loan the necessary funds, at the risk of seeing himself thrown among several heirs? The children will no longer say what their father had said: "These are the trees my father planted, the fields he cleared, the well he excavated." No monument to the labors and intelligence of their father will remain. Those touching reminders that gave birth to and inspired the desire to leave similar ones for his children will be erased, and the children will no longer know where their cradle rocked, nor where their father's ashes lie.

The right of primogeniture in domestic society has the same effects as heredity in political society. And if the monarchy of the father kept the Roman Republic from pitching over the precipice to which democracy had led it, and was, with religion, the anchor that held the ship before the storm, what force of stability and preservation would it not give to the monarchical state, when the domestic power and the public power, the power of morals and that of laws, each constituted like the other, lend each other mutual support?

I have not spoken of one of the most palpable political inconveniences of the equality of division: the progressive diminution of the number of electors and eligible members. The liberal party does not seem to be touched by this, no doubt because it wishes to replace landowning electors with patent-holding electors.

All they desire today is motion: motion of persons, fortunes, and the mind. It is the agitation of a fever that raises the humors and expends strength. But everything should tend to rest, for the force that preserves us is rest.

No doubt, as one journal said, "the earth is no more monarchical than democratic." Who doubts this? Yet who can doubt that men take habits, sentiments, and their cast of mind from their different ways of life or constitutions of social existence? Thus, in the monarchical family the authority of the father passes after his death to the eldest of his children, without the peace among the brothers being troubled, for they see the heir as the support of their name, the representative of their father, and the last resource of their old age. This unites itself naturally to the monarchical government of the state, and the stability, regularity, tranquility, hope of permanence and preservation of government fits well with the weighty, uniform, and laborious habits of the life of the fields. At the same time, but as its contrary, industrial and commercial families with their acquisitiveness and taste for hazardous enterprises, eager for innovation and prospering in revolutions, accommodate themselves much better to the turbulence and mobility of republican governments. All one need do is glance at Europe to see where monarchical sentiments and where republican opinions are found.

The identity of constitution between domestic society and public society, and the harmony of their principles, is thus the most powerful means of strength and true prosperity for both, and it is because one party in Europe is persuaded of this truth that it sets itself to dissolving the family in order to arrive more promptly at the disorganization of the state.

Moreover, the proposed law can be nothing but optional. It leaves the father total liberty to make an equal division among his children, or, what leads to the same thing, to do nothing at all. In the south of France, in the land of Roman law, where families were more landed and more monarchical, everything that brings back the old habits and customs will be received with satisfaction, and at the beginning of the Revolution, the people of the countryside never seemed to me more alarmed than when the Constituent Assembly announced the law of absolute equality of inheritance. Should the proposed law be received less eagerly in the north of France, there will be no need to be astonished. The north was ruled by other customs. The people there were less landed and busier with industrial work.

The mobile fortunes of commerce and industry divide themselves by equal shares among children. These families are not, strictly speaking, political families, for they lack landed property. Landowning families are planted in the soil. The others only rest upon the soil and are ready to abandon it if they find a more fruitful industry elsewhere. Thus, the agricultural family is fixed. The industrial family is mobile, but it tends to fix itself and to pass from the purely civil state to the political state. For this reason, it is in the interest of the state, as it is that of families, that landed property concentrate itself and that mobile property divide itself, in order to leave to a greater number the means to obey their natural tendency and plant themselves in the soil. The contrary obtains today. Immense fortunes are made with capital, and the great fortunes of the land are dissolving. We spin with steam-driven machines that have the force of fifty horses, and soon we will no longer work the fields with the spade and hoe.

I have spoken of the principle of the right of primogeniture, and I have not busied myself with the consequences that the government has deduced from it in its proposed law in the Chamber. We must not forget that this is a proposed law, and that the Chamber could modify and extend it. There are laws on which it is fitting to leave to the Chamber a sort of initiative, in presenting them only with a principle, leaving to their wisdom the care of developing from it and applying its consequences, and I see that this one on the division of families is one of those laws.

JOSEPH de

MAISTRE

- anti-Protestant Revolution
  - anti "individual reason"
  - anti modernity

REFLECTIONS ON PROTESTANTISM IN ITS RELATIONS TO SOVEREIGNTY
(1798)

An anonymous enthusiast for the republic recently made this noteworthy observation: "Whoever has read modern history and observed the convulsions and revolutions of Europe, clearly discerns that since the era of the Reformation there has been a war—sometimes public, sometimes secret, but always real—between republics and monarchies."

This assertion is not literally true, for the republics of Europe are neither numerous nor powerful enough to fight the monarchies and, in fact, have no general antipathy for monarchical sovereignty. Yet by amending this author's words and making his intended meaning clear, a great truth results: in Europe, since the time of the Reformation, there has been a spirit of revolt which "really struggles, sometimes publicly, sometimes secretly, against all sovereign powers and especially against monarchies."

Europe has one great enemy, which must be fought by all legal methods. It is a fatal ulcer that attaches itself to all sovereign powers and eats away at them. It is the son of pride, the father of anarchy, the universal solvent: Protestantism.

What is Protestantism? It is the revolt of individual reason against general reason; consequently it is the worst thing possible. When Cardinal de Polignac said to the too-celebrated Bayle:[1] "You say that you are Protestant, this word is too general; are you Anglican, Lutheran, Calvinist, or what?" Bayle responded: "I am Protestant in all the force of the term: I protest against all truths." This famous skeptic gave the true definition of Protestantism, which is the essential enemy of all belief held in common by men. This makes it the enemy of human nature, because the well-being of human societies reposes only upon these sorts of beliefs.

Christianity is the religion of Europe: this soil suits it even better than the land of its birth. Here it has deeply rooted itself and has entered into all of our institutions. For all the nations of the north of Europe and for all those that have taken the place of the Romans in the middle of this part of the world, Christianity is as ancient as civilization. The hand of this religion fashioned these new nations. The Cross is on all the crowns. All the legal codes begin with the Creed. The kings are anointed, the priests are judges, the priesthood is an order, the empire is sacred, the religion is civil: the two powers are conjoined, and each gives to the other a part of its force. In spite of the quarrels that have divided these two sisters, they cannot live apart.

The boldest men have no idea what we might substitute for this religious system. All our Eratostratuses have destroyed.[2] None have substituted, none have even dared to propose something in place of what they would like to make disappear. It follows that it is necessary to be forever Christian or nothing.

Yet the fundamental principle of this religion, the primitive axiom on which it everywhere reposed prior to the innovators of the sixteenth century, was the magisterial infallibility that results in blind respect for authority, the abnegation of individual reason, and consequently the universality of belief.

[1] Pierre Bayle (1647–1706) was the French Calvinist author of the *Dictionnaire historique et critique* (1695–97), one of the Enlightenment's founding texts.

[2] Eratostratus was a Greek from Asia Minor who burned down the temple of Diana the night that Alexander the Great was born.

Then the innovators undermined this foundation. They substituted private judgment for Catholic judgment. They foolishly substituted the exclusive authority of a book for that of a teaching minister older than the book and charged to explain it to us.

Thence comes the particular character of the heresy of the sixteenth century. It is not only a religious, but a civil heresy as well, for by freeing the people from the yoke of obedience and giving them religious sovereignty, it set our unshackled pride against authority and replaced obedience with discussion.

This is the terrible character that Protestantism has shown since its cradle. It was born a rebel, and revolt is its natural state.

Christian sovereigns have misused their power in order to extend Christianity, but never has Catholic Christianity made war against sovereigns in order to establish itself in their domains, never has it used anything other than persuasion; this has always been its distinctive character. Constantine, once Christian, did wield his scepter against the infidels, but Catholicism, in order to reign in the Empire, did not once take up arms against Constantine. Latterly we have seen this religion established in the extremities of Asia: what arms did it use there in order to vanquish all human prejudice? One monk armed with a wooden crucifix and ignorant of the language of the land when he first touched its shores. And when the sovereign wanted to hunt them, did they resist? Not at all. Thousands of martyrs were made and not a single rebel. When Tertullian said to the pagans of the third century: "We are everywhere, in the armies, in the tribunals, in the palace; we leave you only the people," certainly Christians were in a position to make themselves feared. Yet never did they threaten the sovereign power. The inexpressible firmness that they showed in the face of the most atrocious torments only proved that they should be feared if they did have a mind to topple thrones.

When Christianity finally was elevated to the throne, things changed. Since religion and sovereignty embraced one another in the state, their interests have necessarily united. It is difficult for sovereignty to avoid joining religion in her conquests, and impossible, in the case of an attack on religion, for sovereignty not to take up her defense.

This essential distinction is not made often enough. Sometimes Christianity has the air of a vulgar conqueror because she advances beneath the flags of a conquering prince. Sometimes she is defended by him against her enemies with the temporal arms of sovereigns who reign with her in the same countries. Sometimes, even, she has seemed to serve temporally against rebellious subjects because the two powers defend themselves together. Yet never has Catholic Christianity been established in any land by revolt against civil authority, and never has she employed against sovereignty anything but apologetics, reasoning, and miracles.

This striking truth is precisely the reverse of what Protestantism has displayed since its birth. It was born a rebel. Its very name is a crime because it protests against everything. It submits to nothing. It believes nothing, and, if it pretends to believe in a book, it is in a book that can offend no one.

This makes it the mortal enemy of all sovereignty, even of those who reign with it, because by establishing independence of judgment, free discussion of principles, and contempt for tradition, it undermines all national dogmas, which are, as we have seen, the shield of all great civil and religious institutions.

This indelible and primitive character of Protestantism has made it a civil heresy as much as a religious one. Stronger than the other heresies, it has done what the others were unable to do. Other heresies have won extensive territories but have lacked the power to extinguish the universal belief. The sectary lives beside his enemy, and he insensibly loses his name and his existence to the extent to which the universal principle suffocates the rebel system.

But Protestantism has done more. It has politically divided the empire of Christendom. It has created Protestant sovereignties, and in several countries of Europe it reigns alone.

In order to penetrate to the nature of Protestantism we must examine its two relations with sovereignties: with those it attacks in order to establish itself, and with those who have adopted it as the religion of the state. We must consider its tumultuous actions against those sovereign powers that oppose its establishment and its muffled and noxious action against those that have adopted it.

From the moment of its origins and during a period of time that exceeds the entire duration of Protestantism, Christianity has lived and propagated itself by its own forces. During all this time the civil power has always oppressed it and frequently persecuted it. Nevertheless, she has never taken up arms against the civil power, and her leaders have never preached the doctrine of resistance and insurrection.

But Protestantism was born with weapons in hand: it respected civil sovereignty only long enough to acquire strength, and it rebelled as soon as it had the necessary power. From all sides its apostles preached resistance to sovereigns. To establish their dogmas, they destabilized thrones and vomited forth the most base injuries against any sovereign who resisted them. One cannot recall the horrible tragedies that Protestantism has caused in Europe without trembling. It scorched and bloodied all the lands into which it could introduce itself: Germany, France, England. The Thirty Years War was its work. For thirty years, Germany was put to the torch and knife by Luther's arguments. The detestable Calvin, seizing a reform already so evil, made of it a French work, which is to say an exaggerated work. The infernal character he impressed upon his sect is indelible. It has done greater or lesser evils according to its circumstances, but it has always been and will always be the same. In the last century it preached the sovereignty of the people and the right of insurrection. It shook the throne of Louis XIV to its very core, and the demagogues of our day have not used a single weapon that Jurieu[3] and his fellows had not used before them.

The death of Charles I in England was the work of a ferocious Presbyterianism that still makes all the efforts it can to overthrow a throne it has always detested.

---

[3] Pierre Jurieu (1637–1713), a French Calvinist, was the Huguenot pastor in Rotterdam from 1681. He was a partisan of William of Orange and the Revolution of 1688.

And should it be said to us: "I cannot decide between Geneva and Rome,"[4] I respond that it should not be so anxious a decision. Where was the religious scepter at the beginning of the sixteenth century? At Rome or at Geneva? At Rome, I believe. Geneva was therefore a rebel. Now, in all cases of rebellion, the excesses of the power that defends itself are the fault of the rebel. Humanity as a body has the right of blaming Saint Bartholomew's on Protestantism, for, in order to avoid it, all it had to do was to refrain from revolting. All power, even spiritual, cannot be exercised on this earth except by men, who will defend themselves as men, not as purely rational and dispassionate beings. If a man in this situation exceeds the limits of legitimate defense, his enemy does not have the right to complain. The Protestant who blames the French sovereign for Saint Bartholomew's is like the Jacobin of our century who denounces the inhumanity of the *chouans*.[5] Would Protestantism say that it was in the right? What rebel does not say he is in the right? If this argument were a good one, it would excuse every insurrection. Besides, it is not a question of who was right or wrong, but only who was the sovereign and who the rebel. And on this point there is no room for doubt.

It is sophistry to place in the balance the excesses of those whom certain men ridiculously call *the two sects*, as if Catholicism were a sect, and as if there were such a comparison to make between the *subject* who attacks and the *sovereign* who defends himself.

We will pass quickly over the great questions. The League and the bloody executions of the sixteenth century furnished an inextinguishable mine of righteous speeches and sarcasm to the *philosophes*, who were able to plead for both Henri IV and the Protestants.[6] But

---

[4] Here Maistre quotes from the *Henriade* (1723), Voltaire's epic poem about Henri IV.

[5] The Chouans were Breton peasants who were fighting the Directory about the time Maistre was composing this essay.

[6] Maistre here is referring to the opinions enshrined in the *Henriade*: that the tolerant Henri IV and his Huguenot supporters were in the right, while the Catholic League of nobles that opposed them was fanatical and lawless.

as it is always opportune to seek the truth and to proclaim it, we can return to the path of philosophy.

Without pretending to excuse the criminal excesses that often dishonor and spoil the best causes, and in order to address the essential question, we ask, "Was the principle of the League evil, or at least as evil as it is popularly represented?" Did Henri IV have the right to bring to the throne, in spite of the French, a religion hostile to the French (or one that they so judged)? To pose the question in general: A prince apostatized in a moment of enthusiasm and fanaticism, and moreover embraced an impetuous and anarchic religion which in that very hour was covering the kingdom with ashes and blood: is he not presumed to have renounced the crown? And his subjects, without making a revolution properly so called, have they not the right to consider the act of the king to be a voluntary abdication, according to the hypothesis that Mr. Burke has so ingeniously developed with regard to James II?

And if this sovereign had not yet then ascended the throne, is not the resistance of the people still more reasonable?

I decide nothing. My pen refuses to write about a legitimate case of insurrection. She is much happier when I choose to bring to light the inconsistencies of the *philosophes*.

These men, who are forever mouthing platitudes about the social contract, the primitive pact, legitimate resistance, and so forth, who would permit a revolution in order to abolish tithes and feudal laws, nevertheless uphold passive obedience when it is a question of the greatest and most precious of all rights. If Henri IV had wanted to raise taxes without consent of the people, they would with great erudition prove that the people had the right to resist him. But when it is a question of bringing to the throne an odious and disastrous sect, and thus placing the dominant religion in second place, giving its rival a perpetual and almost invincible means of seducing and conquering, building a wall of separation between the sovereign and the great majority of his subjects, lighting an inextinguishable blaze within the state, they laugh. All at once the rigid defenders of the rights of the people change their tune. Saint Paul himself spoke no stronger than they about the right of sovereigns,[7] and it is an unforgivable crime for the French to make even the merest difficulty for the *Béarnais*.

This is how these men understand their principles. We must not demand that they be reasonable: that is too difficult. But they might at least be consistent.

Montesquieu said in that censorious tone that suited his brilliance: "When the state is satisfied with the religion already established, good civil law will not suffer the establishment of another. Here then is the fundamental principle of political laws in religious matters. When there is a choice whether to admit a new religion into the state, one must not establish it there. When it is already established, one must tolerate it."

If I had lived at the time of this great man, I should have liked to have asked him several questions. First, what does it mean for a religion to be *established* in a state? When a sect wants to introduce itself into a land, it does not wait at the border modestly asking if it be welcome. It slithers in silently like a snake and sows its dogmas in the shadows of the sovereign's ignorance; then all at once it abruptly rises and holds up its head to the heavens. Is it then *established*? This is, doubtless, not what Montesquieu wanted to say, or there would be no distinction to make. This great man thus wanted to speak of admission founded upon public law, or on the tacit concession declared by time and prescription. Up to that point it is not yet *established*, and one must not *suffer* that it establish itself. Thus one must resist it, but how? This would be my second question, and it is an important one. Is it necessary to *pray*, by manifesto, "Would you be so kind as to leave our state?" I fear this would not succeed. So, to conform with Montesquieu's maxim, it is necessary to ordain, to coerce, and to punish. But to what extent is severity permitted, and at what point does it become a crime? Certainly, all useless severity is criminal, and all severity is innocent if it is necessary.

---

[7] Maistre is alluding to St. Paul's Epistle to the Romans, 13:1–7.

Further, the reaction of the sovereignty that defends itself should be proportionate to the action of the enemy that attacks it. On this incontestable principle one is forced to feel less pity for those great acts of rigor, which were really only unfortunate necessities. Seeing a cadaver splayed out on the high road with the murderer standing by would incite all one's indignation. Yet the discovery that the killer is a peaceful traveler and the other a brigand fallen victim to a just defense changes everything. The law, in extending itself, is always the same. The morality of the executions by which an assailed sovereignty defends itself must be judged by their necessity. All that is not indispensable is criminal, but the most severe measures imaginable are licit if other means of defense are lacking. I hope that one would not be tempted to respond, "I see deceit and rage on both sides." No doubt. Human passions are ineradicable, and men fight as men even when they fight for the law. But there is no comparison to make. If in a war of rebellion one hundred thousand men die in one way or another, the side of sovereignty has given one hundred thousand dead and the rebels have *committed* one hundred thousand *murders*. Truths this simple cannot escape anyone.

Thus, in the terrible struggle of the sixteenth century, on one side there was the rebellion that attacked and on the other sovereignty that defended itself. When the excesses were equal on both sides, the party evil by character and essence cannot blame the side that was only so accidentally.

It is easy to forget the evils of our ancestors, but who can describe with enough energy the evils that Protestantism poured out over Europe during the first century of its existence? They were such that men of the highest merit believed that they perceived in them something outside the circle of human events, and they suspected that they might be witnesses to the great calamities that must announce the end of the world according to religious tradition. Wesembeck, a highly esteemed German jurist, a grave and erudite man, made serious excuses for himself because, in 1573, he was engaged in a profane work at a time when one visibly sensed the end of all things. In reading him, one is again moved to pity by his anguish.

"What is, therefore, the fruit of this REFORM?" said Montaigne in his philosophical sneer. "The entire improvement, in my view, boils down to calling oneself Abraham or Isaac instead of John or Claude." If only he were right! But the human species has not and will not pay the debts of its sins for such a small price.

Not only is Protestantism capable of the evils that its establishment has caused, it is antisovereign by nature, rebellious in essence, and the mortal enemy of all national reason. Everywhere Protestantism replaces it with individual reason, which is to say that it destroys everything.

How remarkable that human reason has never made a greater effort nor had a heavier fall than in the establishment of Protestantism.

I agree to speak only politically. I only want to consider Christianity as a political institution. This institution was the national system of a very great number of nations, and never has there existed an institution all at once more ancient, more vast, and more august.

The reformers saw the faults in this ancient edifice, which even they held to be divine. They endeavored to reform it, and this reform consisted in uprooting the old foundations and substituting new ones. Never had human reason made a greater effort, and never had she been more absurd than when she put discussion in the place of authority, and the individual's private judgment in the place of the leaders' infallibility. No system is as great an affront to good sense, not even atheism, for it is more absurd to suppose an absurd God than to deny Him existence. Now, if religion is founded upon a book, if we must become judges of this book, and if all men are judges of this book, the God of Christians is a chimera a thousand times more monstrous than the Jupiter of the pagans.

It is easy to foresee that the abolition of Catholicism would lead straight to the abolition of Christianity. In the last analysis, the system of the reformers reduces to the singular pretension to desire both to maintain the laws of an empire and to overthrow the power to execute them.

Catholics have not ceased to predict this, and the avowals that have escaped from Protestants of good faith have justified their prophecy. Among a thousand avowals of this type, I will choose one that seems to me infinitely remarkable for the time, place, and quality of the person. A professor of theology in the University of Cambridge preached on May 3, 1795, before a respectable body, and with noble frankness outlined the sequence of the reform:

> Scarcely had the right of *private judgment* been assured, scarcely had it been freely put to use, than a group of writers, bearing the imposing title of free-thinkers, boldly established themselves as the preceptors of humanity, and spread their fantastic and foolhardy opinions, especially in matters of religion and govern-ment. . . . Truly I fear that the reformed states have more to blame themselves for on this point than has hitherto been imagined: almost all the impious works and much the greater part of those in which immorality loans its powerful weapons to modern irreligion have been composed and printed by Protestant publishers.

This is all that could be said by a wise man unhappily enrolled under the banners of this sect. He could not have shown more clearly the deadly consequences of a system destructive of all con-stitutions, civil and religious.

When one considers the indelible character of Protestantism, he is less astonished that it has been the object of the avowed hatred of certain Catholic powers such as Louis XIV, whose intolerance has so greatly exercised our *philosophes*. In all governments there is a hidden power or conservative instinct that acts unseen even by the sovereigns and their counselors, and which often makes use of their errors or vices in order to conserve the edifice. The persecutions of

Father Le Tellier[8] against the Jansenists have been cited a thousand times. This man might be guilty in the eyes of God, or he might not. I know no better than those who accuse him. But whether his hatred was reasonable or blind, it is certain that it was *French and politically astute*. By its extreme affinity with Calvinism, Jansenism was the enemy of France. Events have fully justified the famous Jesuit, for Jansenism showed itself to be gravely guilty in the French Revolution, and in this it ran close behind its two brothers, philosophism and Protestantism.

Again, the aversion of Louis XIV for Calvinism was a royal instinct. He could have erred in the means—by forcing certain measures—but his instinct was correct, and he worked for the conservation of the empire. Nothing can reconcile Protestantism with authority; the proofs of this, above all in France, are unforgettable. The Edict of Nantes was wrenched out by force (although perhaps the Protestants remained the beneficiaries of some hidden inclination in the recesses of the heart of that good and great Henri). Yet the concession could not make them loyal subjects. Never did Protestantism cease for an instant to conjure against France: it divided her in opinion while waiting to divide her into *départements*. The duke of Rohan's tomb in Geneva[9] could not eclipse the scaffold he merited in France. It required nothing less than Richelieu's invincible genius to demolish the ramparts of La Rochelle, *bringing the final blow to the head of the rebellion*. But Louis XIII did not dare to be more than a conqueror. Louis XIV arrived, and all gave way before him. He had his way, and in his ascendancy could scorn timid measures with impunity. One day he said to a Protestant of quality: "My father feared you, my grandfather loved you. I neither fear nor love you." He was right. He revoked the Edict of Nantes, and he was right again. It was not a case of confiscation, still less of useless severity, and above all not the tyranny over consciences for which it is everywhere denounced.

[8] Michel Le Tellier, S.J. (1643–1719), confessor to Louis XIV from 1709 to 1715.

[9] Henri de Rohan (1579–1638) was the commander of the Huguenot military during the reign of Louis XIII.

However, to render homage to the truth, it might be necessary to agree that the king was far from knowing all the evil that he did, that the execution of the law, as is almost always the case in great affairs, was followed by abuses that should not be blamed on the legislator, and that in Paris one had only a very false idea of what occurred in the south of the kingdom.

Rarely do these great operations proceed without sadness. The inconveniences consequent to the revocation of the Edict of Nantes do not prevent this revocation from having been very just and very politic.

It has not been often enough observed that this blow was not struck by the despotism of an imperious prince. It was the work of his Council, it was the result of a system conceived and built by the powerful minds that made his cabinet the most feared in Europe. Certainly Louis XIV, devoted to all pleasures, illusions, and dissipations, had other things in mind than a strategy of legislation against the Protestants. He supplied the *royal instinct*; his Council did the rest. Those ignoramuses who accuse him of stupidity, and who believe that the revocation was the result of a fanatical confessor's insistence, do not grasp the facts and forget that in a superior century, everything is superior. Louis XIV's ministers and magistrates were as great exemplars of their kind as his generals, his painters, or his gardeners were of theirs. They perfectly understood France. They were animated by the infallible spirit of great centuries, and knew that they were doing more than would their petty successors. What our miserable century calls *superstition*, *fanaticism*, or *intolerance* was a necessary ingredient of French grandeur. These ministers and magistrates regarded French Calvinism as the greatest enemy of the state. They constantly sought to check it, and each year of the reign of that prince who gives his name to the century was marked by a law suppressing some privilege of the Protestants. The Protestant edifice, which had for so long menaced sovereignty, was gradually cleared away with an imperturbable determination, was deprived of all its supports, and in the end was toppled without the least risk by the revocation of the edict.

Let us suppose that this law cost France four hundred thousand men. The loss is proportionate to taking away one thousand inhabitants from Paris. It would hardly be noticed. With respect to the harm done to France by the loss of the capital taken by the refugees into foreign lands, let us recommend those persons for whom such shopkeeper's objections signify something to go look for answers elsewhere.

Louis XIV trampled on Protestantism. Long did he live, and he died in his bed shining with glory. Louis XVI caressed it, and he died on the scaffold.

The children of this sect led him there.

Would you like to be convinced that Louis XIV was conducted by the most sound policies? Would you like to acquit him of his conduct with regard to French Protestants, at least in its general lines? You need only to consider the conduct of the sectaries during the French Revolution.

Louis XVI had just given a signal benefit to the Protestants. He gave them all civic rights (it is true he did this at the wrong time, but that is another matter). The blind monarch, tricked by his excellent heart and his desire to satisfy a people more blind than himself, did more than pardon the hostile sect, he honored it and allowed it to touch him. How was he thanked?

Rabaud de Saint-Etienne, a Protestant minister, celebrated the acts of kindness of Louis XVI in an eloquent discourse (but more hypocritical than eloquent) that won him universal applause. Before the public, with a pathetic tone of sincerity and gratitude, he had, in the name of his brothers, invoked the blessings of heaven upon the benevolent monarch. He repeated this discourse in a number of other lectures, and while this traitor was traveling through the villages of his province under the pretext of having the people hear the voice of gratitude, he preached the maxims of independence and fanned the flames of insurrection.

Scarcely had the tocsin of the revolt been heard when Rabaud flew to Paris. His actions there are well known. In the first assembly, he figured among the most ardent enemies of the monarchy, and in the third, the mouth that had dared to pray for Louis XVI voted for the death of the virtuous monarch along with Marat, Lebon, and Robespierre.

And when the leaders had undermined the throne in Paris, what was the conduct of the sect as a whole in the south? In vain had tolerance made the greatest progress in France since the beginning of the century; in vain had the public spirit consoled the Protestants for those difficulties to which they were still confined by French legislation; in vain had the parlements, by a large number of interpretive judgments, applied themselves to making the laws lose their former rigor; in vain had the best and most humane of all kings allowed the judgment of opinion to be in favor of Protestants. In their intractable hearts, nothing could extinguish their thirst for Catholic blood and their hatred for the monarchy. Let us dismiss from our minds the horrible scenes of Nîmes[10] and so many other places: they are well known to all. I pray that we make just one observation. It is that among all the French Protestants there is not to be found one single writer who took up the quill for the party of good. You might say that they were few in number with respect to the rest of the population. Yet I do not ask that you cite me the Protestant defenders of the monarchy by the hundred. I ask only that among them and especially among their ministers you show me one man with the courage and nobility to join the many French who consecrated their talents to oppose the principles of the Revolution or to deplore its excesses. We know how the French clergy showed themselves at this time. They did more than write, they flew to their death, and they made themselves immortal. Theirs is an example to make one want to emulate their magnanimity, and all the more because these are recent events. Once more, I know we must make allowances for their small number, but I am only asking for one, and I am not asking for a hero or a martyr. Show me one man who had the courage to raise his voice to say,

---

[10] Nîmes was the scene of street-fighting between Catholics and Protestants in 1789.

"You are doing evil." This French Protestant, this minister, where is he?

Thus the events of our century justify those that preceded them. If you want to see another proof of the wisdom of the revocation of the Edict of Nantes, you will find it in the very character and conduct of the French refugees.

These men, chased from their fatherland by a severe law, should have been full of eternal gratitude towards the generous powers that gave them asylum. Fidelity leading to trust, it seems that in a short time these new subjects should have formed the most loyal and beloved class of subjects of these sovereigns.

Yet just the opposite happened. The title of refugee is not a title of favor, and their conduct further justifies this mixed sentiment. Far from being the best subjects of those sovereigns who had given their fathers asylum, their equivocal fidelity wearied and disturbed the government in several Protestant countries. No one has drunk of the revolutionary poison with more thirst than they. In short, in these lands as in all others there are men distinguished by their attachment to sovereignty and their ancient loyalty: I would not want these men to go looking for models or friends among the refugees.

The universal conscience is infallible, penetrating, inexorable. In spite of all possible prejudices she has graven on their brows a kind of sign, one that cannot be very clearly distinguished, but one for which it would be useless to give a name. It is enough to know that it is displeasing.

In the moral world as well as the physical there are *affinities*, or *elective attractions*. Certain principles attract one another, and others repel one another. The knowledge of these truly occult qualities is the basis of science. I pray, therefore, for observers to reflect upon the truly striking affinity between Protestantism and Jacobinism that has manifested itself before the eyes of the universe.

Since the first moment of the Revolution the enemies of the throne have shown a filial tenderness for Protestantism. Everyone has seen this alliance, and no one has been tricked by it, not even Protestant foreigners.

In the three assemblies that destroyed and dishonored France, has one ever detected, I say not an act, but even a sign of mistrust towards the Protestants? Did these suspicious tyrants who feared everything and who punished those whom they presumed to have the intention of resisting ever dread the doctrine of the Protestant Church? No, never. I defy anyone to find the least trace of it.

What is this? Do not the ministers of the Holy Gospel preach the same Gospel as the Catholic clergy? Is it not written in the Book, for them as much as for us: *All power comes from God, obey your superiors, even unjust ones,* in all that it not unjust, and so forth.[11] How is it then that such maxims never frightened the tyrants of France? Ah! It is because they well knew, as all men know, that there is no more religious sovereignty among the Protestants, that the governing principle is annihilated there, and that a book separated from the authority that explains it is empty.

Men of all lands and all cults, observers of all systems, note well and do not forget it: *The Gospel taught by the Protestant Church never brought fear to Robespierre.*

When the Titans of the National Convention contrived to annihilate the priesthood, to efface the last traces of Christianity, to consecrate the cult of the Goddess Reason, to lead to the bar the ministers of religion and to obtain from them an infamous apostasy, why do we not see Protestants among the afflicted? It is because these odious tyrants did not fear them. They sought the true cult, the eternal cult. They perceived the sacerdotal character where it was and did not seek it where it was not. They madly desired to vilify Catholicism, which alone had effectively opposed the Revolution and alone could end it. Never did they conceive the least suspicion about the Protestant doctors.

England has experienced the striking affinity between Protestantism and Jacobinism. The Anglican Church is more Catholic than she

---

[11] Another reference to St. Paul's Epistle to the Romans 13.

knows, and we believe that her Catholicity has saved the state. Yet is it not among the Protestants properly so called, among the Puritans, that the venom of the French Revolution has done the most damage? Among the innumerable pamphlets that the great event has produced in England, those that are products of the hand of the dissenters are marked with the sign of Revolution: those conservative words *Church and State* send them into convulsions, and the Test oath they call an act of the most insupportable tyranny. They avow and proudly preach the doctrine of the sovereignty of the people, and from it they derive the most appalling consequences.

Their dangerous eloquence is constantly exercised upon the *Rights of the People*, and the imaginary hypothesis in which the three powers conspire to abolish the fundamental laws is the favorite subject of their dissertations.

"Such an act," they say, "would be a conspiracy against the people and the murder of the Constitution; and the people, in their wisdom, would do well to treat their representatives as fools and to chase them not only from the two chambers of Parliament but from the kingdom altogether."

We see that it is no longer a question of knowing what is an attack against the *fundamental laws*: no doubt it is for the people to decide that *in their wisdom*.

According to these principles, the solemn feast that the great nation celebrates annually to expiate the folly of several madmen is only a religious farce for the Dissenters. "Some apology," they say, "may even be made for the conduct of those who brought Charles I to a public trial, and afterwards to the block."

In vain do the Church and state reunite their voices each year to say: *Excidat illa dies!*[12] The mourning of the nation makes the Dissenters smirk. What the nation calls a martyrdom, they call an execution.

We have shown much pity for this sort of Dissenter, famous in the sciences, whom the English people, without respect for physics,

---

[12] "May the day be forgotten!"

have treated as an enemy of the state. I honor these great talents, but I pity them little when I remind myself how their citizen Gibbon, who was not devout, wrote about the works of the exalted puritan: *Tremble, pontiffs! Tremble, judges!*

In fact, they should tremble together and for the same reason, because the intimate nature of Protestantism makes it hostile to all kinds of sovereignty, just as the nature of Catholicism makes her the friend, the conservator, the most ardent defender of all governments.

This is why the English Dissenters have often accused the famous defenders of the British constitution of tending towards Catholicism, which is to say towards a loyalty that even withstands injustice, a crime which Protestantism does not pardon.

Has not Paine reproached the venerable Burke for "facilitating the return of the English to Catholicism and conducting them to religious infallibility by way of political infallibility"?

No doubt this great patriot, this great writer, this celebrated prophet is guilty: he divined the evil of the French Revolution because he would not believe that the people had the right to vote in the hustings to overthrow the constitution; he taught that the united and legally constituted will of the three powers is an oracle at whose voice all must bend; he believed that the English are bound by the vows of their fathers who formed, accepted, and consecrated this constitution, deprived their successors of the right to remake it, and thus insolently claimed *infallibility*. We should take note of Paine's accusation: "*He has shortened his journey to Rome.*"

The great basis of Protestantism is *the right of private judgment*. This right has no limits. It applies to everything and cannot be restrained. Moreover, there is no faction, no enemy of religion or laws who has not praised Protestantism. There is no fomenter of that execrable Revolution who did not praise the Protestantism of the sixteenth century. We can see in the posthumous work of Condorcet to what extent the most odious—and of all French revolutionaries perhaps the most ardent enemy of Christianity—was a friend to the reform. The causes of this inclination are visible, but he did not leave to us the trouble of finding them. "The new sects," he said, "could not restrict the *right of private judgment* within too tight limits without the most obvious contradiction because they had established on the same right the legitimacy of their separation."

We cannot reveal more clearly the secret of the sect: Protestantism appeals from national reason to individual reason, and from universal authority to the right of private judgment. Now, according to this sect, no man and no group possesses religious sovereignty. It follows that the man or body who examines and rejects a religious opinion cannot condemn the man or body who examines and rejects others without contradicting himself. All dogmas will be examined, and by an infallible consequence, sooner or later rejected. There will be no more communal belief, no more tribunal, no more reigning dogma. That is what Condorcet wanted; that is what those similar to him want. Protestantism gives them what they ask for. Once you give them the principle, they will take care of the consequences. They will also make to look ridiculous those pusillanimous men who do not dare to take this principle to its consequences.

Condorcet no less clearly explained the nature of Protestantism with respect to civil sovereignty. "Despotism," he said while exalting the good deeds of the reform, "also has its instinct, and this instinct has revealed to kings that men, after having submitted religious prejudices to the examination of reason, will soon extend it to their political prejudices, that enlightened about the usurpations of popes, they will end by wishing to be so about the usurpations of kings, and that the reform of ecclesiastical abuses, so useful to royal power, leads to that of the more oppressive abuses on which this power is founded."

We have seen that all parties are in agreement about the essence of Protestantism. Whether one loves it or not, whether one praises it or blames it, everyone speaks the truth about it. But, to make it withdraw, nothing is more useful than to show it its friends.

We do not express ourselves with precision when we say that Protestantism is generally favorable to republics. It is favorable to no government; it attacks them all. Yet as sovereignty only exists completely in monarchies, it particularly detests this form of government, and it looks for republics, in which it has less to wear away. There as elsewhere it fatigues sovereignty and cannot uphold the social yoke. It is republican in monarchies and anarchist in republics. In England, it has not ceased to howl about royal prerogative; the constitutional union of the scepter and the Cross makes it roar. It knows it can only break them by separating them, and to this end it toils unceasingly. In republics, the mere image of sovereignty displeases it. It pursues it as if it were real, and, looking always to give authority to the greatest number, it tends towards anarchy. In this regard, our era presents an interesting spectacle. We have seen federal republics, divided in religion, submitted to the venom of the French Revolution, and the least attentive eye has seen the effects. In Protestant states, the sovereigns have trembled, and even the essence of government has been permanently altered. But in the Catholic states, with religious sovereignty fighting for its ally, the people have been unshakeable in their loyalty and have not taken one step towards the French principles.

There is the greatest evidence that Protestantism is hostile in its essence to civil and religious sovereignty, but this thesis must be considered under a particular point of view in order to be placed in full daylight.

I believe I have proved well enough that no institution is solid and durable if it reposes only on human power. History and reason together demonstrate that the roots of all great human institutions are located beyond this world. I have nothing more to say on this score. Sovereignties above all have power, unity, and stability only to the extent to which they are *divinized* by religion. Now Christianity, that is to say Catholicism, was the cement of all European sovereignties. By removing Catholicism from them without giving them another faith, Protestantism has undermined the basis of all those which have had the ill fortune to embrace the reform. Sooner or later, their sovereignty will melt away into the air.

Mohammedism, even paganism, have done less political evil when they substituted their kind of dogmas and faith for Christianity, for they are religions. But Protestantism is not one at all.

There are words that we often repeat, by force of repetition developing the habit of believing that they signify something real, when in fact they signify nothing. *Protestant* is one of these words.

What is a Protestant? At first it seems it is easy to respond. Yet if we reflect, we hesitate. Is he an Anglican, a Lutheran, a Calvinist, a Zwinglian, an Anabaptist, a Quaker, a Methodist, a Moravian, or something else? He is all these, and he is nothing. The Protestant is *a man who is not Catholic*. In this way Protestantism is only a negation. What is real is Catholic. To speak precisely, he teaches no false dogmas, he negates true ones, and he tends to negate all of them. This sect is always trimming.

That the nature and destiny of Protestantism leads it invincibly to negate all Christian dogmas one after another is demonstrated by evidence, metaphysical reasoning, and experience.

No doubt we would laugh at a paradoxical man who upheld the view that once a nation possessed a code of civil law it no longer needed judges, and that for settling all possible disputes it sufficed only to read a book that was intended for all.

By similar reasoning one destroys religious sovereignty. Let us listen to the Anglican Creed, the least unreasonable of all those produced by the reform.

"As the Church of Jerusalem and as those of Alexandria and Antioch fell into error, that of Rome has also fallen into error, not only on morals and rites, but even concerning faith."

Very well. And the other churches taken individually are, no doubt, no more infallible. But if a religious revolt rises up, where are the magistrates, where is the sovereign? No doubt in the unity of these churches? Not in the least: the Anglican Credo rejects this authority.

What is, then, that universal Church to whom its founder made such magnificent promises? *The visible Church of Christ is a congregation of faithful men in which the pure word of God is preached and the sacraments are duly ministered, according to Christ's ordinance, in all those things that of necessity are requisite to the same.*

Yet if one wants to know whether the word is *pure*, and if the sacraments are *duly ministered*, to whom does one address oneself? *To the Book.*

But Jean-Jacques has said that "God himself could not make a book about which men could not disagree." So, if one would continue to disagree about the Book that serves as the rule, what can be done, and how can the dispute be resolved?

Some Indians say that the earth rests upon a giant elephant. And if you ask them what the elephant rests upon, they answer: On a *giant turtle*. To this point, everything is fine, and the earth runs no risk. But if you press them, asking what supports the giant turtle, they clam up and leave the turtle hanging in midair.

Protestant theology is just like this Indian physics. It rests salvation upon faith, and faith upon the Book. But the Book is *the giant turtle*.

Thus, Protestantism is the *sans-culottisme* of religion.[13] The former invokes the *word* of God, the latter the *rights of man*, but they are the same theory, the same movement, the same result. These two brothers have destroyed sovereignty by distributing it to the multitude.

---

[13] The *sans-culottes* were Parisian democratic radicals, so named because they wore breeches instead of stockings.

ON THE POPE (1819)
PRELIMINARY DISCOURSE

It might seem surprising for a layman to presume to treat questions that hitherto have seemed exclusively the province of the zeal and knowledge of the priestly order. Nevertheless I hope that, after weighing the reasons that have led me to enter this honorable combat, every well-disposed reader will approve of me in his conscience and will absolve me of the charge of usurpation.

In the last century our order was eminently guilty towards religion. I fail to see why the same order should not furnish the ecclesiastical writers some faithful allies who will range themselves around the altar to dispel some of the shadows without disturbing the Levites.

I even suspect that such an alliance may have become necessary in our day. A thousand causes have weakened the priestly order. The Revolution despoiled, exiled, and massacred the born defenders of the maxims it abhorred. The old athletes of the holy militia have descended into the tomb. Young recruits advance to take their place, but these recruits are necessarily few in number, the enemy having shortened their lives with the most deadly skill. And if Elijah had thrown down his mantle prior to flying off to his native land, who knows whether the sacred garment would have been able to raise itself up off the ground?[1] It is no human motive that hurries on the young heroes of the new army, and so we may expect great things from their noble resolution. All the same, how much time is needed for the instruction that the coming battle requires? And once they have acquired it, will they be at leisure to employ it? The best works of controversy emerge only during those calm times when tasks can be distributed according to strength and talent. Huet could not have written his *Demonstration of the Gospel* during the exercise of his episcopal functions.[2] And if Bergier had all his life been made to toil in a country parish, he could not have given religion the many works that place him in the rank of the most excellent apologists.[3]

The clergy of Europe, and most especially of France, whom the revolutionary tempest struck most directly and forcefully, finds itself more or less reduced to its holy but burdensome parish duties. All the flowers of the ministry are faded; only the thorns remain. For them, the Church begins again, and by the very nature of things, the confessors and martyrs must precede the doctors. Nor is it easy to foresee the moment when, returned to their former tranquility and numerous enough to make all the parts of their immense ministry march in order, they will astonish us by their learning as well as by the sanctity of their morals, the activity of their zeal, and the prodigies of their apostolic successes.

During this time of reconstruction, I do not see why laymen inclined towards serious studies should not come to range themselves among the defenders of the holiest of causes. When they but serve to fill the voids in the army of the Lord, we cannot justly refuse them the merit of those courageous women who are some-

---

[1] That is, the prophetic office would have failed had Elisha not been present to take up Elijah's mantle. See II Kings 2:13.

[2] Pierre-Daniel Huet (1630–1721), bishop of Avranches, was, with Bossuet, a tutor to the son of Louis XIV. His *Demonstratio Evangelica* (1679) was directed against the skeptics of the day, particularly Spinoza.

[3] Nicolas-Sylvestre Bergier (1715–90), a canon of the cathedral of Paris. He was the leading Catholic apologist in France during the second half of the eighteenth century.

times seen to climb the ramparts of a besieged town to put fear into the hearts of the enemy.

Moreover, every science owes a kind of tithe to the one from whom it proceeds, for "he is the God of knowledge; he prepares all our thoughts."[4] We are beginning the greatest of religious eras, in which all men who have the strength are bound to carry a stone to the great edifice whose construction has been temporarily halted. Our mediocrity should not frighten us. It has not disheartened me. The poor man who sows only mint, anise, and cumin in his tiny garden, may raise with confidence the first stem towards heaven sure of being valued as much as the rich man amidst his vast fields who pours out waves of strong wheat and the blood of the vine in the temple courtyard.[5]

Another consideration encouraged me. The priest who defends religion does his duty and, no doubt, deserves all our esteem. Yet to superficial or preoccupied men, he seems to be defending his own cause, however much his good faith may equal our own. Any observer can see that miscreants are less likely to mistrust a laymen and more likely to let him approach without showing repugnance. Now, all who see this strange and dark bird know that it is incomparably more difficult to come near to it than it is to capture it.

May I say still more? If a man has spent his whole life on an important subject, has consecrated all the time he could give to it, and has turned to it all his knowledge, if such a one senses in himself an indefinable force, which proves to him the need to pour out his ideas, he must of course first fight against all his illusions of self-love. He may, however, have some right to believe that this is a kind of inspiration if he does not lack approbation from strangers.

It has been a long time since I considered France, and I hope that my honorable ambition to be agreeable to her has not compromised my judgment that my work has not displeased her. For if amidst her frightful miseries, she kindly heard the voice of a friend who

---

[4] I Samuel 2:3.

[5] These are allusions to Isaiah 3:1 and Psalm 105:16 (104:16 in the Vulgate).

belonged to her by religion, language, and hopes of a higher order which still live, why should she not consent once more to lend me her ear, today when she has made such a great step towards happiness, and when she has recovered enough calm to examine and judge wisely?

Circumstances have greatly changed since 1796. Then each man was free to attack the brigands at his own peril and risk. Today, all the powers are in their places, but some of the new errors have remained in our policies. Therefore, the writer who does not continually guard himself might suffer what happened to Diomedes under the walls of Troy: to injure a god while chasing down the enemy.

Fortunately, nothing is more evident to the conscience than the conscience itself. If I did not feel myself to be animated by universal benevolence and absolutely detached from every contentious spirit and every polemical anger, even with respect to men whose systems most alarm me, God knows that I would throw down the pen. And I dare to hope that upright men who read me will not doubt my intentions. Yet this sentiment excludes neither the solemn profession of my belief, nor the clear and elevated tone of faith, nor a cry of alarm in the face of a known or hidden enemy, nor, finally, the honest proselytism that proceeds from conviction.

After this declaration, whose sincerity will, I hope, be perfectly justified by the whole of my work, should I still find myself in direct opposition to other beliefs, I will be perfectly tranquil. I know what we owe to the nations and those who govern them, but I do not believe that I fail in duty by telling them the truth with such fitting consideration. The first lines of my work will make it known. He who might fear to be dismayed by it is instantly prayed not to read it. It is proven to me, and I should like with all my heart to prove it to others, that without the sovereign pontiff there is no true Christianity, and that no honest Christian man, separated from him, will sign upon his honor (if he have some knowledge) a clearly circumscribed profession of faith.

All the nations who have separated themselves from the authority of the common Father have, taken in mass, the right (savants do not have it) to complain of the paradox; but none of them has the right to complain of an insult. Every writer who confines himself to severe logic owes nothing to anyone. There is but one honorable revenge to take on him, and that is to reason against him and to do so better.

In my life's work I have treated general ideas as much as has been possible. It is nevertheless easy to see that I have been particularly occupied with France. There is no salvation for her until she has understood her errors. Though France be blind on this point, Europe sees more clearly what we must await from her.

There are nations privileged to have a mission in the world. I have already attempted to explain that of France, which to me seems as evident as the sun. There is, in the natural government and national ideas of the French people, a sort of theocratic and religious element that always asserts itself. The Frenchman needs religion more than other men; if he lacks it, he is not only weakened, he is deformed. Look at his history. To the government of the druids, which was capable of everything, there succeeded that of the bishops who were always—and even more in antiquity than in our day—the counselors of the king in all his councils. It was Gibbon who said that the bishops made the kingdom of France. Nothing could be more true. The bishops constructed that monarchy as bees construct their hive. Their councils in the first centuries of the monarchy were true national councils. The Christian druids, if I may thus express myself, played the leading role in them. The forms have changed, but one always recognizes the same nation. The Teutonic blood that mixed in through conquest enough to give France her name disappears almost entirely at the battle of Fontenay, leaving only Gauls. The proof is to be found in the language. When a people is one, the language is one. And if it is mixed in some way, but especially through conquest, each constituent nation gives its portion of the national language, but the syntax and what is called the genius of the language belong always to the dominant nation, and the number of words contributed by each nation is always rigorously proportioned to the quantity of blood respectively furnished by the diverse constituent nations and mixed into the national unity. Now, in the French language the Teutonic element is barely sensible. Considered in the whole, the French language is Celtic and Roman. There is none greater in the world. Cicero said: "Let us flatter ourselves us much as we please, we will not surpass the Gauls in valor, nor the Spanish in number, nor the Greeks in talent, and so on, but it is by religion and the fear of the gods that we surpass all the nations of the universe."

This Roman element, naturalized in the Gauls, accords well with Druidism, which Christianity stripped of its errors and ferocity while letting remain a certain root that was good. From all these elements resulted an extraordinary nation, destined to play an astonishing role and to become the head of the religious system in Europe.

Christianity penetrated the French so quickly that one must suppose a particular affinity. The Gallican church had hardly any infancy; in being born, she found herself the first of the national churches and the most firm support of unity.

The French had the unique honor of constituting (humanly speaking) the Catholic Church in the world, by elevating her august chief to the indispensable rank that his divine function required, and without which he would have been only a patriarch of Constantinople, a miserable plaything for Christian sultans and Muslim autocrats. It is an honor they have not esteemed highly enough.

Charlemagne, the modern Hermes, elevated (or caused to be recognized) the throne that was made to ennoble and consolidate all other thrones. Just as there has been no greater institution in the world, nor has there been one upon which the hand of Providence has shown itself more visibly. It is beautiful to have been chosen by Providence to be the enlightened instrument of this unique marvel.

In the Middle Ages the French led Europe to Asia, sword in hand, to challenge on its own ground that redoubtable Crescent that menaced all European liberties. One simple private individual, who gave to posterity only his baptismal name decorated with the modest surname the Hermit, aided only by his faith and his invincible will, raised an army, terrified Asia, broke feudalism, ennobled the serfs, transported the flame of the sciences, and changed Europe.[6]

Bernard followed him. Bernard, the prodigy of his century, a man of the world and a mortified monk, an orator, a brilliant wit, a statesman, "a solitary who had more occupations in the world than most men will ever have; consulted by the whole earth, charged with an infinity of important negotiations, pacifier of states, called to councils, carrying speeches to kings, instructing bishops, reprimanding popes, governing an entire order, a preacher, and the oracle of his time."[7]

That not one of these famous enterprises succeeded has been drummed into us. It is true that not one of the crusades succeeded; even children know it. Yet in another way, all of them succeeded, and this is what men do not want to acknowledge.

The name Frank made such an impression in the Orient that it there remains synonymous with the name European. And the greatest poet of Italy, writing in the sixteenth century, did not refuse to employ the same expression.[8]

The French scepter shone at Jerusalem and Constantinople. What could one not hope for from it? It had extended Europe, pushed back Islam, and suffocated the schism. Unfortunately, it did not know how to preserve itself.

A great part of the literary glory of the French belonged to the clergy, especially during the *Grand Siècle* of Louis XIV. Nothing could be more natural than this. The attainment of great knowledge

---

[6] Peter the Hermit was the mysterious leader of the popular pilgrimage to the East that accompanied the First Crusade in 1096.

[7] Here Maistre quotes the *Sermon on Flight from the World* by Louis Bourdaloue, S.J., Bossuet's rival for eloquence as a preacher at the court of Louis XIV.

[8] Torquato Tasso (1544–95), author of *Gerusalemme Liberata*.

is generally incompatible with family life, and so there is an invisible movement of knowledge towards the celibate and priestly state.

No nation has possessed a greater number of ecclesiastical establishments than the French nation, and no sovereignty has used a greater number of priests than the court of France. Ministers, ambassadors, negotiators, tutors, and so on: they are everywhere. From Suger to Fleury,[9] France has gained great advantages from them and can only praise them. We regret that the strongest and most dazzling of all was elevated sometimes to inexorable severity, but he did not surpass it. And I believe that under the ministry of that great man, the downfall of the Templars and other events of this kind would not have been possible.[10]

The highest nobles of France were honored to become the great dignitaries of the Church. What in Europe surpassed the Gallican Church in all that pleases God and captivates men: virtue, science, nobility, and opulence?

Do you require a further explanation of this grandeur? Try to imagine something surpassing Fénelon[11] and you will not succeed.

Charlemagne, in his testament, bequeathed to his son the protectorship of the Roman Church. Repudiated by the German emperors, this legacy passed like a kind of trust to the crown of France. The Catholic Church could have been represented by an ellipse. In one of the foci was Saint Peter, and in the other, Charlemagne: the Gallican Church with her power, doctrine, dignity, language, proselytism, seemed at times to bring these two centers together and to combine them in the most magnificent unity.

O human weakness! O miserable blindness! Detestable prejudices that I will have occasion to treat in this work have totally perverted this admirable order, this sublime relation between the two powers.

---

[9] Suger, abbot of St. Denis, was regent when Louis VII was on crusade from 1147 to 1149. Cardinal Fleury was Louis XV's first minister from 1726 to 1743.

[10] Maistre is here speaking of Cardinal Richelieu. The Templars were suppressed in 1312, thanks to Philippe-le-Bel and his powerful ministers, who were laymen and lawyers.

[11] François de Salignac de la Mothe Fénelon, bishop of Cambrai (1651–1715).

By the force of tricks and stratagems, one of the Most Christian King's most brilliant prerogatives was obscured: that of presiding (humanly speaking) over the religious system and being the hereditary protector of Catholic unity. Constantine used to honor himself with the title of exterior bishop. That of exterior sovereign pontiff did not satisfy the ambition of a successor of Charlemagne; and this job, offered by Providence, was vacant! Ah, if the kings of France had wanted to lend a strong hand to the truth, they would have worked miracles! Yet what could the king do when the lights of his peoples were dimmed?[12] It must be said to the immortal glory of the august house, the royal spirit animating it was often more wise than the academies and more just than the tribunals.

At last overturned by a supernatural storm, this monarchy so precious for Europe has raised itself by a miracle that promises further ones and should imbue all French with a religious courage. But let them not believe that the Revolution is over and that the column of the state is stable because it has been raised up again. On the contrary, it must be understood that the revolutionary spirit is much stronger and more dangerous than it was a few years ago. The powerful usurper made use of it. He knew how to contain it in his iron grip and reduce it to a kind of monopoly to the profit of his crown. Yet since "justice and peace have embraced," the evil genius has no longer been afraid, and, instead of agitating a single mind, it has spilled its roiling spirit over the land.

I beg leave to repeat it: the French Revolution resembles nothing in history. It is satanic in its essence. It will never be totally extinguished except by the opposing principle, and the French will never again fill their proper place until they have recognized this truth. The priesthood should be the principal object of royal thought. If I had before my eyes the table of ordinations, I should be able to predict great events. Once again the French nobility finds an occasion to make a worthy sacrifice to the state. Let her offer her sons to the altar as in days gone by! Today it will not be said that her ambition

---

[12] This is a pun at the expense of the *philosophes*, who called themselves the "lights" (*lumières*).

is for the treasures of the sanctuary. The Church used to enrich her and make her famous. Let the nobility give to the Church all that it may. The brilliance of great names with all their weight of reputation and appeal will make a crowd of men follow their standard. Time will do the rest. By thus upholding the priesthood, the French nobility will acquit itself of the immense debt that she contracted towards France and perhaps even towards Europe. The greatest mark of respect and profound esteem that we may give her is to remind her that the French Revolution (which she would have no doubt ransomed with all her blood) was nevertheless in large part her work. While a pure aristocracy—that is, one that believes and exalts the national dogmas—surrounds it, the throne is unshakeable, even when weakness or error sits upon it. But if the nobles apostatize, the throne is lost, even if it carry a Saint Louis or a Charlemagne. By her monstrous alliance with the evil principle during the last century, the French nobility has lost everything; it belongs to her to repair everything. Her destiny is sure, provided she doubt not, provided she is well persuaded of the natural, essential, necessary, and French alliance of the priesthood and nobility.

At the Revolution's darkest hour, we said, "this eclipse of the nobility is merely what she deserves. She will regain her place. Then she will have paid the price for having embraced children to whom she had not given birth."

What was said twenty years ago is verified today. If the French nobility has been enlarged, then it is up to her to remove all that might trouble the ancient families. When she knows why this was necessary, then she will not be able to complain—yet this should be discussed only in passing and not in great detail.

I return to my principal subject and observe that the irreligious rage of the last century against all Christian truths and institutions was particularly directed at the Holy See. The conjurers knew better than the mass of well-intentioned men that Christianity reposes entirely upon the sovereign pontiff. They therefore directed all their efforts against him. If they had proposed directly anti-Christian measures to the Catholic governments, fear or shame—absent more noble motives—would have sufficed to repulse them. Therefore they devised a more subtle snare for the princes.

Alas, they have taken away wisdom from the kings!

They alleged the Holy See to be the natural enemy of all thrones. They calumniated and defied it. They labored to bring the papacy in conflict with *raison d'état*. They neglected nothing that would make independence seem necessary to dignity. By usurpation, violence, chicanery, and trespasses of all kinds, they painted Roman politics as shadowy, heavy, and underhanded. They accused it of their very own faults. Their success staggers. The evil is such that the spectacle of certain Catholic countries has been able at times to scandalize even Protestants. Without the sovereign pontiff, the whole edifice of Christianity is undermined and will soon crumble entirely.

The facts of the non-Catholic world speak for themselves. Do Protestants amuse themselves by writing books against the Greek, Nestorian, or Syrian churches, which profess dogmas that the Protestants detest? They refrain from doing so. On the contrary, they protect these churches; they address compliments to them and show themselves ready to unite with them, holding every enemy of the Holy See as a true ally.

The unbeliever, for his part, laughs at all the dissidents, and makes use of all of them, perfectly sure that they advance his great work: the destruction of Christianity.

Protestantism, philosophism, and a thousand other perverse and outrageous sects have greatly diminished truth among men. The human race cannot remain in such a state. It is agitated, ashamed of itself, and searching with convulsive movement to ascend against the torrent of its errors after abandoning itself to them with the systematic blindness of pride. In this memorable time, it has seemed useful to me to unfold in all its plenitude a vast and important theory, and to clear away from it all the clouds with which we have obstinately enveloped it for such a long time. Without presuming too much on my own efforts, I hope nevertheless that they will not be absolutely in vain. A good book is not one that persuades the whole world, for none would pass this test. It is the one that satisfies completely the class of readers to whom the work is particularly addressed and leaves no one to doubt either the author's good faith or his indefatigable labor to gain mastery of the subject. I naively flatter myself that every just reader will judge me acceptable on this score. Never has it been more necessary to surround a truth of the first order with all the light of evidence. I also believe that the truth has need of France. I hope, therefore, that France will read me once again with goodness; and I will count myself happy if the great personages of all the orders, in reflecting upon what I hope for from them, will attempt to refute me.

ON THE POPE (1819)
THE OBJECTIVES OF THE POPES IN THEIR STRUGGLES WITH EUROPEAN SOVEREIGNS

If one examines the conduct of the popes during their long struggle against the temporal power, he will find that they unswervingly pursued three ends with all their powers, spiritual and temporal: first, to maintain unshaken the laws of marriage against the attacks of an ever-dangerous libertinism; second, to preserve the rights of the Church and the morals of her priests; third, to secure the liberty of Italy.

THE SANCTITY OF MARRIAGE

A great adversary of the popes,[1] who complains about the *scandal of excommunications*, observes that it was always *the making or breaking of marriages that added this new scandal to the first.*

On this view, public adultery is a *scandal,* and the act intended to repress it is also a *scandal.* Never have two more different things born the same name. Yet let us restrict ourselves, for the moment, to the incontestible assertion that *the sovereign pontiffs principally employed their spiritual arms to repress the anti-conjugal license of the princes.*

---

[1] Maistre is here referring to an anonymous French jurist, the author of *Lettres sur l'histoire* (1803).

Now, never have the popes, and the Church in general, rendered a more signal service to the world than that of repressing in the princes, through the authority of ecclesiastical censure, their access to the terrible passion that constantly wreaks havoc with the holy laws of marriage wherever it is left to itself. When not tamed by civilization, love is a ferocious animal capable of the most horrible excesses. If one does not wish to see it devour all, it must be chained, and it can only be chained by terror: but what will strike fear into him who fears nothing upon the earth? The holiness of marriage, the sacred basis of public happiness, is of the highest importance in royal families, in which disorders of a certain kind bring incalculable consequences. If in the youth of the northern nations the popes had not possessed the means of frightening the passions of the sovereigns, the princes, running from caprice to caprice and from abuse to abuse, would have ended by establishing the law of divorce and perhaps even polygamy. This disorder would then spread to the lowest classes of society, and no eye can see the limits at which such a development will stop.

Emancipated from that uncomfortable power, so inflexible about morals and marriage, Luther had the effrontery to write in his commentary on Genesis, published in 1525, that on the question of knowing whether one could have several wives, the authority of the patriarchs leaves us free, that the thing is neither permitted nor denied, and that he decides nothing: an edifying theory that soon found its application in the house of the Landgrave of Hesse-Cassel.[2]

Should the indomitable princes of the Middle Ages have been left free, they soon would have had the morals of pagans. Even the Church, in spite of her vigilance and untiring efforts, and in spite of the force that she exerted over minds in those backward centuries, only obtained equivocal and intermittent successes. She never conquered without afterwards losing ground.

The noble author whom I cited above has astutely reflected upon the repudiation of Eleanor of Aquitaine. "This repudiation," he said,

[2] Maistre alludes to the bigamy of Philip of Hesse, approved by Luther in 1539–40.

caused Louis VII to lose the rich provinces she had brought to him. . . . The marriage of Eleanor had rounded out the kingdom and extended it to the sea of Gascony. It was the work of the celebrated Suger, one of the greatest men to have lived, one of the greatest ministers and benefactors of the monarchy. While he lived, he opposed a repudiation that must call down so many calamities upon France; but, after his death, Louis VII listened only to the motives of personal discontent that he had against Eleanor. He must have supposed that the marriages of kings are something other than the acts of a family: they are—AND THIS WAS TRUE ESPECIALLY THEN—political treaties that cannot be changed without leading to the greatest dangers for the states for whose destiny they had been the rule.

It could not have been better said. Yet elsewhere, when it was a question of marriages in which the pope believed himself to have a duty to intervene, the same author saw the issue in another light; and the action of the sovereign pontiff to prevent a solemn adultery was but a scandal added to that of the adultery. Such is, even in the best minds, the captivating force of the prejudices of our century, nation, and class. It would, however, be easy to see that a great man capable of stopping an impassioned prince, and an impassioned prince capable of letting himself be led by a great man, are two phenomena so rare that there is nothing so rare in the world as the happy encounter of such a minister with such a prince.

The writer whom I cite above rightly said ESPECIALLY THEN. Remedies were then necessary that may *today* be dispensed with, and may even be ineffective. The highest civilization tames the passions. By rendering them more abject and more corruptible, it takes from them at least that ferocious impetuosity that distinguishes barbarism. Christianity, which does not cease to work upon man, has especially deployed its forces in the youth of nations. But all the power of the Church would have been nil had it not been concentrated upon one head alone, a foreigner and a sovereign. The priest who is a subject always lacks force, and perhaps he should lack it with respect to his sovereign. Providence may raise up an Ambrose (*rara avis in terris!*) to frighten a Theodosius; but in the ordinary course of things, good example and respectful remonstrances are all that should be expected from the priesthood. May it please God, I do not wish to deny the merit and real efficacy of these means! Still, for the great work, others are required; and to accomplish it, as much as our feeble nature permits, the popes were chosen. They have done everything for the glory, the dignity, and above all for the preservation of the sovereign races. What other power could see the importance of laws of marriage, particularly over the thrones, and what other power could make them be enforced over the thrones? Has our puffed-up century been able to occupy itself with even one of the deepest mysteries of the world? It would not, however, be difficult to discover certain laws, nor to show them sanctioning current events, if respect permitted it: but what is there to say to men who believe that they can make sovereigns?

As this book is not a history, I shall not pile up examples. It will suffice to observe that the popes have struggled, and alone could have struggled, endlessly to maintain the purity and indissolubility of the marriages of those enthroned, and that for this reason alone they could be placed at the head of the benefactors of the human race. "For the marriages of princes"—it is Voltaire speaking—"forge the destiny of the European peoples; and never has a court given over entirely to debauchery lacked revolutions and sedition."[3]

It is true that this same Voltaire, after having so brilliantly testified to the truth, elsewhere dishonors himself by a striking contradiction that he rests upon a pitiable observation.

"The adventure of Luther," he says, "was the first scandal touching marriage of the crowned heads of the West." Here again

---

[3] This is the first of a series of quotations from Voltaire's *Essai sur l'histoire générale*, also known as the *Essai sur les moeurs* (1756).

the word scandal is applied with the same justice that we have admired above; but it is what follows that is exquisite: "The ancient Romans and the Orientals were more fortunate on this point."

What matchless idiocy! The ancient Romans had no kings at all; later, they had monsters. The Orientals have polygamy and all that it produces. We would today have monsters, or polygamy, or both, without the popes.

Having repudiated his wife to marry his mistress, Lothair had his marriage approved by two assembled councils, one at Metz, the other at Aix-la-Chapelle. Pope Nicholas I quashed it, and his successor, Adrian II, made the king swear, while giving him communion, that he had sincerely given up Waltraud (which was, however, false), and he required the same oath from all the lords that accompanied Lothair. Almost all of these died suddenly, and the king himself expired only a month after his oath. Voltaire did not forget to tell us that all historians have called this a miracle. In the end, we are often astonished by less astonishing things. Yet this is not a question of miracles. Let us be content to observe that these great and memorable acts of spiritual authority are worthy of our eternal gratitude and could only have emanated from the sovereign pontiffs.

And when Philip, king of France, decided in 1092 to marry a married woman, were not the archbishop of Rouen and the bishops of Senlis and Beauvais good enough to bless this strange marriage, in spite of the opposition of Yves of Chartres?

When a king wishes to commit a crime, he is too often obeyed.[4]

The pope alone was able to mount opposition; and, far from employing an exaggerated severity, he finished by contenting himself with a promise that was most poorly executed.

In these two examples can be seen all the others. Opposition could not have been better placed than in a foreign and sovereign power, and a temporal one. For majesties, in disagreeing, balancing, and even attacking one another, do not injure one another, because no one dishonors himself by fighting against his equal. Whereas, if

---

[4] This is a line from Voltaire's *Henriade*.

the opposition is in the state itself, each act of resistance, whatever form it may take, compromises the sovereign.

The time has come when, for the good of humanity, it would be well to ask the popes to restore their enlightened jurisdiction over the marriage of princes, not by a dreadful veto, but by a simple refusal that should appease the reasonable European. Deadly religious schisms have divided Europe into three great families: the Latin, the Protestant, and the one we call Greek. This schism has tightly restrained the circle of marriages in the Latin family. With the others there is, doubtless, less danger, as their indifference to dogmas lends itself without difficulty to all sorts of arrangements. Yet with us the danger is immense. If we are not ceaselessly vigilant, all the great families will rapidly march to their destruction, and it would be a criminal weakness to hide the truth that the evil has already begun. Let us hasten to consider this while there is still time. Each new dynasty being a plant that grows only with human blood, the disdain for the most evident principles now exposes Europe, and the world, to interminable carnage. O princes whom we love, whom we venerate, for whom we are ready to spill our blood at the first call, save us from wars of succession. We have espoused your families: preserve them! You have succeeded your fathers. Do you not wish for your sons to succeed you? What good will be our devotion if you make it useless? Let truth come near, and since the most senseless counsels have reduced the high priest to no longer daring to tell you, permit at least your faithful servants to introduce it to your presence.

What law in nature is more evident than that which dictates that all that germinates in the world desires a foreign soil? The seed grows only with regret upon the same soil that carried the stem from which it fell. The wheat of the plain must be sowed in the mountain, and that of the mountain in the plain. From all sides we call for seed from afar. In the animal kingdom the law becomes more striking, and all legislators pay homage to it by more or less extended prohibitions. Degenerate nations forget themselves even to the point of allowing marriage between brother and sister, and these infamous unions produce monsters. The Christian law, one of the most distinctive characteristics of which is to take hold of all general ideas in order to combine and perfect them, greatly extended the prohibitions. If there were sometimes excesses in this respect, they were the excesses of the good, and never did the canons equal the severity of the Chinese laws. In the material order, the animals are our masters. By what deplorable blindness does the man who would spend an enormous sum to breed an Arabian horse to a Norman mare give himself without the least difficulty to a wife of his own blood? Fortunately, not all of our sins are mortal, but they are, nevertheless, our sins, and they will all become mortal through continuation and repetition. Each organic form carries in itself a principle of destruction, and if two of these principles come together, they will produce a third and incomparably worse form, for all powers that unite themselves are not merely added together, they are multiplied. Does the sovereign pontiff happen to have the power to dispense from physical laws? A sincere and systematic partisan of his privileges, I nevertheless admit that this power is unknown to me. Is not modern Rome surprised when history teaches us what was thought in the century of Tiberius and Caligula about certain unheard-of unions? Did not the accusatory verses that echoed on the ancient stage and are repeated today by the voice of the wise find some feeble echo within the walls of St. Peter's?

It cannot be doubted that extraordinary circumstances sometimes require, or at least permit, extraordinary dispositions. Yet we must remind ourselves that every exception to the law admitted by the law demands nothing more than to become law.

When my respectful voice has lifted itself towards those high regions where prolonged errors might have such deadly results, it cannot be taken for the voice of audacity or imprudence. God gives to frankness, fidelity, and righteousness an accent that can neither be counterfeited nor mistaken.

THE PRESERVATION OF
ECCLESIASTICAL LAWS AND MORALS

We may say—begging pardon for the hackneyed expression—that in the tenth century, the human race in Europe went mad. From the combination of the corruption of Rome with the ferocity of the barbarians who had inundated the Empire, there finally resulted a state of things that, fortunately, we are not likely to see again. Savagery and debauchery, anarchy and poverty were everywhere. Never has ignorance been more universal. To defend the Church against the frightening excesses of corruption and ignorance, no less than a power of a superior order was required, and this was completely new in the world. It was the power of the popes. In this miserable century, they too paid a fatal tribute to the general disorder. The pontifical chair was oppressed, dishonored, and bloodied. Yet soon she recovered her former dignity, and we are indebted to the popes for the new order then established.

I must be permitted to be irritated with the bad faith that so bitterly insists upon the vices of a few popes without saying a word about the appalling excesses of their day.

Moreover, I have always had an idea about this sad era that must be placed here. When the all-powerful courtesans, monsters of license and shamelessness, profited from the general disorder to grab power, dispose of everything at Rome, and raise their sons or lovers to the See of St. Peter by guilty means, I deny most expressly that these men were popes. Those who attempt to prove the contrary proposition will certainly find their work very difficult.[5]

After this observation, I turn to the great question that resounded throughout the world: investitures. This issue was contested by the two powers with a warmth that even well-instructed men have difficulty understanding today.

The quarrel over investitures was not trivial. The temporal power openly threatened to extinguish the ecclesiastical one. The dominant feudal spirit would have made the Church in Germany and

[5] Maistre retracted this claim in the edition of 1821.

Italy a great fief belonging to the emperor. Words, always dangerous, were particularly so on this point. The word benefice belonged to the feudal language and signified equally a fief and an ecclesiastical title, for the fief was the benefice or benefit par excellence. It was even necessary to have laws to prevent prelates from giving ecclesiastical lands as fiefs, because the whole world wanted to be vassal or sovereign.

Henry V demanded either that investiture be given over to him or that the bishops be obliged to renounce all the wealth and rights they held from the Empire.

His confusion is manifest. The prince only saw temporal possessions and the feudal title. Pope Calixtus II proposed to regulate these matters as it had been done in France, where investitures were not made either with the ring or the crosier and the bishops lacked nothing to acquit themselves perfectly of their duties for their temporalities and fiefs.

At the council of Reims, held in 1119 by this same Calixtus II, the French had already proven that they understood this point. For when the pope said, "We absolutely prohibit the reception of investiture from a layman for churches or ecclesiastical lands," the whole assembly cried out because this canon seemed to reject the princes's right to give the fiefs and royal rights dependent upon their crowns. Yet when the pope had changed his expression and said, "We absolutely prohibit the reception of investiture of bishoprics and abbeys from a laymen," they approved both the decree and the sentence of excommunication with one accord. There were at least fifteen archbishops, and two hundred bishops from France, Spain, England, and even Germany at this council. The king of France was there, and Suger approved of it.

This famous minister never spoke of Henry V except as a parricide stripped of all human sentiment, and the king of France promised the pope to assist him with all his power against the emperor.

This was not the caprice of the pope, it was the opinion of the whole Church, and it was also that of the most enlightened temporal power of the period.

Pope Adrian IV gave a second example of the extreme care required to distinguish things that seemed similar, but really were distinct. When the pope, perhaps without much reflection, had said that the emperor (Frederick I) held the imperial crown from him as a benefice, the emperor believed it to be his duty to contradict this in a circular letter. Then the pope, seeing how the word benefice had raised such an alarm, explained himself by declaring that by benefice he had meant benefit.

Nevertheless, the German emperor publicly sold ecclesiastical benefices. The priests carried arms; scandalous concubinage soiled the priestly order; all that was required to destroy the priesthood was an evil mind to propose the marriage of priests as the remedy to their greatest evils. The Holy See alone was able to oppose the flood, avoid the total subversion of the Church, and await the reform that must operate during the following centuries. Let us again listen to Voltaire, whose natural good sense makes one regret that his passion caused him at times to lose it.

"We see in the history of these times that society had few rules in the Western nations and that states had few laws. The church wished to give them to them."

Among all the pontiffs called to this great work, Gregory VII stands forth majestically. The historians of his time, even those whose birth could have led them to take the side of the emperors, have rendered full justice to this great man. "He was," one of them said, "a man profoundly instructed in the holy letters and shining with all sorts of virtues." "He expressed," said another, "in all his conduct the virtues which he taught to men through his mouth." And Fleury,[6] who as we know does not spoil the popes, did not refuse to recognize that Gregory VII "was a virtuous man, born with great courage, raised in the most severe monastic discipline, and full of ardent zeal to purge the Church of the vices with which he saw her to be infected, particularly those of simony and clerical incontinence."

[6] Claude Fleury, a French historian of the seventeenth century, was a Gallican, that is, he championed the religious prerogatives of the French crown.

The meeting at Canossa in 1077 was a superb moment and would furnish the subject for a lovely painting. Holding the Eucharist between his hands, the pope turned to face the emperor and called him to swear, as he would swear himself, upon his eternal salvation, never to have acted except with perfect purity of intention for the glory of God and the happiness of the people. The emperor, oppressed by his conscience and the influence of the pontiff, neither dared to repeat the formula nor to receive Communion.

Gregory did not presume too much when, with the intimate conviction of his power, he attributed to himself the mission to instruct European sovereignty, at that time still young and in the throes of its passions, and wrote these remarkable words: "We have had care, with the divine assistance, to furnish to emperors, kings, and other sovereigns the arms of humility they need to calm the furious tempests of their pride."

This is to say, I will teach them that a king is not a tyrant. And who would have taught them this if not he?

Maimbourg makes the serious complaint that the "imperious and inflexible mood of Gregory VII did not permit him to accompany his zeal with that beautiful moderation of his five predecessors."[7]

Unfortunately, the beautiful moderation of these pontiffs corrected nothing, and we still criticize them. Violence has never been stopped by moderation. Powers are not balanced except by contrary efforts. The emperors committed unheard of excesses against the popes, yet we no longer speak of them. The popes, in their turn, sometimes passed the bounds of moderation with respect to the emperors, and we make a great deal of noise about it, turning little exaggerations into serious crimes. But human affairs happen in no other way. Never has a constitution been formed, never has a political amalgam been able to operate other than through the mixture of different elements which, being first thrown against one another, end by penetrating and tranquilizing one another.

[7] Louis Maimbourg, another Gallican historian of the seventeenth century, was expelled from the Jesuits by Pope Innocent XI.

The popes did not dispute with the emperors about investiture by the sword, but only investiture by the ring and crosier. We say that this was to trifle. On the contrary, it was essential. Why were both sides so heated if the question was unimportant? The popes did not even dispute about elections, as Maimbourg proves by the example of Suger. Moreover, they consented to investiture by the sword, that is, they did not oppose the custom that prelates, considered as vassals, received from their sovereign lord, by feudal investiture, that mother and mixed empire (to speak the feudal language), the true essence of the fief, which supposed on the part of the feudal lord a participation in the sovereignty paid towards the sovereign lord who is the source of it by political dependence and military faith.

Yet they did not allow investiture by the crosier and ring, lest the temporal sovereign, in making use of these two religious symbols for the ceremony of the investiture, might take the air of conferring the spiritual title and jurisdiction and thus change the benefice into a fief. And on this point the emperor in the end was forced to submit. Yet ten years later, Lothair returned again to the charge and labored to obtain from Pope Innocent II the reestablishment of investitures by the crosier and ring (1131), which proves how important a goal it was to him!

On this point, Gregory VII doubtless went further than the other popes, as he contested with the sovereign for the purely feudal oath of the vassal prelate. Here we may see one of the exaggerations spoken of above; but we must also consider the excesses that Gregory VII had in view. He feared that the fief would eclipse the benefice. He feared warrior priests. We must put ourselves in the true vantage, and thus find less dismissive this reason alleged by the Council of Châlon-sur-Sâone (1073) to protect ecclesiastics from the feudal oath: "that the hands that consecrate the body of Jesus Christ should not be placed between hands so often soiled by the effusion of human blood, and perhaps also by rape and other crimes." Each century has its prejudices and its manner of seeing, according to which it must be judged. It is an insupportable sophistry of our own to suppose that what would be condemned in our day also was in times past, and that Gregory VII should have acted towards Henry IV as Pius VII acted towards his majesty the Emperor Francis II.

We accuse this pope of having sent too many legates. Yet this is only because he could not trust provincial councils. And Fleury, who is not suspect, and who prefers councils to legates, nevertheless agrees that if the German prelates so strongly feared the arrival of the legates, "it was because they sensed themselves guilty of simony" and saw in this the arrival of their judges.

In a word, it would have been the end of the Church, humanly speaking. She would have had no more form, no more police, and soon no longer a name without the extraordinary intervention of the popes, who took the place of weakened and corrupt authorities and governed in a more immediate manner for the restoration of order.

It also would have been the end of European monarchy if detestable sovereigns had not found a terrible obstacle upon their path. And, to speak at this time only of Gregory VII, I do not doubt that all just men will agree with this perfectly disinterested judgment of the historian of the German revolutions: "The simple exposition of facts shows that the conduct of the pope was such that all men of firm and enlightened character would have held in the same circumstances."[8] However much we should like to fight against the truth, in the end all good minds must return to this decision.

THE LIBERTY OF ITALY

The third goal that the popes ceaselessly pursued as temporal princes was the liberty of Italy, which they desired to uphold absolutely against the German power.

---

[8] Here Maistre quotes Carlo Denina's *Rivoluzione della Germania*.

"After the three Ottos, the struggle between German domination and Italian liberty remained the same for a long time. It seems to me that the true basis for the quarrel was that the Popes and the Romans did not desire the emperors in Rome,"[9] which is to say that they did not desire any masters in their own home.

This is the truth. The line of Charlemagne was extinct. Neither Italy nor the popes owed anything to the princes who replaced them in Germany. "These princes lived by the sword. The Italians certainly had a more natural right to liberty than did the Germans to be their masters. The Italians never obeyed the German blood except in spite of themselves; and this liberty, of which the Italian cities were then idolaters, had but little respect for the German caesars." In these unfortunate times, "the papacy and practically all of the bishoprics were for sale to the highest bidder: if the authority of the emperors had been severe, the popes would have been naught but their chaplains, and Italy enslaved."

"Pope John XII's imprudence in calling the Germans to Rome was the source of all the calamities by which Rome and Italy were afflicted during the many centuries." The blind pontiff did not see what kind of pretensions he would set loose, and the incalculable force of a name borne by a great man. "It does not appear that Germany under Henry the Fowler had pretensions to be the Empire; nor did it under Otto the Great." This prince, who knew his own strength, "had himself anointed and obliged the pope to swear fidelity to him. The Germans thus held the Romans subjugated, and the Romans broke their chains as soon as they could." Here is the entire public law of Italy during those deplorable times in which men absolutely lacked principles to guide their conduct. "Even the right of succession (that talisman of public tranquility) was not then established in any state in Europe. Rome knew neither what she was, nor to whom she belonged. The custom was established of giving the crown not by right of blood, but by the suffrage

---

[9] Here Maistre quotes Voltaire's *Essai sur les moeurs*. A series of quotations from the same work follows.

of the lords. No one knew what the Empire was. There were no laws in Europe. They recognized neither the right of birth, nor the right of election. Europe was a chaos in which the strongest rose up upon the ruins of the weakest, only to be followed in the same way by others. The entire history of these times is that of a few barbarian captains disputing with the bishops for the domination of ignorant serfs."

"There really was no more Empire, neither by right, nor in fact. The Romans, who gave themselves to Charlemagne by acclamation, no longer wished to recognize the bastards and foreigners who were barely masters of a part of Germany. This was a peculiar Roman empire. The German body called itself the Holy Roman Empire, while truly it was neither holy, nor Roman, nor an empire. It seems evident that the grand design of Frederick II was to establish in Italy the throne of new caesars, *and it is certain that he wished to rule over an undivided Italy without internal frontiers.* This is the secret of all his quarrels with the popes. He made use of subtlety and force by turns, and the Holy See fought him with the same arms. The Guelfs, those partisans of the papacy, AND STILL MORE OF LIBERTY, always balanced the power of the Ghibelines, the partisans of the Empire. The divisions between Frederick and the Holy See NEVER HAD RELIGION AS THEIR OBJECT."

Whose head is Voltaire using when, forgetting these solemn avowals, he manages elsewhere to tell us that "from Charlemagne to our days, the war between the Empire and the priesthood was the principle of all revolutions; *it is the thread that leads us through the labyrinth of modern history.*"

First of all, in what sense is modern history more a labyrinth than ancient? For my part, I see more clarity in the Capetian dynasty than in that of the Pharaohs. But let us leave behind this false expression, which is less false than the idea behind it. As he expressly admits that the bloody struggle between the two parties in Italy was absolutely foreign to religion, what can Voltaire mean by his *thread?* It is false to say that there was a war, strictly speaking, *between the*

Empire and the priesthood. This is endlessly repeated in order to make the priesthood responsible for all the blood spilt during this great struggle. In truth, it was a war between Germany and Italy, between usurpation and liberty, between the master who brought chains, and the slave who rejected them, a war in which the popes did their duty as Italian princes and wise politicians by taking the side of Italy, for they could not honorably take the side of the emperors, nor plead neutrality without courting disaster.

When Henry VI, king of Sicily and emperor, died in Messina in 1197, a war for the succession broke out in Germany between Philip, duke of Swabia, and Otto, son of Henry-Leo, the duke of Saxony and Bavaria. The latter descended from the princes of Este-Guelf, and Philip from the Ghibeline princes. The rivalry of these two princes gave birth to the two all-too-famous factions, and these—neither the popes nor the priesthood—were the cause of the long desolation of Italy. The civil war once ignited, the popes were forced to choose a side and fight. By their greatly respected character and the immense authority they enjoyed, they naturally found themselves at the head of the noble party of right conduct, justice, and national independence. Thus we are accustomed to see only the popes, instead of Italy; but, at bottom, it was Italy, and *in no way religion.* This cannot be too often repeated.

The poison of these two factions penetrated so deeply into Italian hearts that at length they lost their original meaning, and these words, Guelf and Ghibeline, ended by signifying no more than groups of people who hated one another. During this dreadful fever, the clergy did what it always does. They ignored none of the means in their power for reestablishing the peace. More than once, we see bishops, with their clergy, throw themselves with crosses and relics of the saints between two armies ready to charge one another, and implore them, in the name of religion, to avoid the spilling of human blood. They thus did very much good, without being able to extinguish the evil.

"There was no pope," and here again we listen to the express avowal of a severe critic of the Holy See,[10] "who did not fear the

---

[10] The Italian historian Muratori.

aggrandizement of the emperors in Italy. The ancient pretensions . . . would be made good on that day when they would be judged in a better light."

Thus, there was no pope who did not oppose them. Where is the treaty that gave Italy to the German emperors? Where was it learned that the pope is not to conduct himself as a temporal prince, that he must be purely passive, let himself be attacked, despoiled, and so on? Never shall this be proven.

In the era of Rudolph (in 1274), "the ancient rights of the Empire were lost . . . and the new house was not able to assert them without injustice; nothing is more incoherent than to wish to uphold the pretensions of the Empire by reasoning according to how they were under Charlemagne."

Thus the popes, as the natural heads of the Italian confederation and the born protectors of the peoples that composed it, had every imaginable reason to oppose themselves with all their powers to the rebirth in Italy of that nominal power which, in spite of the titles affixed at the head of its edicts, was nevertheless neither *holy*, nor *Roman*, nor an *empire*.

The sack of Milan, one of the most horrible events of history, *alone suffices*, in Voltaire's judgment, *to justify all that the popes did*.

What shall we say of Otto II and of his famous banquet of the year 981? He invited a large number of lords to a magnificent banquet, during which an officer of the emperor entered with a list of those proscribed by his master. Those on the list were conducted to a neighboring chamber and were slaughtered. Such were the princes with whom the popes had to deal.

And Frederick, with the most abominable inhumanity, deliberately hanged relatives of the pope who had been imprisoned in a captured village. Was it not reasonable to take some efforts to free oneself from this kind of rule?

The greatest evil for a political man is to obey a foreign power. No humiliation, no torment of the heart may be compared to this. The subject nation, if it be not protected by some extraordinary law, does not believe that it obeys the sovereign, but the sovereign's nation. No nation wishes to obey another for the simple reason that no nation knows how to command another. Observe the peoples who are the wisest and best governed at home. You will see them absolutely lose their wisdom when it is time to govern another people. The rage of domination is innate in man, and the rage to make domination felt may be no less natural. The foreigner who comes to command a subject nation in the name of a faraway sovereign, instead of informing himself about the national ideas in order to conform to them, seems too often to study them in order to contradict them. He believes himself more a master to the extent that he applies his hand more rudely. He takes arrogance to be dignity and seems to believe this dignity better attested by the indignation he excites than by the benedictions he might obtain.

Thus, all peoples agree in placing in the first rank of great men those fortunate citizens who have had the honor to wrench out their land from under the yoke of the foreigner. Heroes if they succeed, martyrs if they fail, their names last through the centuries. Modern stupidity wishes to exclude only the popes from this universal apotheosis and to deprive them of the immortal glory due to them as temporal princes, for having tirelessly worked for the liberation of their fatherland. Thus it is that certain French writers refuse to render justice to Gregory VII. Their eyes clouded by Protestant, philosophical, Jansenist, and parlementarian prejudice, what can they see through this quadruple blindfold? The despotism of the parlement even extended to the point of refusing to allow the national liturgy to attach a certain pomp to the feast of Gregory VII. The priesthood, to avoid serious damage, found itself forced to submit, thus confessing the humiliating servitude of that Church whose fabulous liberties we have so highly touted. Yet you, strangers to all these prejudices, you, inhabitants of those beautiful lands that Gregory wished to liberate, you who should be enlightened by gratitude, harmonious inheritors of Greece, illustrious descendants of the Scipios and of Virgil, you who lack only unity and independence, you should build altars to the sublime pontiff, who has wrought miracles in order to give you a name.

We have seen that the sovereign pontiff is the natural head, the most powerful promoter, and the great *demiurge* of universal civilization. His civilizing powers are limited only by the blindness and ill will of princes. The popes have also served humanity by the extinction of servitude, which they have ceaselessly fought and infallibly extinguished without upheavals, divisions, or danger wherever they have been allowed to work.

It was a singular folly of the past century to judge everything according to abstract rules and without regard for experience. This folly is all the more striking because this same century constantly complained about all the philosophers who began with abstract principles instead of seeking them in experience.

It is curious that Rousseau begins his *Social Contract* with the resounding maxim: *Man is born free, and everywhere he is in chains.*

What does he mean? He surely does not speak about the facts as they are, inasmuch as in the same sentence he affirms that EVERYWHERE *man is in chains*. It is therefore a question of *right*; yet this is what must be proven *contrary to the fact*.

The contrary to this mad assertion, *man is born free*, is the truth. In all times and places prior to the establishment of Christianity, and even until that religion had sufficiently penetrated our hearts, slavery had always been considered as necessary to the government and political estate of nations, in republics and in monarchies, without it ever having occurred to any philosopher to condemn slavery, nor to any legislator to attack it by fundamental laws.

Everyone knows that Aristotle said that *there were men who were born slaves*, and nothing could be more true. I know that in our century he has been blamed for this assertion. But it would be better to understand it than to condemn it. His proposition is founded upon the whole of history, which is experimental politics, and upon the very nature of man which has produced that history.

The one who has sufficiently studied this sad nature knows that *man in general*, if he is left to himself, *is too evil to be free*.

Let each man look into his heart. He will see that wherever civil liberty belongs to everyone, there is no longer any means, *without some extraordinary help*, of governing men in the body of a nation.

Thence it follows that slavery has constantly been the natural part of a very great part of mankind until the establishment of Christianity; and as universal common sense saw the necessity of this order of things, it was never contested by laws or reasoning.

A great Latin poet put this terrible maxim in the mouth of Caesar: "Mankind is made for a few men." In the sense that the poet gives it, this maxim presents itself under a shocking and Machiavellian aspect. Yet, from another point of view, it is most true. Everywhere the very few lead the many, for without an aristocracy the sovereign power cannot be strong enough.

The number of free men in antiquity was far less than the number of slaves. Athens had forty thousand slaves and twenty thousand citizens. At Rome, which at the end of the Republic had about 1.2 million inhabitants, there were barely two thousand property owners, which by itself demonstrates the immense quantity of slaves. At times one lone individual had several thousand in his service. Once four hundred from a single house were seen to be executed together in virtue of the appalling law that decreed that when a Roman citizen was killed in his own house all the slaves who lived under the same roof were to be put to death.

And when it was a question of giving the slaves a particular uniform, the Senate refused, *from fear that they could no longer be numbered.*

Other nations furnish more or less the same examples, but they must be abridged. In any event, it would be useful to prove at length what everyone knows: *that until the era of Christianity the world had always been covered with slaves, and that the wise had never condemned this custom.* This proposition is unshakable.

Then at last the divine law appeared upon the earth. All at once it seized the heart of man and changed it in a way that excites the eternal admiration of all true observers. Religion began by working without rest for the abolition of slavery, a thing that no other religion, legislator, or philosopher had ever dared to undertake or even to dream. Christianity, which acts divinely, for the same reason acts slowly; for all legitimate operations, of whatever manner they be, are always accomplished insensibly. Wherever we find noise, confusion, impetuosity, and destruction, we may be sure that crime or folly is at work.

Religion waged a continual war with slavery, acting sometimes here and sometimes there, in one manner and another, yet never flagging, and the sovereigns, sensing without being able to give a reason for it that the priesthood relieved part of their pains and fears, insensibly yielded to them and accepted their beneficent views.

"At last, in the year 1167, Pope Alexander III declared in the name of the council *that all Christians must be exempt from servitude.* This law alone *should render his name dear to all peoples,* just as his efforts to uphold the liberty of Italy should render his name precious to the Italians. It is in virtue of this law that, a long time afterwards, Louis X declared that all the serfs remaining in France should be freed. . . . Nevertheless, men returned only by degrees and with much difficulty to their *natural right.*"[1]

---

[1] Maistre here quotes again from Voltaire's *Essai sur les moeurs.*

There is no doubting that the memory of the pontiff should be dear to all peoples. The initiative for such a declaration truly belonged to his sublime office. Yet note that he spoke only in the twelfth century, and that even then he proclaimed the right to liberty rather than the liberty itself. He permitted neither violence, nor threats: nothing that is done well is done quickly.

Wherever reigns a religion other than our own, slavery exists by right, and wherever our religion is weakened, the nation becomes proportionately less able to support general liberty.

We have just seen the social order shaken to its very foundations because there was too much liberty in Europe and not enough religion. There will be other commotions, and the good order will only be solidly affirmed when either slavery or religion is reestablished.

The government cannot govern alone. This maxim becomes more incontestable the more one meditates on it. The government needs, as its indispensable minister, either slavery, which diminishes the number of wills acting in the state, or the divine power which, by a kind of spiritual healing, removes the natural bitterness of these wills and allows them to act together without destroying one another.

The New World provides an example that completes the demonstration. What have the Catholic missionaries, that is, the envoys of the pope, not done to extinguish servitude, to console, heal, and ennoble mankind in these vast countries?

Wherever we let this power work, it operates to the same effects. Let not those nations that disdain her—be they still Christian—decide to abolish slavery, if it still exists in them: a grave political calamity will be the infallible consequence of such blind imprudence.

Let it not be imagined that the Church—or the pope, for they are one and the same—has the perfecting of human politics as its aim in the war against slavery. To this power, there is something higher: the perfecting of morals. Political refinement is only a simple derivative of this. Wherever servitude reigns, there will never be true morals, because of the disordered empire of man over woman. Mistress of her rights and actions, she is only too weak with respect to the seductions surrounding her on all sides. What would she be if her own will could not defend her? The very idea of resistance vanishes. Vice becomes a duty, and man, gradually undermined by the ease of his pleasures, would no longer be able to raise himself above the morals of Asia.

Mr. Buchanan,[2] whom I cited above, and from whom I willingly borrow an equally correct and important thought, has remarked that in all the lands where Christianity does not reign, we observe a necessary tendency towards the degradation of women.

Nothing is more evidently true. It is even possible to assign the reason for this degradation, which can only be combatted by a supernatural principle. Wherever our sex can command vice, it will not be able to have true morals, nor truly dignified customs. Woman, who can do everything with the heart of man, reinforces all the perversity she has received from him, and the nations languish in a *vicious circle*, from which it is radically impossible for them to escape on their own power.

By a completely contrary operation, and also one completely natural, the most effective means of perfecting man is to ennoble and exalt woman. It is towards this that Christianity alone has worked without ceasing with an infallible success differing only in degree according to the kind and number of obstacles that oppose its action. Yet the immense and sacred power of Christianity is nullified when it is not concentrated in the hands of one unique hand who can exercise it and make it valued. Christianity is disseminated throughout the globe as one nation which only has existence, action, power, consideration, and a name in virtue of the sovereignty that represents it and gives it a moral personality among the peoples.

[2] Maistre here cites Claudius Buchanan (1766–1815), a priest in the Church of England who became a missionary in India.

Woman is more indebted to Christianity than is man. From Christianity she holds all her dignity. The Christian woman is truly a *supernatural* being insofar as she is raised up and maintained by it in a state that is not *natural* to her. Yet by what immense services has she paid for this species of ennobling!

Thus, mankind is *naturally* in large part serfs, and can only be lifted from this state *supernaturally*. With servitude, there is no more morality properly so called. Without Christianity, there is no general liberty. Without the pope, there is no true Christianity, that is to say no Christianity working, powerful, converting, reigning, conquering, *perfecting*. Thus it belongs to the sovereign pontiff to proclaim universal liberty. He has done it, and his voice has echoed throughout the world. He alone makes this liberty possible in his quality as unique head of that religion which is alone capable of making our wills tractable, and which cannot deploy all its power except through him. Today, one must be blind not to see that all the sovereign powers weaken themselves in Europe. On all sides they are losing the confidence and devotion of the people. Sects and the private spirit are multiplying in a frightening manner. Our wills must either be purified or bound: there is no middle. The dissident princes who have servitude in their kingdoms will preserve it or perish. The others will be brought back to servitude or to unity.

Yet who will tell me that I will live another day? I therefore want to write today a thought that comes to me on the subject of slavery, even if I depart my subject, which, however, I do not believe that I do.

What is the religious estate in the Catholic countries? It is ennobled slavery. To the ancient institution, useful in itself under a number of headings, this estate adds many particular advantages and removes all the abuses. Instead of lowering man, the religious vow sanctifies him. Instead of making him serve the vices of another, it frees him. By submitting him to a person he chooses, it declares him free with respect to others, with whom he no longer has anything to do.

Whenever one may deaden wills without degrading the subjects, he renders society a priceless service by discharging the government from the care of looking after these men, employing them, and paying them. Never has there been a better idea than that of bringing together peaceful citizens who work, pray, study, write, give alms, cultivate the earth, and ask nothing of authority.

This truth is particularly evident today when from all sides all men fall in mobs upon the arms of the government, which does not know what to do with them.

An impetuous, numberless youth, free for its own misery, greedy for distinctions and riches, flies in swarms into government jobs. Every imaginable profession has four or five times the number of candidates that it needs. You will not find a bureau in Europe in which the number of employees has not tripled or quadrupled in the past fifty years. We say that there is more work to do; but it is men who create work, and too many men mix themselves up in it. Everyone is looking for power and rank. They force all the doors and necessitate the creation of new places. There is too much liberty, too much movement, too many unchained wills in the world. *What good are religious?* so many imbeciles have said. How then? Cannot a man serve the state without being given an office? Is it no longer an achievement to subdue the passions and neutralize the vices? If Robespierre, instead of being a lawyer, had been a Capuchin, would we have also said of him, seeing him pass by: *Good God! What use is this man?* Hundreds of writers have brought to light the services that the religious estate renders to society. I think it useful to look at it from a less often seen perspective as the master and director of a great many wills, as the unappreciated supplement to the government, whose greatest interest is to moderate the internal movement of the state and to increase the number of men who ask nothing of it.

Today, thanks to a system of universal independence and the immense pride that has taken hold of all classes, every man wants to fight, judge, write, administrate, and govern. We are lost in the whirlwind of affairs. We groan under the burdensome weight of memoranda. Half the world is busy governing the other half, and they are unable to succeed.

FRÉDÉRIC

LE PLAY

SOCIAL REFORM IN FRANCE (1864)
INTRODUCTION: PREJUDICES AND FACTS

> The Romans became masters of the world because,
> having conquered the nations, they renounced
> their own customs when they found better ones.
>
> — Montesquieu, *The Greatness of the Romans*

ANTAGONISM AND INSTABILITY WITHIN
FRANCE PROVE THE URGENCY OF REFORM

Today two books could be written about France, both true but with opposite conclusions. One would describe the customs and institutions that make our nation better than others, and would explain why she keeps her leading position in Europe down to the present in spite of so many trials and reverses. The other, enumerating the vices of our social constitution, would reveal how these causes of superiority are paralyzed by the revolutions that have become regular occurrences for us.

France must be considered from the first point of view at those critical times when she needs confidence in herself. Yet she should be regarded from the opposing point of view when, as today, a time of calm and security returns. Noting the evils from which we suffer, good citizens will then react against our imprudent tranquility and stop the country's descent down the slope on which it has been sliding for two centuries. It is with this end in mind that I have published this book.

I should first justify the use of the word *reform* in the title, for this word is rejected by those who, discouraged by the sterile theories and fruitless attempts of recent years, desire only to preserve the status quo. The word also offends those who attribute an imaginary superiority to France because they know nothing of foreign nations.

The word reform is frequently used with the same meaning as the word revolution: to designate a violent and temporary remedy for some transitory evil. I use it with another one of its accepted meanings: to indicate a slow and regular improvement. Observation teaches that corruption tends constantly to invade societies under the power of our inescapable evil instincts. History even teaches that this danger is greater precisely when a happy combination of circumstances creates exceptional prosperity. To this permanent propensity towards evil, societies must oppose a permanent spirit of improvement.

Among the social vices that a reform should combat, I will here cite two, the danger of which can be seen immediately and without recourse to the arguments that follow. Until today they have not been seen united in France with such grave characteristics. These vices began to exist under the Valois when our civil discord broke out. They were but little developed in the seventeenth century. On the other hand, they are no longer found in some nations who cruelly suffered from them in the past, but now successfully contend with us for preeminence.

The formidable vice that heralds the fall of empires is the antagonism that divides our society into different enemy camps. The struggle to which I refer is not the one that arises from personal questions or incidental quarrels between a few great persons or ruling classes disputing for influence and power. Rather, it exists in the smallest subdivisions of the social body, in village, workshop, and family. The evil consists above all in this, that the superior classes, instead of acting together to lead society into a better path, mutually neutralize one another by attempting to make contrary political principles prevail by force at the risk of destroying the social order. This antagonism rages both in private and public life. It has developed to the point where persons attached to the same enterprises in industry and commerce believe themselves to have diametrically opposed interests, while others, who might be in a position to devote themselves to the common good, refuse to cooperate, even unofficially, with a government that lacks their sympathy. This last sentiment presents a source of greater danger. If it were to spread, it would eventually destroy our most precious heritage: the national spirit we owe to the genius of our fathers.

The second vice from which we suffer is instability, an even more evident symptom of the decline of a nation. While we inadequately perceive the disorders that this evil produces in private life, no one fails to see those of public life. This instability is dangerous because it has been continually increasing for the past two centuries, precisely during the period when, in the case of our principal rivals the English, private fortunes and political power have become more firm and stable with each new generation.

While in the past France found the means to recover from the greatest of disasters in the regular movement of her institutions, today, even amidst prosperity, she cannot succeed in preventing revolutions. The public peace which during so many centuries was more or less independent of the person of the sovereign has since 1789 twice been reestablished by the temporary intervention of a dictator.

The French people can no longer restrain abuses by the force of tradition, nor escape them through intelligent reforms. In their attitude before authority, they know no middle ground between passive submission and revolt. They have rejected those habits of respect and independence with which their rivals honor themselves now more than ever, and they seem to have lost all initiative by destroying the old customs that the English proudly preserve. In vain will the French seek to found upon the ruins of the past a regime that will rally all men of good will. Each new constitution invariably raises the same hatred and attacks, and these efforts have led to violent changes in the principles of the constitution or the personnel of the government ten times in the last three-quarters of a century.

This antagonism and instability have relentlessly undermined private lives and political power. These scourges are thus permanent causes of weakness, and they alone suffice to demonstrate the urgency of reform.

To overcome either the despair or the exaggerated confidence that counsels the status quo it is not enough to point to these two national vices. Before indicating the way to return to a more just point of view through the comparative study of the European peoples, we must examine several ideas, thought by many to be axiomatic, which tend to discourage our efforts or lead them astray. In this introduction I will not pretend to refute them by a direct appeal to reason and justice without recourse to the facts set out in the seven chapters that follow. I will attempt only to establish that these so-called axioms do not have the evidence attributed to them, and therefore that they authorize no one to reject the results of the method of observation without having examined them.

MORAL DISORDER INCREASES IN
SPITE OF OUR MATERIAL PROGRESS

Some are persuaded that our social disorders are compensated for by the striking material prosperity we enjoy. Some even think that the progress of the sciences and the arts, the first cause of this prosperity, will remedy not only these disorders, but also other, no less evident, evils. Experience and reflection, however, soon lead to a different conclusion.

The recent progress of the sciences and the arts and the rapid growth of our wealth naturally give rise to this oversight and effectively obscure the perils of our social organization. An unprecedented combination of circumstances has led to the renowned discoveries of the last hundred years: the steam engine; machines that comb, thread, and weave textile materials; machines to fashion wood, leather, and metals; machines to aid the farm laborer with the harvest and use of agricultural products; the use of coal in metallurgy; the steamboat; the railroad; the telegraph; photography; and the numerous innovations that flow from these primordial inventions. These discoveries have modified the procedures of agriculture, industry, and commerce. They have reduced the costs of production to an unprecedented extent, increased the demand for labor, and improved the well-being of the population in myriad ways. While acquiring this deeper knowledge of material facts, we have also taken better account of the general laws that govern them. The domain of the physical sciences has markedly grown and has furnished new strength to the human mind.

These conquests that subject the physical world to the rule of man are surely a source of legitimate glory to him. Yet they do not lessen the moral disorders that have been growing in Western nations during the past two centuries.

The teachings of history and the observation of contemporary societies refute the doctrine that considers the perfection of morals to be intimately linked to that of the sciences and the arts. I will show repeatedly in the course of this work that we must weigh against the many advantages of material progress the fact that it is commonly a source of disorder. The development of art and labor has for its first consequence the progress of wealth, and this soon engenders corruption if it is not countered with a more assiduous observation of moral laws. Experience and venerable precept both establish that an exclusive devotion to material interests is a source of decadence. Changes provoked by developments in the sciences and the arts in the situation of persons and things often damage social relations. Thus, in England, for instance, the new organization of manufacturing has temporarily subjected patrons and especially workers to evils that have never weighed upon less advanced nations.

Finally, the same devotion of our leading men to the discovery of physical truths and the importance that opinion attaches to the agricultural and industrial improvements that flow from them has made us lose sight of the progress that humanity obtains through the cultivation of moral truths. A people grows less by perfecting the production of objects necessary to its needs than through the effort to contain its appetites and to put the good into practice. The developments of physical activity are always limited by the extent of the soil, human strength, and the quantity of materials, while the growth of the faculties of the soul is truly unlimited. When we study the life of those useful men who daily raise themselves from the lowest ranks of society into the superior classes, we almost always note that their successes are more due to a moral energy that triumphs over their passions and the fatigue of work than to the knowledge of scientific laws and the latest methods of production. In the same way, we find that the decline of those who traverse life in the opposite direction results less from their ignorance of the truths of science and art than from the forgetfulness of moral laws and the invasion of the vices that develop in the womb of sloth and wealth. If the ruling class of one of the nations placed at the head of civilization inculcates to each citizen under its influence the sentiment of his duties towards God, family, and fatherland, if they succeed only in destroying drunkenness and the other base vices that degrade the greater part of the population, they will have done more for the strength of their country than if they had doubled its wealth through labor or its territory through conquest.

Moreover, the physical sciences, which have discovered so many truths, and from which I have borrowed the method that I apply to social science, are not truly fruitful in a society that loses its attachment to the moral order. Today the savants cannot excel except by sequestering themselves within a narrow specialty. Consequently, in the use of their faculties there follows a phenomenon analogous to that which results for artisans from the extreme division of the manufacturing art. The savant grows, but the man is diminished, especially if a preoccupation for moral truths does not preserve in him a certain breadth of mind. From this point of view, a too-exclusive application to the physical sciences is not without peril for society, and, far from healing the evils that produce moral disorder, it may aggravate them.

The cultivation of moral truths is certainly not without its difficulties, and it has often been the source of deplorable abuses. This cultivation has never been separated from religion, even in the present day, and therefore we have had to confide the higher direction of souls to clerics who, abusing this power, have sometimes become active agents of corruption or antagonism and have pushed societies to their ruin. Yet this kind of disorder is not reserved to religious authorities. We find it also in governmental authorities who have through their vices still more frequently provoked the decadence of peoples. The propensity to egoism and tyranny is so pronounced in man that we will never have enough authorities who are strictly submitted to their duty. Even paternal authority, imbued by God with a special affection, love, and devotion, has its own failings. He who fails to take account of these organic infirmities of human nature will always be led to erroneous conclusions about society. Those who err the most in these matters are those who adopt the idea of original perfection, and consider moral progress to be the necessary consequence of material progress.

These two errors are refuted for all right minds by the experience of life and the government of men. There is hardly reason to believe that they will become the principal obstacle to reform. The most dangerous error seems to come from those who, admitting the preponderant influence of the moral order, seek progress not in a more perfect practice, but in the change of doctrines.

THE REFORM OF MORALS DOES
NOT REQUIRE NEW DOCTRINES

The improvements introduced in our day in the material order have led ardent or inattentive minds to think that similar successes have been reserved to them in the moral order. At a time when more true and more complete physical laws replace, with the unanimous assent of the wise, the laws admitted since the time of Aristotle, some willingly persuade themselves that an analogous revolution should be accomplished in moral laws.

This confusion is one of the errors of our day, and it is easy to see that it is in no way justified by the facts.

The various labors in the physical sciences all converge towards certain new truths that the public adopts with deference and are not slow to work to our profit. The innovations brought today in the domain of the moral sciences, however, remain entirely sterile and are all condemned to be forgotten after a brief period of agitation or scandal.

Civilized peoples ordinarily make use of inventions made in the physical sciences and under their influence develop the scope of intelligence, the resources of industry, and the well-being of the population. Yet, in spite of lengthy researches, I have not been able to discover a society in Europe that has adopted and put into practice a single one of the innovations proposed for the moral order. If any result can be noted after such efforts, it is always a weakening of productive forces and a recrudescence of social antagonism. Such was, notably in France and Germany, the consequence of the doctrines propagated during the period that preceded the revolutions of 1848.

From another point of view, this contrast can be explained by considering the radical differences between the physical and moral sciences. The physical world contains a multitude of primordial elements that group themselves according to numerous combinations that are themselves modified to infinity under the influence of vital forces. Finally, all these phenomena produce themselves in a space to which our imagination cannot assign limits. Thus we cannot perceive limits to the field of observation, nor to the useful consequences that can be taken from them, either for the process of the physical sciences or for human well-being. The moral sciences, on the contrary, have but one object: the study of the soul and its relations with God and humanity. Each of us may find within himself the rigorous means of observation in the sentiments that develop during the different phases of life. We understand that so simple a subject contains only a small number of essential truths and that the knowledge of the greater part of these has been revealed since the origins of civilization. The savants devoted to the study of the living species of animals and plants already count these by hundreds of thousands, and each day they add to their catalogues and taxonomies. The physicists and chemists see no limit to the phenomena or combinations they might try to produce, and, finally, the astronomers who carry their investigations outside our globe have before them a still more extended field. Nothing similar presents itself in the domain of moral science: the innumerable thinkers who, in all civilizations, have recommended the analysis of the virtues and vices have added nothing to the Decalogue of Moses.

Still more sharp are the differences in circumstance that, since the beginnings of civilization, have accompanied the propagation and preservation of these two kinds of truths. Only with difficulty do people act against their passions and appetites. Thus, they frequently refuse to do their duty even when moral truths have been revealed to them by the precepts and examples of those whose superiority they recognize. On the other hand, they are inclined to take utility from physical phenomena without having any idea of the scientific laws that allow them to do so. Thus, for instance, the art of smelting silver ore is, in fact, the application of laws that chemistry has only recently revealed, and which until recently were not understood at all. Nevertheless, when one observes the slag from the fusion of this ore obtained on the coasts of Murcia in Spain, one is astonished to note that it does not show a more advanced practice than what the Phoenicians used centuries ago. In the material order, man willingly adopts the useful practice not founded upon a doctrine, while in the moral order, he frequently rejects one even when it reposes upon the most respectable authorities.

Physical truths once gained are preserved with ease in those peoples who maintain public peace and moral order. No instinct or interest counsels to reject their use, and we could not imagine how civilization could henceforth be deprived of the telegraph, photography, or even of the knowledge upon which these applications of science repose. On the contrary, we sense in ourselves the germs of the bad instincts that lead to the forgetfulness of moral laws by smothering the fear of God, the hope of a future life, the respect for parents, and the love of neighbor. The history of our country teaches us only too well how moral truths are obscured amidst the material progress of civilization. Since the end of the seventeenth century we have seen the influence of three bad princes gradually pervert the court and the ruling classes and provoke the social catastrophe the consequences of which weigh so heavily upon us.

Several ancient nations offer us more conclusive examples. Their forgetfulness of moral laws destroyed their material prosperity, and all that remains of once-illustrious regions are buried treasures.

These considerations all combine to put in relief a final contrast that dominates all the questions raised by the reform of morals. While in the material order practice almost always advances beyond doctrine, in the moral order it only follows it at a great distance, and can even take a backwards march. Thus, in the first rank of Christian nations we see numerous classes falling into a state of degradation unknown in the great nations of antiquity and from which the pagan tribes of Asia have preserved themselves. This degradation not only affects the moral life, it also acts visibly upon the physical organization of the race. The deplorable condition of this part of the population is not balanced by the condition of the superior classes. We do not see that these have made substantial steps towards that moral perfection sketched out in a perfect model eighteen centuries ago by the Gospel. If the interior practice of the European peoples is far from responding to the moral doctrine, their exterior lives do not leave less to desire. In their mutual relations they continue to be inspired by barbarous habits, and in their four centuries of relations with the pagan populations of the new worlds, they have only too often been agents of ruin and corruption.

In sum, if the Europeans are to preserve their preeminence, they must pursue the discovery of the innumerable physical laws that remain unknown. But they will accomplish a still more useful work and acquire a more lasting glory by devoting themselves to better understanding and better practicing the moral laws revealed so long ago by divine goodness. It would be a sterile effort to seek in a change of doctrine the progress that should arise from the better practice of the truths we already know.

NATIONS DO NOT RISE
AND FALL FROM NECESSITY

Now I shall refute two theories—mutually opposed and equally erroneous—that would compromise social reform either by giving us exaggerated confidence or by casting us into despair.

According to the first opinion, man is naturally led to the good, and it suffices to leave human societies freely to follow their propensities for progress to manifest itself. And because the facts daily deny this theory, it is supplemented by declaring the government to be the source of evil and always inclined to pervert the individual tendency to good. This view concludes by declaring that we can throw ourselves confidently into those revolutions that periodically remove the popular masses from the influence of the ruling classes.

The two connected ideas on which this first theory is founded—the original perfection of individuals and the beneficent influence of revolutions—seem to me to be refuted by the observation of human

nature and the events of the past two centuries. Evil is not introduced to the world only by governments, for the people who are
best preserved from evils are precisely those who have made the least
recourse to revolutions. Evil is born primarily in the ignorance and
depraved instincts of the younger generations. It is incontestable
that the nations in whom the movement of progress is the most
marked in our day are those whose social organization permits them
effectively to combat this permanent source of corruption through
education and the ascendancy of the mature and the elderly.
Progress can only be obtained under these conditions. Surely it is
retarded or compromised when the ruling classes cede to the causes
of corruption brought on by prosperity, especially the influence of
wealth, and do not rest upon the heights of their mission. Yet this is
impossible in any society in which the new generations are abandoned to their natural propensities. The state of nature, so highly
extolled at the end of the last century, is a chimerical idea conceived
outside of all methodical observation. As to revolutions, they can
be, from time to time, a heroic remedy for the people when the
ruling classes have fallen into corruption. But they are only fruitful
upon the condition of being immediately followed by a long period
of good morals and stable government. This truth is to be seen in
the success that the English have attained since 1688 and by our
hard trials since the end of the last century.

Unlike the first, the second opinion does not spring from a false
principle, but it deduces false consequences from a true principle.
Accepting that the propensity to evil is inseparable from human
nature, it infers that the nations are, in the long run, condemned to
decadence and destruction as fatally as our individual lives are
bound to decrepitude and death. This analogy is found in the literature and in the common speech of the majority of people.
According to the common expression, there are *young* nations with
a long future before them, and there are *old* ones that have accomplished a certain mission in the work of universal civilization and
must now be extinguished. The former have firm religious beliefs,

leadership by elders, frugal and simple customs, physical strength and martial courage, and, finally, a power of expansion that makes their race overflow its native region through conquest or colonization. In the latter, the opposite characteristics are found: religious indifference, disdain for elders and relaxation of family bonds, the abuse of luxury and wealth, sterility and the physical weakening of the race, and the inability to populate its colonies and recruit for its armies. A fatality that man cannot master obliges nations to pass successively through these two states, just as water from a spring must travel past all the banks of the river until it reaches the ocean. This image is frequently reproduced in our common language to affirm that no nation can swim against the tide of civilization.

While at first sight this theory is more in conformity with history than the first, it is nevertheless falsified by reason and experience. In the first place, it is evident that the equation made between individuals and societies cannot be adopted in its literal sense, because societies do not age, but remain in absolute conditions of stability so far as the age of their members is concerned. Yet the state of equilibrium that is spontaneously produced in physical organization always tends to be upset in the moral and intellectual order. For death harvests from among the mature and elderly, and therefore constantly deprives society of the treasures of wisdom and experience, while birth tends constantly to infuse these same societies with original barbarism. This cause of decadence acts equally upon all peoples, while the first weighs especially upon the most advanced. How many times have those of us who have lived a half-century had to groan to see extinguished by death those good men who are the principal vital forces of the country! The most perfect societies are evidently those which, under this double influence, have the most to lose and the least to gain; they are, consequently, the most exposed to decline. Yet this difficulty is not insoluble, and it does not increase with the number of centuries in a nation's history. To the extent a people elevates itself, it is more exposed to decline, but it will find in its successes new forces by which to resist corruption and thus preserve itself from decadence. Many populations without histories or recently implanted upon a virgin soil cannot escape barbarism, while the oldest European nations are able to keep themselves in the first rank. Others, such as Spain and Italy, after having languished for centuries, give new testimonies to their youth and vitality. The possession of a glorious past, far from being a cause of weakness in them, is, on the contrary, a source for renewal. The special object of this work is to seek the forces that allow nations to progress and reform, and I will prove that these are especially found in those social regimes in which each citizen has the power to overcome the original vice of his children and to transmit to them the habits of work and virtue created by their elders. For the moment I will merely note that this task is no more difficult for the old imperial nations than it is for their newest colonies.

In conclusion, nations, like individuals, enjoy freedom of the will. They are fatally bound neither to good nor to evil, and we cannot discern in the history of any nation the necessary succession of youth or progress by old age or decadence. Whatever their past may have been, they remain the masters of their own future. They may always expect success, even after a long period of abasement, if they once again observe the moral laws, while their prosperity will come to an end as soon as they let these laws fall into neglect.

**VICES CAN BE REFORMED
BY INSTITUTIONS AND MORALS**

Another widespread prejudice helping to discourage the spirit of reform is the view that would subordinate the destiny of a nation to the physical organization of the race. Like the other errors, it can be disproved by observation. I do not absolutely deny that the diverse human races take their leading characteristics from certain traditional habits and the conditions of their soil and climate. Yet the spirit of system has singularly abused this theory, which each father of a family can refute from his own experience. The most palpable proof is the extreme diversity of characters and aptitudes of children issued from the same marriage. Among the different members of the same family we find the calm tastes that lead one to seek the joys of the paternal hearth and the ardor that pushes another to faraway enterprises; the sweetness that disposes one to obey and the firmness that makes another desire to command; the moderation that makes virtue easy to one, and the passions that lead another to vice or crime; in one, the insufficiency of mind that allows success to be found only in a common profession, and in another the eminent aptitudes which make it possible to fill the highest social functions. The regular generation of these contrasts and of the two sexes is a providential law that everywhere preserves harmony in the family and society. It always dominates and frequently effaces the characteristics that are claimed for this or that race.

A second refutation of the theory of races is found in the preponderant influence that education exerts on the destinies of individual, family, and nation. To change the direction children will take it suffices to modify the ideas and customs given by the head of the family. Our history presents many variations of this nature. It is manifest, for example, that the similarity frequently claimed between the Gauls and the Frenchmen of our day disappears before the transformations that the national character has seen during the brief intervals that separate the eras of the Catholic League and Henri IV, Descartes and Voltaire, Louis XVI and the Directory.

Since the middle of the seventeenth century, medical science has frequently propagated this error by exaggerating the influence of physical organization upon man. Yet here a more correct direction to minds is given by the precepts and practice of the art. It has been known for a long time that the surgical operations of the civil and military hospitals in England succeed in a greater proportion than in France, and the discussions of this subject tend to confirm that this result is due not to the superiority of the English surgeons but to the greater quietness of spirit of their patients. On the other hand, when one analyzes the causes that make men peaceful in the face of death, he finds them in inferior peoples in the animal propensities that smother the love of neighbor and the idea of a future life, in religious peoples in the institutions and beliefs that give to the death all guarantee of the actual well-being of those they love and of the coming reunion in a better life. This opinion has been advanced by the surgeons who have operated amidst the populations in which the moral sentiments are but little developed. I have found it myself in the German and French surgeons established in Russia and Siberia, who attribute the comparative success of their operations to the serenity maintained, notwithstanding the imminence of death or the attacks of sorrow, by firm beliefs and the organization of the patriarchal family. I have been assured that one of our leading surgeons believes the success of certain risky operations to be assured by first making an appeal to religion and assuring the invalid about the future of his wife and children. If moral forces can play such a great role in the most grave lesions of the human organism, they must eventually triumph over egotistical passions and base appetites.

Let us then reject this deadly doctrine that would have us accept error and vice as the fatal consequences of our physical organization. Let us understand that the grandeur of humanity consists precisely in the subordination of material forces to moral ones dominated by our will, and that consequently each nation can find in itself the resources necessary to raise itself as high as its rivals. Assuredly, the influences that we wrongly seek in the physical order can be exerted in the moral order. Yet progress and decadence have their source in the practice or neglect of these principles and not in the race itself. We suffer cruelly today from the faults of our fathers, yet we remain the arbiters of the destinies of our children. This destiny will be great, if we are able to again take up the good principles of our elders and transmit them to our descendants.

History, moreover, confirms these inductions based upon the daily observation of facts. It refutes the allegation of the inferiority of the French to the Anglo-Saxons, and it proves that the ascendancy of the two races has followed the same changes as the development of their moral forces. It was long ago that our ancient Celtic races, mixed with those from the North and Germany, and under the influence of their old traditions made fruitful by Christianity, acquired all the virtues that distinguish great nations. Already in the seventeenth century, the French were classed in the first rank by the unanimous opinion of other peoples. Arrested in her growth by the sovereigns to whom they gave unreserved devotion, France has been able to preserve herself from the abasement to which the other races have fallen. She resisted the religious persecution that in 1685 exiled to our rivals that industrious part of the nation which, following the example of the first Christians before the pagan persecution, did not fear to sacrifice their temporal interests to their religious convictions. Notwithstanding the corruption propagated by three successive reigns and the dangerous remedies that our fathers sought in the Revolution, she has preserved amidst hard trials the love of justice and patriotism. She has raised herself from unprecedented reverses, the fatal conclusion of the greatest military successes of the modern era. Having broken a regime discredited by the corruption of its ancient ruling classes, she sought with a determined will a new regime that would not involve a return to the abuses from which she had so much suffered. To arrive at the end of the reforms begun in 1789, she resigned herself to calamities, and above all to an instability that would have already led a weaker nation to absolute decadence. Finally, in spite of the critical situation created by her revolutions, in spite of the national antipathies raised by the wars of the First Empire, it suffices to our race to find peace and security again in order to take up a part of her ancient leadership.

To what height will France be called the day on which she frees herself by a generous effort from the vices and errors that have hindered her march for so long, when to the desire for progress and the sentiment of justice and love of humanity so happily preserved amidst the corruption of the Old Regime, she joins anew the respect for good traditions, the source of her ancient grandeur, and the principal cause of the present growth of her rivals!

FALSE THEORIES OF HISTORY
OBSCURE THE CONDITIONS OF REFORM

Among the principal factors that obscure the true conditions of reform are the false theories of history that surround us.

All who have treated this branch of the social sciences in depth have recognized the false judgments of our so-called universal histories. For my part, when I had studied the true sources of the subject, I found that the judgments of our classical historians on the fundamental questions are in poor conformity to the truth. It is not necessary to possess great knowledge or to devote oneself to lengthy researches to see the falsity of these historical judgments. It suffices to inspect the texts on which they were based. Every writer who has observed human nature has given precious insights about older civilizations, but history properly so-called, history founded upon manuscript documents and archaeological evidence, was born in our time. In spite of its literary grandeur, the century of Louis XIV had barely any understanding of past ages. Its histories denatured the mind of antiquity and the Middle Ages by lending its own sentiments and ideas to them, just as on stage they dressed up their own personalities in ancient costumes. The Revolutionary school also spread falsehoods, especially in what concerns social relations. It attributed to the six preceding centuries a social antagonism that only existed then as an exception and which did not become widespread until our day. These false impressions accelerated the work of destruction that French opinion gloried in, but today they weigh heavily upon us by misleading us about the origin of our present evils and discrediting the remedy offered us by the good traditions of our fathers.

Fortunately, the modern historians of Germany, England, France,

Spain, and Italy are beginning to react against these errors and prejudices. The convictions they have formed by returning to the original documents are precisely those I have acquired by directly observing the numerous European families that have preserved the instincts, habits, and social relations of the Middle Ages. Like one of our most able historians, I have often been indignant to see contemporary literature pervert public opinion by affirming that our old France was only composed of tyrants and those oppressed by them. While admitting that on many points the Middle Ages were inferior to our time, I have more and more perceived that social harmony was then better established in parish, workshop, and family.

I would quit my proper subject were I to attempt a methodical exposition of the errors that are accepted in France about the history of social relations. Moreover, the enterprise would be premature, for social science must first be established upon a solid foundation by the study of our own time before it is extended to treat past ages. To this end, I can contribute only to the extent of my own strength. I foresee that this work will be immediately condemned by certain minds nourished by the prejudices of history or imbued with the hateful instincts of the French Revolution. I will therefore attempt to put them on guard against their inveterate convictions by showing them that a people excellent in the culture of the arts and letters can temporarily lose awareness of the most manifest truths of its national history.

The Middle Ages were not merely a time of social organization. They also created several original branches of art and industry. Notably, they founded a school of architecture that compares favorably with those of better periods. The society that built admirable monuments at such great cost makes one take note of its value and forces later generations to admire it. Nevertheless, from the sixteenth century, this sentiment disappeared amidst our admiration for the art of the Greeks and Romans, and soon there was no one to admire the monuments that so profusely covered our own soil. Our great men of the seventeenth century, who raised the human mind to so great a height in so many directions, completely lost their affection for French art. They did not suspect that one might see the least merit in the dwellings of their fathers or the edifices in which they daily practiced their religious duties. The eighteenth century and the Revolution also contributed to the growth of these false impressions. In this connection, we cannot be grateful enough to those writers, artists, and archaeologists who have finally opened our eyes to the light and restored our national tradition to its place of honor.

Yet, if under the sway of an elite aesthetic the public ignored the value of the material objects before its very eyes, what errors must they commit under the influence of new doctrines and political passions when it comes to the ideas and customs of generations that long ago descended into the tomb? The more I study contemporary facts and the traces of the past, the more I am assured that we are mistaken in the judgments we make daily about the social relations of preceding centuries. If this is true, what moral and material disorders must be provoked by a theory of history that leads us to disdain our traditions and deny the origins of our nationality!

According to established opinion, the ruling classes of the Old Regime caused an intolerable oppression to weigh upon the inferior classes. In the countryside, the lords abused their power in order to keep for themselves all the fruits of their vassals' work and intelligence. Political orators, the press, and the theater incessantly repeat these assertions in a variety of forms. More recently, this thesis has been taught to the rural classes in scientific textbooks. There they discourse on the anarchy that gave rise to the slavery of feudalism. We have even seen it affirmed that the feudal lords, having to divide certain domains, were careful to divide the bodies of their peasants in order to arrive at an exact measure. The public is thus persuaded that at the time of the Revolution of 1789 the French nation was composed only of victims and executioners. Again, renouncing here all methodical discussion, I will limit myself to pointing out several facts that disprove the regnant opinion and show the condition of our fathers in its true light.

Many documents preserve a faithful description of the relations between lords and the rural populations from the origins of the Middle Ages until 1789. I wish to speak of the titles that, having accumulated in chateaux and abbeys or in the offices of the parlements, tribunals, and other jurisdictions of the police that escaped revolutionary vandalism, are today held in the public collections under the direction of the able paleographers who form our School of Charters. I have never neglected an occasion to glean the impressions of these learned men who know of these treasures of social science, and I have always learned with astonishment that they have found no trace of that permanent oppression which, according to common opinion, was the characteristic trait of our Old Regime. Some even say that the inferior classes enjoyed a well-being and repose that left them little to envy in their patrons.

The French lawyers, who so much contributed to the rupture of ancient social relations and who since the Revolution have sung the praises of the new regime, are beginning to perceive its weakness. By studying the past, they are noticing that their ancestors habitually exemplified virtues that are now rare. Thus, an honorable judge, in the history of a great judicial family, recalled that the sixteenth century had been the heroic age of the French bench. A young lawyer, recently publishing a valuable correspondence found in the archives of the former parlement of Provence, cast in relief the extraordinary contrast produced before and after the reign of Louis XIV between the noble views preserved by the lawyers of the seventeenth century and the corrupt ones of the eighteenth.

Manuscripts and monuments are not the only sources for understanding former days: men and the soil have preserved the faithful imprint of the past more than is generally thought. For instance, the Basque peasant families inhabit the same dwellings in which their ancestors lived in the Middle Ages. They have preserved the same language, occupations, and customs. Finally, the regime of inheritance that transmits these traditions is the same one that a Latin author described in this country twenty centuries ago. Old men still living who received directly from their fathers the traditions of the Old Regime testify unanimously that their situation has been unaffected by our political revolutions. Now, the study of this situation reveals an excellent social organization, much superior to several of ours created since the reign of Louis XIV and especially to those of our own day. The study of present-day sharecropping also furnishes precise data about the former relations of landowners and their tenants. This kind of contract, still in use in our day in the central and southern provinces, was in the fifteenth century the foundation of rural organization in almost all of France. Now, it is easy to see by the old leases that the relations of master to servant have not changed for four centuries. From another perspective, this kind of contract identifies the two interests in such a way that it excludes all charge of oppression by the landowner. It is even manifest that the disadvantages of sharecropping, which, as in any social relation, result from human imperfection, weigh heaviest upon the owner. Our sharecroppers of the center and south of France incontestably had in the past and maintain today a happier and more worthy situation than that enjoyed today by the rural workers attached to the farms of the east, west, and north. Assuredly, improvements have been introduced since the Middle Ages in the condition of the small holders and tenant farmers. Yet they have been balanced by many new disadvantages. The particular evil from which we have suffered for two centuries and especially since the Revolution is that our prejudices and passions have not allowed us to see the facts from their true point of view and rightly to distinguish good and evil.

Another consideration particularly struck me during the course of my research on the customs of my fellow citizens. If the French Revolution had truly released the inferior classes from the oppression of the Old Regime, we should have seen the mutual affection of masters and servants slowly take the place of the old antagonism. But even the dullest observer can see that the change that has taken place and continues under our eyes is the opposite. The writers who have acquired a just celebrity by describing the social relations of the last six centuries provide touching examples of the solidarity that existed between the landowner and the tenant, between the patron and the worker, and especially between the master and the domestic servant. On the contrary, the antagonism of these same conditions has become, as I have remarked above, the most obvious trait of modern French morals. The old men of our day have all seen, during their youth, domestics in many families identifying with the ideas and interests of their masters. Only vestiges of that state of affairs remain. And if there be no salutary reaction against this trend, I doubt whether the generation that follows us will see even one example of that ancient solidarity. Certainly social antagonism is not a new thing, reserved to our day. In the past, civil discord even had a violent character that it now lacks. Yet between the two eras there is the essential difference that in the Old Regime each patron went into combat upheld by his workers and domestics, while today he finds them facing him armed. In the past, after the struggle, one found in the workshop and in the house a restorative peace and repose. Today, the struggle is in the house itself, and it continues silently when it does not break forth openly. In this way it ceaselessly undermines society by destroying every chance of domestic happiness. The writers who propagate subversive doctrines today are refuted by their own household. And I see in the trials that afflict our families today one of the most severe lessons that will lead us back to the truth about social relations.

The study of Europe has helped to destroy my inherited prejudices and to show me the social relations that the revolutions, with their mixture of good and evil, destroyed on our soil. The European Old Regime, even with its feudal forms, still exists in eastern Europe, Russia, Poland, Turkey, Hungary, the principalities of the Danube, and the Slavic provinces contiguous with the German states. Now everyone will testify, as I have done myself, that notwithstanding the disturbances that have spread from the West into the East, the solidarity of the different classes of society remains the characteristic trait of these countries, while the antagonism of these same classes propagates itself more and more among the populations of the West that adopt our ideas. I testify to this fact without proposing a doctrine. I do not pretend to uphold, contrary to the evidence, that the civilization of the East is better in principle than those of the West that have renounced regimes of privilege and remain free of the two vices from which we suffer. I wish only to make felt, while waiting for a more complete demonstration, that we go astray in taking a false notion of history for our guide, and that our growth finds itself hindered in several directions by disorders unknown to our fathers.

These historical errors are generally founded upon certain exceptional facts falsely presented as normal and regular. There is no paradox that cannot be established upon such foundations. If some historians one day decided to discredit maternal love, they would be able to produce a long enumeration of cruelties exercised by heartless mothers upon their young children. Thus, some cite disorders such as the Jacquerie,[1] those of Auvergne of the seventeenth century, and several other popular agitations as testimonies of a former state of antagonism. Yet these were manifestly local and accidental. They are few in number and cannot support the presumption of a general and permanent state of struggle between lords and vassals. Moreover, one must note the provocation exercised upon these events by royal power and the lawyers interested in disorganizing the feudal regime: the massacres that took place in 1846 in a Slavic province subjected to Austria have shown similar results in our own time.

Nor do I admit that one can condemn the social relations of the Old Regime by reference to several popular movements, or by citing the pillages of chateaux in several of our rural districts between 1789 and 1793. These disorders were not extended beyond the localities where the old relations of landowner and tenant had been broken for more than a century by habits of absenteeism engendered in the richest families by the life of the court. We have not enough sensed

[1] The Jacquerie was a peasant rebellion in northern France in 1358.

the implications of the provinces such as Brittany, Anjou, the bocage of the Vendée, and the mountains of the center and south, where the landowners continued to reside amidst their tenants. Today there still exist hundreds of ancient families who never left the lands of their ancestors and were protected by the local population against the enterprises of the revolutionary committees organized in the towns and villages of their surroundings. The Revolution of 1789 only took the character of a social war in a few places. It was, like many of the agitations of the Old Regime, a struggle justified by the corruption of the ruling classes. Those who see in this great event revenge against the so-called tyranny of the two privileged classes, those above all who consider the pillages and spoliations of this era as a national movement, should observe attentively the passions and appetites that today are developed among the lower reaches of society. The attempts made here and there in December of 1851 reveal enough to us the scenes of violence that are produced if—God preserve us—the systematic enemies of property arrive in power and maintain themselves by a second Terror. Will not the theoreticians of this new revolution justify their doctrine by pointing to these disorders as a testimony of the oppression that must have been exercised by the landowners over the poor part of the nation?

I no longer see any political school disposed to conclude from these reflections that the regime of privilege destroyed in 1789 should be preferred to the regime of equality under the law that is now adopted with preference in all the free and prosperous nations. By founding my doctrine upon the facts laid out in the seven following chapters, I have proved in some measure that the solution of our social problems will henceforth be found less in the institutions that systematically maintain inequality among men and more in the sentiments and interests that create harmony among all classes. Yet before beginning this demonstration, I had first to protest against an unjustified belief in a former state of antagonism. I had to indicate, moreover, how we may be sure that our fathers were neither oppressed nor tyrants, that before 1789 they formed a nationality worthy of respect, and, finally, that the study of their patriotic acts will be more profitable to us than will discussion of the utopias of our day.

Our successive revolutions, in compensation for so many evils, have definitively meted justice to the principal abuses of the Old Regime. We may henceforth point out the virtues of it without fear of giving rise to a spirit of reaction. It is not only in the interest of art that we must with several eminent writers propagate respect for the past, it is also in the name of the great examples of social harmony that science has led us to discover. The historian or novelist who adopts this point of view based on the study of facts and customs will transport us to an unknown land. He will help us honor the sane practices of our ancestors. He will habituate us to seek in the experience of our race the elements of the new regime we desire, and he will thus exercise a beneficent influence on social reform.

It is time to put an end to the disdain that has led so many of our writers systematically to glorify all the actions and tendencies of the French Revolution with a view to establishing the ascendancy of our nation in the world. It is in vain that we wish to attain this goal by altering history, by pulling the wool over the eyes of Europe, and by affirming that they admire what, on the contrary, they severely condemn. Our rivals will never affirm the facile reasoning by which we convince ourselves. They blame with liveliness, even with a malign or hostile insistence, the attacks and ignorance of our revolutionary school. Unfortunately, we have but one solid argument to oppose to these critiques: that the French Revolution put an end to the disorders of the regimes of Louis XIV, the Regent, and Louis XV. To attain this end, it appealed more to passion than truth. Today the abuses have partly disappeared, but we preserve the errors of our passions. We should leave behind these preoccupations and return to the truth by an impartial study of the past. We should seek the true conditions of reform in the best practices of our fathers. We are more likely to regain the moral leadership that Europe gave to us in the seventeenth century by doing this than by continuing to propagate the paradoxes of the Revolution. The only sure way to glorify the Revolution of 1789 is to end it.

SOCIAL REFORM IN FRANCE (1864)
ON THE FAMILY

> *Gratia super gratiam mulier sancta et pudorata.*[1]
> *Ecclesiasticus* XXVI:15

THE MODERN FAMILY IS
THE ESSENTIAL UNIT OF SOCIETY

As with all social institutions, the family is today the subject of lively controversy, and the errors that have been published about it greatly trouble our minds. I shall attempt to refute the most dangerous of these in this chapter. Yet it is also true that the family remains the only institution whose essential elements have not been officially proscribed in the name of science, justice, or natural right. In all regular social organizations, the family imposes itself even more imperiously than property. With respect to the family, I will follow the plan previously adopted for the discussion of property and will not address the arguments of the skeptics. I simply take it as given that those who refuse to see the family as a direct creation of God must nevertheless admit that it is a necessary consequence of the natural laws He has instituted.

[1] The holy and chaste wife adds grace upon grace.

Today there still exist social organizations in which the existence of the isolated individual is materially impossible, for instance, the nomadic shepherds of the East. There are other societies in which the law prohibits individuals from separating from the family, which was the case with the Russian peasants until the most recent reforms. The sedentary people of the West have removed these obstacles by changing their laws to favor the individual. Careful inspection, however, reveals that the extent of individual independence is more apparent than real. Wherever individualism becomes the dominant form of social relations, men rapidly descend towards barbarism. Wherever, on the contrary, society is progressing, individuals eagerly seek the bonds of the family and unhesitatingly renounce the independence that law and the nature of things allow them. The nations that European opinion chooses as guides leave complete latitude for the exceptional tendency of the few towards isolation. Yet even those individuals who go the farthest in this direction remain, according to the law, subordinate to the fundamental needs of the family. This tendency of the law is in harmony with the general interests of the modern family and in particular with the view of those who demand the concentration of authority in the hands of the father. Reminding ourselves of the principles set out in the previous chapter concerning the possession and transmission of property, we may already sense that the best means of assuring the well-being of the family is to confer unlimited power to its head. Moreover, I have shown that the liberty of testament that seems to give individualism its final sanction is not truly fruitful except when it is completed by a law of inheritance inspired exclusively by the interests of the family.

Ancient civilizations often found it advantageous to constitute more sizeable social groups in which the individuality of the family was absorbed, and this is today the condition of the Russian peasant towards his commune and landowner. Modern constitutions all encourage associations of numerous individuals, the characteristics of which I shall indicate in a subsequent chapter.

Yet whether they regulate these large human groups or, on the other hand, write statutes for isolated individuals, the legislators of our day always have in view that intermediate group which, by a signal favor of Providence, possesses all the beneficial aspects of the individual and the association. When we closely examine the reforms in religious institutions and in the regime of property that are today being introduced by the experts, we soon perceive that they have as their principal end the strengthening of the family. For the moderns, more than ever, the family is the essential unit of society.

Like religion and property, the family is an unchangeable institution when considered in its essential principle. Yet also like them it submits to considerable modifications of form. The principal forms given to these three institutions are not independent of one another, and together constitute one of the essential characteristics of each social organization. In this way we may distinguish two extreme types, the patriarchal family and the unstable family, and then an intermediate type, the stem-family.

The first type of family is common to the shepherds of the East, the Russian peasants, and the Slavs of eastern Europe. The father keeps all his married sons with him and exerts extensive authority over them and his other children. Other than a few furnishings, property remains indivisible among the members. The father directs all the work and accumulates as savings the produce not required for the family's daily needs. In nomadic shepherds, this community endures throughout the father's life. In sedentary farmers, it divides when the family property is no longer sufficient to provide for the children of the young married couples; and, according to the existence or lack of available land, the swarm that leaves the mother-house establishes itself nearby or leaves the area. Thus it is that the father, with the help of thrift and common work, presides over the creation of a new establishment or the equipping of emigrants. The father also designates the member of the family charged to exert the new patriarchal authority. Among nomads, the inclination that moves young married couples to desire an independent situation is neutralized by the necessities of life, which do not permit these couples to survive in isolation. Among settled farmers, the same is accomplished by the feudal organization of property, and, in all patriarchal families, by moral influences rooted in tradition. This cast of mind has its source in firm religious beliefs that come more from faith than reason. In work and social habits, it maintains respect for the established order more than it develops the spirit of initiative. In this state of material or moral constraint, the community arrests the rise of eminent individuals to an independent situation. On the other hand, it allows the least moral, least able, and least hard-working individuals to participate in the common good.

The second type, the unstable family, now dominates the populations of workers that live under the new industrial regimes in the West. It also spreads among the wealthy classes because of a variety of influences, the most important of which is forced equality of inheritance. Created by the union of two spouses, at its beginning the family grows through the birth of children. Later, it shrinks when these children, lacking obligation toward parents and kin, establish themselves elsewhere, either as celibates or by creating a new family. These families are finally dissolved by the death of the parents, or, in case of the premature death of the parents, by the dispersion of the younger children. Each child gains his inheritance upon leaving the paternal house, and, in any event, enjoys the fruit of his labors himself. The precocious use of reason, propagated by the teaching of the schools, by the advice of parents, and by the example of the superior classes, shapes his beliefs in the latest views of good and evil. The taste for novelty often triumphs over the spirit of tradition. In this regime, because the individual no longer has any care for the needs of his kin, if he is skilled he will soon gain a higher social position. On the other hand, since he is unable to rely upon his family for help, if he is unskilled or vicious he will quickly fall into misery. Unfortunately, once this condition is produced, it tends to become permanent, either because the parents can no longer contribute by savings to the establishment of the children, or because the children are abandoned to their bad tendencies or are perverted by bad example while still young. In this way the unstable family creates new fortunes alongside a new social state, unheard of in prior ages, for which we have today created the word pauperism.

In discussing the stem-family with reference to the law of inheritance, I have sufficiently indicated that it unites the advantages and avoids the inconveniences of the first two. The stem-family shows itself superior to the others by two manifest traits: it develops spontaneously wherever there is liberty of testament balanced by a strong custom of handing on the inheritance whole and entire, and it remains precious even to those who go abroad seeking fortune with their inheritance. If the designated heir dies prematurely, the younger children are always ready to renounce a brilliant future and to return to their family home to fill the void that has opened. This regime can be established under the traditional influence of the patriarchal life, but it does not acquire all its fecundity except when joined to religious liberty and individual property. It at once satisfies those who are content with the situation in which they are born and those who wish to rise in the social hierarchy by bold endeavors. Under these diverse headings, it conciliates, in a just measure, the authority of the father and the liberty of the children, the inclination to innovate and respect for tradition.

In the following paragraphs, when indicating the conditions of moral and material order for the principal elements of the family, I generally have in view this third type, when I do not explicitly make mention of the first two.

THE FAMILY HOME IS THE FAMILY'S ESSENTIAL PROPERTY

One of the most fruitful traditions on the European continent is the one that assures the private possession of its residence to each family, rich or poor.

The customs and institutions that preserve this salutary practice are among the most definite signs of a progressive civilization. Even in a relatively backward social order, they give families a dignity and independence not found among peoples more advanced in other respects, in whom prevails the deplorable custom of living in rented rooms. The possession of the family home seems to have been one of the general traits of the European Old Regime. Other than rare exceptions, it still obtains among the Russians, the greater part of the Slavs of central Europe, the Hungarians, and others. As I will explain below, the too-sudden invasion of the industrial regime has partially destroyed this protective organization in the West. It is, however, still maintained in many rural districts. There the populations wisely continue to reject the ease of private establishment that might be offered by the renting of houses. The self-respecting head of the family refuses to give his daughter in marriage to a suitor who does not possess his own home. On this point, the peasants, still imbued with the old European spirit, have a more correct sense of their dignity than do those who in our urban agglomerations satisfy themselves not by raising themselves to the possession of a home, but by refusing to pay respect to social superiority. I am thus led to think that the spirit of innovation that today agitates Europe will be less useful to social reform than will be the pure and simple return to tradition.

Some distressing signs have pointed to the danger of the regime that infiltrated the West in the middle of the last century, and into which it progresses more than ever during this peaceful era after the great wars of the Revolution and the Empire. In England, where there is no fear of examining social ills, many leading men have already reacted against an unreflective tendency: they have taken upon themselves the mission of helping workers acquire ownership of their residences. By appealing to the initiative of patrons and creating special corporations known as Land Societies, they have already obtained results that we cannot praise enough. These societies propose to stimulate workers' spirit of thrift by enabling them to acquire the land necessary to build a dwelling. They are made up of patrons whose assistance is freely given and of subscribers equal in number to the available building sites. The annuity is low, so that its payment might be within the workers' reach. They are put in possession of the land when they have paid a part of their subscription, and they are generally freeholders within ten to fifteen years.

On the Continent, several centuries-old mining corporations, notably those of the Hartz mountains, find the workers' progress towards the ownership of their dwellings to be a means of improving their intellectual and moral condition. When, at the death of a worker, his house and garden are to be sold, the other workers take precedence over capitalists, merchants, and local political leaders in the ensuing auction. The worker borrows a sum equal to the cost of the house from the mining corporation and then pays through a reduction in his salary, plus interest on the debt at the rate of four percent. If he is sufficiently provident, he may amortize the debt by means of supplementary payments. In reality, the Hartz miner in these conditions is more a renter than a freeholder. Yet experience proves that this combination, by elevating the social condition of the worker, leads him better to understand both his duty and his dignity and fortifies his habits of work and temperance.

In France, the ownership of a residence remains one of the most characteristic traits of rural families, while, as in England, the regime of renting has unfortunately introduced itself into the cities and manufacturing centers. Yet to the same social disorder, we have begun to oppose the same remedy. Some societies of patronage, among which we should note the one in Mulhouse, have given a better direction to ideas and morals. As recently as 1853, a society of worker cities was founded in Mulhouse under the inspiration of Jean Dollfus; it has already built 630 houses, of which 560 have been sold and fifty entirely paid for. These houses are worth from 2,650 francs to 3,300 francs. They can be acquired by an initial payment of three hundred to four hundred francs, to which is subsequently added regular payments of 18 to 25 francs per month over thirteen to fourteen years. The passion for ownership has given the spendthrift population a powerful incentive to save. Moreover, the workers who have become property owners understand the danger of political agitations. They now dream only of bettering their condition and raising themselves into the ranks of the bourgeoisie.

The observations of the Society for Social Economics give reason to hope that the initiative of individual patrons has equaled that of these collective undertakings. These initial steps certainly constitute the most difficult part of the reform that the worker population requires. In view of these efforts, we take confidence in the future. We are persuaded that when this reform has been understood by the ruling classes, it will easily triumph over the obstacles that seem to pose a fatal limit to the progress of civilization. We may even see many fruitful sentiments and generous habits of mind develop in those individuals least disposed to obtain property through work and thrift. The sovereign who progresses in this direction with the help of peaceful subjects will obtain great successes. He will found his dynasty still more firmly than did that great king who promised to put a chicken in every pot. This success will be even more permanent if it is more fruitful in the moral progress that is its means than the material progress that is its end.

In England, the regime of leasing to the middle and inferior classes seems to have begun long ago. The common practice by which it was created and is maintained is a system of extremely long leases. The persons who wish to construct a dwelling obtain from the property owner the cession of the land, while agreeing that the land and its improvements will be returned to the heir of the owner after a period of ninety-nine years. By this means, the urban and rural dwellings owned by the great owners of the soil tend to multiply, and so the owners, to make some profit, give them out to lease. Yet the dependence imposed by this regime upon the large class of renters is made less burdensome in practice by excellent traditions. The most honorable property owners are reluctant to change abruptly the conditions of the ancient leases held by their tenants, nor do they believe themselves authorized to expose them to the competition of new bidders without regard for their long-standing relations. Nor is it even rare to find that generations of property owners have held it to be a point of honor to maintain, without being bound by a lease, the price that generations of renters have enjoyed for a century. These traditions, so favorable to the maintenance of social harmony, were equally widespread in our Old Regime. Vestiges of it can be seen here and there in the provinces. Even in Paris, we still see owners of houses who, keeping the paternal tradition, protect their old tenants by refraining from raising a price established thirty years previously. According to the belief in the sanctity of the family home that the French used to hold, the expulsion of a family incapable of paying increased rent would have been considered extremely harsh. •

In the large cities, and notably in Paris, I only find these old ideas among those of greatly advanced age. There now remain few land-lords who do not believe it fitting and right to base their rents on the going rate and to change their tenants as frequently as they would their holdings on the stock exchange. The rigorous applica-tion of the economic principle of supply and demand disorganizes social relations, whether it be applied to rents or salaries. This system is rejected both by our former tradition and by the current practice of those few owners who have perceived the dangers of the new regime.

The complete isolation of the family dwelling is one of the fun-damental conventions of every civilization. The rural populations rightly seen as models satisfy this convention and also the condi-tions of the best agriculture by placing their dwellings at the center of their properties. The condition of isolation is even fulfilled in many European towns, where the high price of land next to public roads makes the contiguity of houses necessary. The English respect this principle religiously. In London, where land brings a consider-able price, the poorest bourgeois and even often simple workers each occupy a separate house. In this regime, an urban dwelling

presents the arrangement that we see in Paris today in the neigh-
borhood of St.-Marceau, in the Cité, and in several other ancient
quarters. They form massive row houses subdivided by floors connected by a common staircase, giving each a bedroom with a closet
and rarely more than three rooms in all. Surely these little frontages,
in which there is frequently but one window per story, are not
found on the monumental boulevards that we have been pleased to
multiply for some time in our cities. Yet the English are not affected
by this supposed inferiority noticed by unreflective tourists, for they
love the aspect of their towns, where respect for the laws of the
family is preserved. They are moreover persuaded that private
dwellings have for their chief end not the pleasing of the eyes of
passers-by and the curious, but the sheltering of chaste women,
obedient children, hardworking servants, and, what sums it all up,
citizens enjoying their homes in complete sovereignty.

Wherever fertility and the other essential laws of the family are
preserved, the most modest dwellings contain at least four rooms:
the first for the head of the family and his wife, the second for the
designated heir, his wife, and their youngest child, the two others
for the children, the single adults, and the servants, separated
according to sex. The hearth at which the food is prepared, near
which the meals are taken and reunions and vigils held, is generally
found in the room of the head of the family. Even in cities, where
there is less space, there are always joined to this principal part several other rooms destined for the conservation of household provisions, the laundry, and other domestic tasks. In the regions of
Europe where grains are consumed as bread, there used to be
included among these little rooms a small workshop for the win-
nowing, sifting, and baking. The miller and the baker have generally, in the West, removed this task from the family home; the
extreme simplification brought on by the use of coal in the construction of bread ovens has, however, begun to move things in the
opposite direction, giving back to families in Belgium and England
one of their essential functions. In the country and the urban neigh-

borhoods, dwellings also generally have a garden in which vegetables and fruits are produced, as well as several buildings dedicated to the raising of domestic animals. Among these, we see successively appear, according to the family's degree of wealth—even when these families are little inclined towards agriculture—turkeys, pigs, goats, milk cows, asses, and horses. Finally, when the trade practiced by the couple requires working with some important material, the family home is completed by the annexation of a workshop. In spite of the concentration of manufacturing that has ceaselessly developed for a century, this organization is still very common among rural artisans and, in general, among those who work with textiles, metal, wood, and leather.

The inferior classes have maintained this organization of the family home in the greater part of Europe, and especially in the East, but it is too often weakening in the industrial regions of the West. In a few great cities in England and France, the family home is even at times reduced to a single room, stifling and dim, in which both sexes and all ages languish in utter destitution. I need not here dwell upon these lamentable miseries, already described by the official inquiries of England and pointed out by many writers, both English and French. At a later juncture, I will explain how these two peoples of the first rank of civilization nonetheless have disorders unknown to less advanced civilizations. This is one of the social problems that comes most directly under the plan of this work. I shall return to this anomaly when I treat the question of pauperism. I will then indicate the reasons that prevent me from considering this sad condition of certain families to be an inevitable part of the constitution of society, and I will at the same time point out the reforms that it demands.

On the other hand, when the progress of wealth is combined with the understanding of social laws, the family home is lifted above the level I have just described and given conveniences of a higher level. The number of rooms dedicated to the lodging of the various members of the family is multiplied, and special rooms are dedicated to the preparation of food, the taking of meals, and the gathering of the family.

In the families of the superior class, we see rooms devoted to family prayers, intellectual exercises, and to objects recalling the memory of elders and the family's heritage. In all these cases, the number of outbuildings increases in proportion to the size of the principal dwelling. Finally, in every civilization where the moral order rests on a profound belief in the life to come, near these various buildings is found the family tomb.

Furnishings—including the furniture itself, silver, and linens— are one of the characteristic elements of the family home. They are naturally found to be in agreement with the general organization of the dwelling and the habits of the family. The needs and conveniences to which these furnishings correspond are more variable than are those of the primary dwelling. They acquire an excessive value in those families given over to refined luxury, and they are reduced to nothing in those families threatened by poverty. For these, the total absence of furnishings is ordinarily the most visible sign of their destitution. For all peoples who strongly preserve their morals there is in this respect a certain minimum of comfort or well-being below which families will not consent to descend. Imbued with certain traditional requirements that are but the expression of centuries-old experience, young women refuse to enter into an engagement until, with the help of their future spouse and their parents, they have assembled the normal furnishings of a family home, without which the new family could claim no public consideration. The same remark applies equally to the acquisition of the bride's trousseau. The more opinion requires of them, the more that our youth, attracted by marriage, will be led to hard work and thrift. I will have occasion to make further comments on this topic. Basing my argument on the experience of the most prosperous peoples, I will prove that customs imposing severe conditions upon those who would marry are the surest way to relieve workers from the threat of poverty, and, in general, to raise the condition of all social classes.

The most commendable traits concerning the organization of the family home were habitually found both in the city and the country in our Old Regime; that is to say, each family, even those of modest means, lived alone in its own house. Unfortunately, since the end of the seventeenth century, the relaxation of morals, and since 1793, the forced equality of inheritance, have profoundly injured this tradition. The resulting evil is already great and is daily made worse.

Today, as in all other times, the natural tendency of every man who has raised himself in the social scale through hard work and intelligence is to build himself a dwelling that suits his fortune. Yet his children, even if they be but two or three in number, do not prefer to live there together even during the life of the father, and still less after his death. As ordinarily none of them will be in a situation to live in it alone with his family, the customary solution consists in selling this dwelling to a capitalist who will make a profit by letting it out. Thus, many among the rural and urban populations rent houses constructed by their elders and become tenants of the newly enriched.

Forced equality of inheritance tends by a wholly material cause to reduce the level of private existence. Moreover, it makes families less numerous, either because the children leave the paternal home when they marry, or—and this especially—because the number of children issuing from each marriage becomes smaller and smaller. Then each family requires less space, and consequently the landowner of an old property finds it in his interest to subdivide it in order to rent it to several tenants. Yet this investment of capital in a collective residence requiring extensive oversight soon leads to another deviation from true principles. The costs of such an enterprise are lowered by multiplying the number of renters in each location, and thence come those immense apartments that are being built before our very eyes, and which seem to have been built for the sake of violating all the conveniences respected by other peoples.

A modern house in Paris destined to families in a middling condition is ordinarily built with a monumental luxury that was heretofore restricted to palaces. It is subdivided into six levels linked by large staircases to an interior courtyard, various outbuildings, and the street. It extends over a considerable surface, so that each level contains several apartments—inhabited by distinct families—opening either on to the courtyard or street. These are linked up with their neighbors by the common use of the stairways, but also by the division of each dwelling into two or three parts. The principal subdivision is occupied on one of the intermediate levels by the head of the family, his wife, and their young children. Often some of the domestic staff is lodged on the ground floor, and in any event the servants, and sometimes the young men of the family, are relegated to the garret rooms. The owner rarely lives in the house, nor does he watch over the cleaning tasks imposed upon the tenants for the common areas of the stairs and outbuildings. He delegates his authority to a special agent named the concierge, a type almost unknown in the rest of Europe, who unites his harassing oversight with the performance of menial domestic tasks. We cannot enough deplore the profound injury that this sort of promiscuity brings to domestic morals and the authority of masters and parents. Thrown together apart from all surveillance, the servants of the two sexes mutually corrupt one another. They form a sort of clan, to which the concierge is the natural ally, where the spirit of insubordination ferments and the art of deceiving masters is perfected. These morals and sentiments in turn act upon the children, who are always in contact with the servants, and they are a continual source of malaise and weakness for the family. No doubt these evils are linked to another that I will describe in the paragraphs to follow, but they derive especially from the vicious disposition of these family homes.

The English and, in general, all people who preserve firm morals and traditions, enjoy the proper sense of what is required in furnishings and dwellings. They are correct to attach themselves to material arrangements that are in some sense founded on human nature, and not at all to give way, in the presence of equally permanent interests, to the spirit of speculation, the caprices of style, and architectural fads. From this point of view, I needed first to point out that the rational establishment of the family home is the first condition of social progress to be accomplished by the family. It remains now for me to indicate the other elements of reform that are found in the good organization of marriage, paternal authority, the education of children, and celibacy and domesticity.

**THE WISE AND MODEST WOMAN IS
THE PRINCIPAL AGENT OF SOCIAL PROGRESS**

The situation held by women in the family and society influences the morals and progress of a nation more than any other cause. Amidst the shocks to our minds caused by our successive revolutions, reformers have often treated this delicate subject. Yet in seeking the good outside of tradition, they have left us a utopian vision. On this subject, as on all others relating to the foundations of the social order, the human mind has explored most of the useful possibilities and cannot fruitfully innovate. Several ancient peoples held an exalted idea of the social role of the woman. The Bible, which furnished me with the epigraph for this chapter, presents almost all the excellent aspects of this subject. In the Middle Ages, several European peoples raised the respect owed to women to the level of a social dogma. To assure women of the happiest and worthiest situation, we need, then, less to innovate than to take heed of the successes gained by certain nations through these age-old practices.

The errors committed on this difficult subject derive principally from the opinions that would place the two sexes in conditions of equality. This idea of equality, which appears so simple and so intimately linked to our common notion of justice, easily imposes itself upon our minds. It is, however, very complex. Thus, those for whom the making of distinctions is difficult, do not hesitate to derive false consequences from this premise. For seventy-five years, this kind of error has been responsible for limiting the progress of liberty in the social order. The same consideration, when applied to the relative condition of the two sexes, leads to the most deadly consequences in the moral order. To speak candidly, there is here no pretext for error for those who will take note of experience. We have often improved the condition of peoples by diminishing the inequality between different families, but we have always failed when we tried to establish equality amongst all of them. The attempts made in this direction have always cast in stronger relief the radical difference in aptitudes and the necessity of maintaining inequality of station.

The English and the North Americans may run into this problem in the organization of labor, yet they have the correct idea of the true destiny of woman. According to the prevailing opinion in England, the two sexes have roles to fill in the social order that are no less different than they are in the physical order. Legislators inspired by an abstract theory of justice who would establish absolute equality between the sexes produce an intolerable situation for both. This misplaced independence always turns to the detriment of women, who gain rights of little use while remaining shorn of the advantages and guarantees they most desire. The existing contrast between English and French opinions is most visible in the institutions and customs related to the right of women to property, the contracting of marriages, and the penalties for seduction.

The rules adopted in England for the law of property have arisen spontaneously from a principle the practice of which is firmly maintained. The English desire unity of action in a family as well as a judicious division of responsibility. They think that the true function of the woman is to govern the family home, and that in this clearly circumscribed domain the father should delegate his authority without reserve to the mother of the family. This delegation is indicated by the nature of things, for where marriages are fruitful, the mother is kept at home by the duties of maternity. It is therefore the man who must look after the exterior property and defend it against encroachment, exercise the duties of a profession and fight for the interests related to it, and, finally, uphold the rights of the family before commune, province, and state. Even in the most modest household, the work of the family home has a considerable importance. Often it contributes to the family's prosperity as much as the father's profession. In all cases, it exerts a decisive influence on individual happiness. It is, moreover, manifest that the affectionate direction impressed by the mother of the family on the habits, minds, and sentiments of the child exerts a sovereign influence on the future of the race and truly constitutes a high social function in every civilization having moral progress for its principal end. Providence has doubtless traced the path of more or less all human societies, and, in this special goal, has given admirable natural aptitudes to woman. Nevertheless, for this mission to be fulfilled, there must be both apprenticeship and organization. The young girl should be prepared for it early on by helping her mother. Once become a woman, she should consecrate all her solicitude and activity to it. To take the woman away from this natural domain in order to give her cares in the world outside is to disorganize the family home. Today she is fatally pushed in this direction by being obliged to share the works of men and by being conferred a personal right over goods and industry. Yet the greatest evil of this assimilation of the two sexes is to lower the social dignity of woman and to denature the august character of the mother of the family by making her into a manufacturer, merchant, or property-owner. Such are the dangers that the law and customs of England have wished to avoid by preserving women from the cares of exterior life and by restricting as much as possible to men the rights and duties of property.

The English law does not, however, go as far as formal exclusion. It leaves the father of the family free to give a legacy to his daughters, even to the detriment of his sons, for it seems evident to our neighbors that no law can foresee the innumerable factors that the father of a family appreciates with so much intelligence and solicitude. Yet the law of inheritance counsels fathers to give the family dwelling and business with all their furniture to the eldest son and, in addition, to call upon the sons to divide the remaining household possessions equally with the daughters. Testaments, however, often leave the daughters only with a trousseau and the nest egg necessary for them to enter into a household according to the needs of their condition. This was our ancient Norman custom, and it obtains today among the populations of the south of France, while it is also widely adhered to by both peasants and nobles in certain countries in the north of Europe. Moreover, the law restrains the daughters without instituting a principal male heir. Thus, in Savoy, the old customs, replaced from 1792 to 1815 by forced equality of inheritance and then reestablished to general satisfaction until the recent annexation,[2] attributed to the sons a part double that of the daughters, and testaments continued for the most part to exceed this proportion.

The beneficent character of laws that keep property together is particularly visible in English sentiments and ideas about the negotiation of marriages. Provided with the greater part of the goods on which they exert their agricultural or industrial work, men need only to seek in marriage the means of increasing their fortune or completing their establishment. They can thus devote themselves to the search for a companion unburdened by material cares. They believe themselves to have committed an indelicacy if they subordinate to a calculus of interest an engagement that should be the result of affection, conformity of taste, and harmony of character. And if, by exception, a man is led by such a calculus, he must hide it out of respect for opinion, just as he would any other shameful thought. Such a regime clearly gives women solid guarantees of domestic happiness. Thus made independent of questions of fortune, marriages are less generally contracted between persons belonging to the

[2] The French Revolution forcibly annexed Savoy in 1792. In 1815, the Congress of Vienna restored it to the Kingdom of Piedmont-Sardinia. Finally, in 1860, Napoleon III regained Savoy for France in exchange for his role in the *Risorgimento*.

same families and the same social situations, from which results a fruitful mixing of the various classes of society. This organization of property reduces the number of consanguineous marriages, which are so frequently concluded in the regime of forced equality of inheritance so as to prevent the division of belongings. It places in the first rank of society those women who are gifted with the most eminent qualities of their sex. Thus, it produces, from high to low in the social order, a selection favorable to the progress of the entire race, the happy results of which have always been seen in England and in our ancient province of Normandy. The harmony that reigns among the parents, and the good examples that are its result, exert a happy influence on the moral development of children. Finally, the ease of the household has for its unique source the husband's fortune and labor, and thus his family home enjoys a dignified situation that is necessarily lacking when this ease results from the woman's personal fortune. The order of things established in England thus contributes beneficially to the social place of women, the dignity of husbands, and the physical and moral improvement of the race.

The first desire of the Englishman or North American who achieves some success in his enterprises is to build his own house or at least to bring some level of comfort into his home, to make it an agreeable place for his wife and children. As soon as he raises himself above the level of subsistence, he relieves his wife from all work outside the home and spares her the cares brought by the exercise of a profession. He thinks that she fulfills all her tasks when she makes good order reign in the home and succeeds in raising many graceful, healthy, and obedient children. The spouses see a numerous posterity as a testimony of divine favor. It gives them rights to public consideration, and it is a lasting support for the family business. This fertility is both physically and morally beneficent, and it seems also to exercise the best influence on the health and longevity of women. Kept in the home by the most lively affections and the most cherished bonds, the father of the family is not inclined to spend away from the home any time that the duties of his profession leave free. The meeting places and places of pleasure that play such a large role in the lives of certain peoples on the Continent are foreign to the habits of the English middle class, for whom the exercises of worship are the only regular diversion to life inside the home. These severe morals have often been criticized as antisocial by those who claim to direct public opinion in France. Nevertheless, they better assure individual happiness than do those unbridled pleasures that, in certain southern peoples, result in the abandoning of wives and children. Until this day, whether among the ancients or the moderns, only morals such as these have been able to create strong families and found civil liberty on its true basis.

Every nation that has enjoyed progress and stability has given women the power to exercise beneficent influences by ennobling the role assigned to her in the family home. They have rejected the utopias of those modern authors who would give women functions in civil life. In this decision they have been correctly inspired by the principles of association and the division of labor, the essential forces of humanity, of which the family always offers the most perfect model. The family home is in certain respects a complete world whose government demands all the solicitude of the mother, yet which cannot subsist without the assistance of some exterior activity, which in turn cannot fill up the whole life of the father. He finds the charm of a well-ordered life in the alternation of the joys of family life with the public duties and labors of a profession. Citizens accomplish these labors and duties better when they are more assured of finding rest and well-being at home. Thus it is that affection, virtue, and intelligence in women act most directly upon civil and political life. Some nations, profoundly imbued with these truths, have taken care to proclaim publicly that the woman who stays at home contributes to the exterior successes of the family more effectively than she would by her activity outside the home. In China, for instance, when a public servant has given extraordinary proof of zeal and ability, the sovereign not only rewards him, but at the same time gives an honorary distinction to his wife. This certificate conferring the sign of the imperial satisfaction also testifies that the wife has given an important service to the state by providing her husband with a sweet and happy life that doubles his strength for public functions. Such traditional practices shed light on the political and social role of the family home. The custom of deep-rooted respect for elderly parents explains the vitality that a civilization takes from the organization of the family; however, this custom is imperfect if considered from the religious perspective, because the domestic ministry of the woman and the anniversaries preserving the memory of ancestors partially supplant the worship of the gods.

The testimony of many documents and the example of several families who preserved the national traditions prove that some of these excellent customs were still habitual with us in the first half of the seventeenth century. The fertility of marriage and the severity of domestic habits were held in common by Catholics and Protestants, by the nobility and the middle and lower classes. They could still be seen at the end of the last century in the peasants, the bourgeois, and the provincial nobility, while the nobility of the court had lost them. Thence came the success of that sudden social revolution which displaced the influence of older customs and gave power to the classes that were more worthy of governing. Unfortunately, the bad morals of the eighteenth century continued to spread among us into the classes they had not hitherto penetrated, and the forced equality of inheritance aggravated the disorganization of marriage in all classes.

Marriage in France no longer displays the disorders that reigned at court in the eighteenth century, nor more recently in certain parts of Italy, yet nevertheless it is far from demonstrating the purity and dignity that is one of the conditions of existence for a free people. The principal source of the evil is the absolute equality that has been established between the sexes on this important matter of the division of property. Each man must, in effect, repair by his marriage the damage done to his own family by the division of property. His wife must bring furnishings for the home and also return to the husband the property his own sister took from him. Such a calculation in the selection of a wife is generally seen as an act of wisdom, so that if a man marry an exceptionally gifted but penniless girl, he is considered imprudent and socially inferior. Moreover, the wife's fortune and the joint expectations of the couple to an inheritance from their parents are generally considered to constitute a claim to public notice, and this claim is heightened if the death of the parents is likely to be soon. Every day worthy families conclude marriage negotiations in a matter of minutes, just as they would a purchase at the market, by seizing the best bargain. The analogy is not an exaggeration. We speak only of the reciprocal convenience of the two fortunes that are brought together without having any way to tell whether the tastes and characters of the principals are similarly well disposed. These customs have become widespread in the wealthier part of society, and the wealthy are no longer aware of how they debase their character and sentiments. Yet it is only too clear that marriages subordinated to material interest cannot constitute a regular social order. One need only look around to see the consequences that generally follow: dissension between the spouses, bad examples given to the children, and the soiling and finally abandonment of the family home.

Another direct consequence of our practice of the forced equality of inheritance is the systematic sterility of marriage. After having repaired the division of the paternal household by the search for an ample dowry, the new head of the family is naturally inclined to spare his son the burden of a similar trial. Yet, faced with the prescriptions of the law, there is but one prudent means to obtain this end: to limit his offspring. Lengthy research undertaken with the help of my friends and many conversations with doctors and men of the cloth have demonstrated the daily worsening consequences caused by this disorder among all classes of the French. Every new study of this subject condemns with irresistible evidence the systematic ideas governing the transmission of property. These studies reveal the weakening of society, which I shall discuss below with regard to work, colonial enterprises, and defense. Even those with little interest in these great public questions cannot deny the deadly consequences of sterility for individual happiness.

The whole family is injured by the violation of the essential laws that command fertility, but the deplorable consequences of this disorder weigh heaviest upon the wife. The last generation of French women has been strongly affected in body by this sterility, and doctors have perceived in it the cause of a general weakening that is not seen in those countries that preserve fertility. In the moral order, the consequences of this rebellion against the laws of marriage are still worse. Deprived of the functions assigned to them by nature during the best part of their lives, those women who are not forced to work for their livelihood are condemned to an idleness that their lively spirits find insupportable. They busy themselves creating futile occupations and imaginary duties outside the home. Thus we see in the leisure class, and even in the middle class, indiscretions formerly known only at court. Women give themselves over to all the attractions of mindless luxury. They surround themselves with costly furniture that is more gaudy than tasteful. They have no shame in spending more on one outfit than would suffice to clothe an entire family. They doll themselves up in the latest fashions and, in general, are busy destroying the distinction hitherto maintained, even in dress, between vice and virtue. Their favorite occupation is to meet regularly in groups much larger than their circle of family and immediate friends to discuss the theater, light reading, the events of the day, and especially whatever offers occasion for scandalous and malicious gossip. They thus adopt the habits of low friendship that were last seen in the declining years of the Roman Empire and in recent years have been seen, outside the court of Louis XIV and his successors, only in those idle men who are separated from the family home either by celibacy or unlicenced tastes. These new morals gradually destroy the character of rich women, and thus dry up at its source the influence of the ruling classes upon society. This leads us to disquieting reflections on the future of our society. In truth, women cannot remove themselves from the beneficent influence of the family home without impunity, for as soon as they have left the straight and narrow, they quickly outstrip men in perversity and become the most active auxiliaries to the spirit of evil. Unless one has collected, as I have done, the complaints of those families thus afflicted in their dearest interest, one cannot imagine the social disorders that result from several thousand Parisian women in open rebellion against the duties of their sex. Amidst our frivolous habits, our public good sense seems to have taken note of this danger. Our songs and popular caricatures today take their examples from the plight of disordered women, just as in the wake of the Revolution of 1830 they targeted the cynicism and base sentiments of men. The remedy to these disorders is to be found in the return of women to their natural place, that is, by modifying the laws of inheritance that are manifestly the first cause of the vices of marriage. Fertile unions founded upon the spontaneous choice of spouses can alone preserve woman from these ills and assure her happiness: in her youth, by nourishing her faculties and affections according to the will of nature, and in her old age, by surrounding her with the devotion and love of a numerous posterity.

The social disorganization that gradually invades the leisured class is less common in the working classes, even though these are in contact with the corruption of the cities. In some of our bourgeois families, those women little busied with maternal duties take an important and sometimes leading role in the management of the family business. We see them successfully engaged in outside work, buying and selling, hiring workers, managing the workshop, and carrying out business and legal discussions. Such work, in which women at times show great finesse and ability, sometimes becomes a source of material prosperity for the family. The English, however, when they are even but a little raised above the condition of wage-earners, refuse to follow this example and profit from its advantages.

They love to receive the counsels of an active and intelligent wife in the intimacy of the home, but they are loath to have her charged with the execution of tasks outside of it. To their eyes, a woman working outside the home causes three problems: it lessens the dignity of the husband, disorganizes the family home, and imposes labors and cares on the wife that she should be spared. They do not wish to sacrifice one of the essential laws of the moral order for the sake of material profit.

This happy situation, we cannot say it enough, is assured to the English woman by the law of succession, which, according to our false theory of forced equality of inheritance, seems to be unfavorable to her. Her happiness also results from the customs that are the natural consequence of this law. The young girl, prematurely deprived of her parents, finds welcome and protection beside her brother, and when he keeps the family home she often retains the place that she held in it before the death of her parents. The wife enjoys the fortune of her husband in community, and it might even be said that she disposes of it more than he does, for the money is used for the needs of the family home. The widow does not generally enjoy the worthy situation made for her by the stem-families of the Continent. Her situation is nevertheless often guaranteed by the dowry stipulated in the marriage contract. Other than the case of widowhood, women are, in the diverse situations that they successively occupy, able to enjoy the property of both their first and second families without ever submitting to the cares of property or profession.

The contrast between the Anglo-Saxons and the French is still more marked with respect to their attitudes towards seduction. Here the firm maintenance of the distinction between the sexes does not seem to be an advantage to the stronger sex: the weight of inequality falls directly upon the man. On this issue, the North Americans in particular are motivated by a profound sense of justice and a delicate appreciation of the interests of women.

According to their opinion, a woman's power cannot be based, as is a man's, on the right to property and the influences that follow from the exercise of a profession in the administration of a city. A woman's power is found in the devotion that she constantly inspires, in that incomparable grace to which the epigraph of this chapter points, and in the ensemble of moral qualities by which she effortlessly subjects brother, husband, and children to her rule. The wise and modest woman glorified by the Holy Book exercises an ascendancy upon those around her that does not need to be confirmed by legal prescriptions, and which would be infallibly weakened by them. However, a woman neither possesses this authority, nor completely develops these powers, nor, finally, achieves a happy domestic life unless she finds guarantees in the character, tastes, and affection of her husband. Therefore, a woman is even more concerned than a man to obtain intimate knowledge of her intended prior to settling the marriage. It is thus essential for good morals to allow the young girl the necessary liberty to choose the one who best corresponds to her own sentiments.

Yet this liberty accorded to young girls to look after their primary interest themselves would become illusory and damaging to morals if, during the course of this search for a spouse, it left girls defenseless in the face of seduction. Here is found the just compensation for the apparent superiority given to men in the regime of property. The woman, thought to be too weak or too trusting to preserve the wealth of the family from violence or fraud, is equally incapable, according to a legal fiction, to defend her honor against the tricks of libertinism or the assaults of passion. Because according to this same fiction the ascendancy of women is founded upon chastity and the virtues that derive from it, it is correct to protect their greatest good against rape and fraud. The honor of young women is thus placed under the protection of the law, the courts, and all honest men in the same way as is the weakness of childhood. In the common opinion, to injure a woman's honor is to commit an act that is both guilty and dishonorable. The demands of women who have been seduced are thus heard by judges with sympathy and solicitude, and when they are recognized as legitimate, the guilty are punished with inexorable severity and often lose their entire fortune. The most admirable trait of Anglo-Saxon morals, a trait which compares favorably to the deplorable habits of the Latin people, is surely this protection given by the law to women who are accidently taken from the family home and deprived of the protection of their family by some unexpected event. Men, in truth, must take great care lest their relations serve as a pretext for false accusations or unjust lawsuits. This reserve is especially imposed on men of high rank and may even pose some difficulties for them. Yet, in compensation, they assure the security of poor girls, and give a guarantee to good morals that is singularly able to raise the moral character of a nation. The laws that protect women are less formal and less effective in England than they are in the United States, but the private associations that constantly work for the moral progress of the country have already taken steps towards reform, and the local judges think it honorable to take from the law all the good that the text will allow. The laws and morals that thus protect the poor man's daughter against the passions of the rich are, I repeat, the most respectable trait of a civil organization in which the dominance of the superior classes is, in some respects, more marked than it is in the French constitution.

The principle of the equality of the sexes that has been so poorly introduced to the greater part of our modern laws has naturally led us to see seduction under a different light. Contrary to ancient tradition, relations injurious to morals are no longer considered to be a crime whose guilt weighs exclusively upon the man. When such relations are not complicated by rape or violence, they are considered to be a sort of natural right of both sexes, the usage of which cannot be punished in the man alone. This theory was first set forth in France in September of 1791. Yet what is more damaging than the doctrine itself is the strange language by which the compiler of our new penal code has tried to justify it.

This legal indifference has borne its fruit. During the last century of the Old Regime, seduction belonged only to the morals of the court. It has since spread to the very mass of the nation. Today this disorder has become almost an habitual trait of our private morals. No father, unless constrained by hard necessity, dare confide his daughter to the faith of the world at large. In well-off families, the girls are kept cloistered in the family home, so that they would be unable to choose their own husband, even if it were the case that the choice was not wholly subordinated to a question of money. As to poor families, in which all the members must work, they must expose their daughters to a corruption that invades the whole country. Seduction exerted to the detriment of young working girls is today common in the cities and the countryside. The most deplorable circumstances are to be seen in the factories of Lille, Amiens, St-Quentin, Reims, Sédan, Mulhouse, Lyon, Limoges, and other cities. Many property-owners and manufacturers look indifferently upon a degradation that even the nomadic peoples of the East would find inconceivable. This shameful tolerance even exists in those manufacturing towns where the leaders of industry show a true solicitude for the material well-being of their workers. Public opinion, here failing in the mission assigned to it among a free people, has neither the delicacy nor the necessary energy to preserve these poor girls from the most harmful moral torture. In several manufacturing districts, this social disorder has attained its most extreme limits. The corrupt belong not only to the working class, they are also the employees of the factory, the men of the leisure class; at times even the leaders of industry themselves, that is to say, those who, according to divine and human laws, are charged with the preservation of the social order. This depravity is so bad that it is more often known because of the vain indiscretion of the guilty parties than the just reproaches of the upright. Finally, in several places, this evil has progressed to the point that the protests of those who are aware of the shame brought upon French civilization by such morals are met only with ridicule.

All the social forces habitually used to do good among us should be brought together in order to begin a reform. In the first place, the law should give a first impulse to our minds and return them back to a sense of justice. Without returning to the principle, still followed in Prussian law, that makes seduction a crime, the law should consider it a civil damage for which the seducer can be held liable upon the demand of the seduced, with the level of damage being set by the judge. To this end, we must abolish article 340 of the Civil Code and extend the protection of article 1382 to girls who have been seduced. Second, the leaders of industry who have a sense of duty should protect the female workers they employ by means of such practices adopted by the weavers of Lowell, Massachusetts, and since imitated in France by several honorable employers.

I do not deceive myself so as to think that such a reform would be easy to accomplish in a country that, led astray by unhealthy literature, glorifies seducers and mocks cuckolds and seduced girls. I also know that our judges, making use of the discretionary powers that must be given them, have for a long time issued judgments different from those in England and America. Yet these same considerations show the opportunity for a reform that should not be imposed by the public authority, nor be overly legalistic, but rather gradually accomplished as the moral sense of the nation is rehabilitated.

The repression of seduction and the rehabilitation of institutions that would lift the moral character of women are more necessary for modern peoples than for those who preserve the characteristics of the Old Regime. Among the latter peoples, a strong government imbued with a sense of duty can sometimes effect social progress in spite of the failures of private morals. It is not the same with the moderns, for whom progress is more and more a question of the initiative of citizens. The people who aspire to civil and political liberty thus have a particular interest in stemming the disorder of concubinage and illegitimate births, not by formal repression, but by all the indirect means that are able to increase the respect owed to women.

Thus, with good reason the chastity of women is considered to be the principal element in the morals of a nation, and the simplest analysis proves that it is one of the principal sources of individual happiness and public prosperity. Wherever this virtue reigns, young men are particularly inclined to marry. The girls thus sought after, further assisted by the natural laws that exaggerate the number of male births, find themselves in a situation to choose, and will naturally give themselves to those who excel in virtue, talent, and wealth. In the regimes where chastity reigns and where girls are given a simple trousseau, the most lively attraction of humanity thus becomes, for the youth, a powerful lead to follow. By accepting the most worthy men and condemning the unworthy to celibacy, women exercise a moralizing action of considerable power and thus in a certain way preside over the social hierarchy. This influence is manifest in those populations that have preserved firm morals founded upon work. I have frequently noted it in Europe in those regions where the rude populations find their principal means of subsistence in periodic emigration. Local customs require the young emigrants to send back some savings to the family each year as a sign of their temperance and success, and marriage is prohibited to those who during these years of apprenticeship do not display these proofs of application and virtue.

The law that prohibits divorce, like the one that makes marriage a venerable institution, is one of the most solid foundations for the morals of a nation. Fortunately, this part of social reform was accomplished a long time ago after some deplorable experiments and has, in part, healed the wound of the social vices I have just mentioned. The benefits of the indissolubility of marriage reveal themselves everywhere by their excellent traits. The conjugal bond shows itself in a more august character to the people; the engaged are apt to reflect before entering into a lifelong commitment, and they are more inclined to reduce through mutual concessions those troubles that arise from the contrast of their characters; persons bereft of those qualities that make marriage happy cannot provoke new scandals by contracting new marriages; and, finally, the children can count more surely on the care and affection of their parents. Moreover, the approbation given by the most eminent women to the laws prohibiting divorce has always seemed to me to be, in this delicate matter, the most fitting basis for the convictions of the legislator.

On this same authority I have always seen the strongest justification for the principles set out in this paragraph. However, in giving this approval, the women who inspire the respect and devotion of those who surround them have habitually made a qualification of which we should take note. They recognize that their domain is limited to the family home, but they intend to join to the affections and material cares that occupy the greatest part of their time an understanding of the interests of the world and a knowledge of the great results of social activity. This legitimate pretension must be satisfied, not only to raise the dignity of women as much as possible, but also to encourage men to give the most complete development to their own faculties. In European civilization, the men who distinguish themselves by their talents and virtues for the most part owe their superiority to the instruction of their mothers and the counsels of their wives. Moreover, they find in the approbation of these distinguished women the highest reward for their success. The cultivation of the intellectual aptitudes of women is therefore a social need as imperative as the cultivation of their domestic aptitudes. The most eminent families attain this twofold end by keeping their daughters within the family home until their marriage, by delaying their engagement until their twenty-first year, and by filling the many hours of leisure that remain after their domestic chores with the instruction that can be given them by mother, father, and brothers, assisted by special masters. The education of the married woman is completed by the high ministry of the family home, by the community of thought that exists between the two spouses, and finally by the relations established with leading men of the same condition, relations whose principal attraction is found in their wives' sociability and incomparable grace.

In conclusion, the classification of men by marriage and, as I shall indicate later in more detail, the action of the mother upon the intellectual and moral development of children, is in the first rank of social principles. Women will see these beneficial influences grow to the extent that they are less busied with the duties of property and profession and give themselves exclusively to the administration of the family home. The sovereignty that they thus obtain by their grace and devotion is not limited to the family home. The chaste woman with a cultivated intellect creates good morals in the group of which she is the center. In this way, and beyond the legal sphere, she often proves herself to be the principal source of social progress.

ÉMILE

KELLER

THE ENCYCLICAL OF THE
8TH OF DECEMBER AND
THE PRINCIPLES OF 1789 (1865)
THE ULTIMATUM OF CHURCH AND STATE

PREFACE

There are times and nations that satisfy themselves with a small number of religious, political, and social truths. Justifying their egoism and apathy by their own narrow views, they are rooted in a shameful immobility. It is the privilege of Catholic nations—especially France—and it is the glory of modern times to pursue the ideal of perfection in all things and to have an unquenchable thirst for morality, justice, truth, progress, and liberty. Today, from the princes and ministers in power to the workers engaged in ceaseless labor, each of us is moved ardently by the problems of our destiny, and each of us examines the foundations of religion, politics, and society. The more we look into these diverse questions, the more we see that they are intimately united, and with the growing solidarity that binds all nations and souls, and with the legitimate influence that France exercises upon the world's opinion, we may say that from our minds' agitation will come a decisive and universal solution for the present generation. *Questions → Unity → Solution (s)*

At this solemn hour when indifference is permissible to no one, the vicar of Jesus Christ, heir to 250 popes and spiritual head of two hundred million Catholics, could not remain silent. On the contrary, his duty is more compelling than any other's. By inalienable right he defends the sacred interests now at stake and reminds us how the Church understands those interests and that it has a mission to protect, serve, and save them.

Pius IX has spoken. The indescribable emotion stirred by his encyclical[1] proves that he was at the very heart of the difficulty. The memorable document was immediately attacked with lies and calumnies. Yet these disorderly and contradictory efforts have only made the victory of the papacy more evident. In spite of material obstacles, his voice has carried to the ends of the earth, and to those who pretend that the pope spoke alone and who would trick bishops and the faithful into disagreeing with him, the whole Church has responded with a unanimous cry of conscience that no human power could either produce or stifle: "We adhere with all our heart to what the new Peter has just taught. Most holy Father, you are for us the teacher of sane doctrine, you are the center of unity, you are an unfailing light to the people prepared by divine wisdom; you are the foundation of the Church herself, against which the powers of Hell shall never prevail. When you speak, it is Peter we hear; when you decree, it is Christ we obey."[2]

There is a second victory yet to win, to which this one is but a prelude, and an edifice to raise, for which the adherence of the episcopacy and the faithful is but a foundation, and to which each of us today must carry his stone. The doctrine of the Church has been clearly affirmed and defined. It remains to seek it, to pursue it, and to put it into practice, each in his own sphere: political, scientific, or social.

The politics and economics of society as a whole must now accord with Catholic teaching. By this teaching, theology does not close but opens the way to progress. Far from being an obstacle, the

---

[1] The encyclical *Quanta Cura* of December 8, 1864, to which was appended the *Syllabus of Errors*.

[2] Keller here quotes from the Declaration of Bishops of June 9, 1862.

faith is a torch in light of which the liberty and duty of the citizen are exercised.

In accomplishing the doctrinal mission reserved to them, the bishops have been careful to warn us that the Church in no way pretends to constrain us to apply these principles in a violent, absolute, or chimerical manner, or, still less, to put us back under the hateful yoke of an outdated absolutism. Yet if they have rightly replied to those extravagant critics who falsified and calumniated the encyclical, they have condemned no less severely those who have seen in it only a platonic expression of immutable doctrines that can be freely and indefinitely abandoned in practice as long as they are respected in principle. We are thus invited to see how each of us, in the times and countries in which we live, can work in a peaceful and regular fashion—but also firmly and perseveringly—to realize the true liberty proclaimed by the Church.

What are, on the one hand, the invariable laws of all societies, and on the other, the particular necessities, tendencies, passions, prejudices, errors, and dangers of the one in which we live? Are the principles that our society upholds really in conflict with those of the encyclical? If our society is mistaken on such a serious matter, does it not compromise its future and its existence? To what degree can our society escape this peril and return to the path of true progress? Here is a most urgent problem for anyone who loves his fatherland and liberty, and the Christian loves them more than anyone. On such a matter, neither doubt nor indifference is possible. And when, after mature reflection, one sees what is required for the common good and salvation of all, nothing in the world can dispense or prevent one from speaking out.

This is not a theological work. That would be beyond my competence and superfluous in light of the bishops' teaching. Rather, this is a political and practical exposition in response to the call of the Church and is, I hope, in conformity with her doctrine. I submit it to the public's good sense.

THE ENCYCLICAL OF DECEMBER 8, 1864,
AND THE CONVENTION OF SEPTEMBER 15TH,
OR, THE ULTIMATUM OF CHURCH AND STATE[3]

The encyclical of December 8, 1864, is addressed neither to one man, nor to one party, nor to one isolated people. It is addressed to the nineteenth century as a whole.

Regardless of those human interests that might have kept him silent, the Holy Father, with a heroism admired even by his adversaries, has stood alone against the impetuous and universal current of the illusions of our time. To seek in his words a response to the Convention of September 15th would be to reduce a calm and solemn teaching directed to mankind to the minute scale of a personal discussion.

The only connection between the two acts is that the convention gives us a rough measure of the errors and dangers pointed to by the encyclical. In truth, the encyclical was anterior to the convention, for it merely reproduced and more clearly affirmed truths belonging to all times and all popes. Moreover, in the convention there is nothing new, nothing surprising, nothing unexpected. It was but a step already traced on the road we have followed for a long time. The line of the Holy See does not change; modern society only diverges more and more from it. The convention timidly took note of this. The encyclical categorically declared it. Now what is needed is a frank explanation that will result either in a reconciliation or a definitive rupture.

Let us not avoid the question. We are no longer in the initial moments after the encyclical when it was necessary to hasten to refute the calumnies that the encyclical was an attack on existing governments and a condemnation of liberty. With the rapidity of light, an illustrious bishop descended into the arena of polemic and

---

[3] The Convention of September 15th (1864) was an agreement between France and Italy by which Napoleon III tacitly abandoned support for Pope Pius IX's rule over the city of Rome. In the event, Napoleon III secured Rome for the pope until 1870.

reassured the alarmed by showing them clearly what the encyclical was not.[4] Today it remains to be seen what it was, and to find in it not only what must not injure, but what must attract, satisfy, and captivate all honest and generous souls. It would be a small thing merely to be inoffensive. The encyclical must be of sovereign efficacy, benevolent and timely, and—to princes as well as peoples, to authority as well as liberty—it must offer the only true security and only possible reconciliation.

Our goal is to show that this is so.

To attain it, we must neither antagonize nor flatter, and we must avoid the sterile temptation to reduce all the faults of the government to its ability to compromise and to subdue opinion for its own protection. In France our minds are exaggerated and fickle, and the prestige of the government and its opposition are alternately all-powerful. We must navigate the narrow channel between these two shoals.

France has lived in fear of liberty since 1848. A Catholic cannot share this sentiment. Separated from the Church, modern hopes have gone awry and been condemned to sterility, because it is the Church that makes men capable of conceiving and realizing—in the measure of their virtue—the generous perspective of universal emancipation. And many are beginning to realize that neither was the reactionary chain of events of 1852 profitable for Catholics.[5]

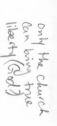

[margin note: Only the church can give true liberty (God?)]

While appearances have changed since the war in Italy, at bottom the situation remains the same. The completely superficial alliance of Catholics and Liberals now being attempted will be neither more intimate, nor more profound, than that of Catholics and the political power in the wake of the 10th of December.[6]

---

[4] This is a reference to Félix Dupanloup, bishop of Orléans, whose *La Convention du 15 septembre et l"Encyclique du 8 decembre* was the leading episcopal response to the *Syllabus*.

[5] This is a reference to those Catholics, such as Louis Veuillot, editor of *L'Univers*, who supported Napoleon III in the 1850s and then moved into a guarded opposition in the 1860s as Napoleon III progressively abandoned his support for Pope Pius IX.

[6] That is, of Napoleon III's coup d'état in 1851, when the then-president of the Second Republic declared himself to be the hereditary ruler of the restored Empire.

Instead of joining the government to fight religious despotism, the great party of 1789 has provisionally joined the Church in claiming political liberty. Now, it seems, we shall prove that the government misunderstands modern ideas and attempt to create a great opposition party by momentarily bringing together all manner of Catholics and Liberals under the banner of vague sentiments of independence, justice, and political honor. This may be a clever tactic, but it will enjoy no lasting achievements.

Let us abandon this ephemeral strategy. It is a simple matter to hide its weakness, to gain a kind of popularity by joining the opposition. In this way have the best governments been overturned in the past, and we have learned nothing from the process. It is time for another strategy. It is time to see that the form of government is a mere detail. Today, under all regimes, the people have the dominant share of the power of those who seem to conduct it. Absolute princes and free assemblies are but the echo of the thoughts that summoned them, and, in these high regions, the man who believes that he obeys only his personal passions and interests will be, without knowing it, the slave of the interests and passions of his age.

Let us then leave political power and its counselors to their responsibilities. We should first busy ourselves with our own, with policies that reflect our doubts, incertitude, and griefs. Let there be no illusions on this subject. The official documents have only followed the trail blazed by other governments. They are bound to register the complaints that travel from mouth to mouth. They have displayed one of the deepest wounds of the age, which is the apparent contradiction between religious truth and political and social truth, between religious truth defined and represented by the Catholic, Apostolic, and Roman Catholic Church, and the political truth that we believe to be defined by the principles of 1789 and represented by the modern state. This, in a word, is what weighs on our souls. Whether we follow the standard of political power or that of liberty, or whether we shift from one to the other, we will have done nothing unless we put an end to this antagonism. For—why pretend?—the regime and its current policies are merely the natural and necessary result of the state of our minds. In separating itself from the Church, modern liberalism has vowed itself to powerlessness, and by achieving the secularization of society it leads us inexorably to the worst of despotisms, in spite of the good will of those governing and those governed.

goodness cannot be achieved w/o Church

The evil grows in plain view. The same blindness and passion are found among the adversaries of political power and its most intimate counselors. In the press, at the rostrum, on the lips of Prince Napoleon, in Ajaccio and the Senate, from the pen of a minister or that of a simple pilgrim, it is always the self-styled democratic or Napoleonic idea, in the end despotic and caesarist, which provokes and exploits our divisions, making its way in the world at the expense of peoples and sovereigns and on the ruins of the Faith and liberty.

Contemporary society, whose worst prejudices are thus flattered, has nevertheless made a great step towards the Church. It no longer wants to destroy her; on the contrary, it wants to preserve her, to protect her, and to live in peace with her. It regards her as one of the necessary means with which to fight the doubt and immorality by which it is undermined. Yet this incomplete return makes the situation more delicate and perilous. Under the pretext that its advances are rejected, society accuses the Church of ingratitude and menaces her with a new rupture.

What then is the agreement that has been sought for long years and that has been presented today in a more pressing manner than ever? What place would we give to the Church in an edifice from which she was at first completely excluded? Liberals and the government would accept her willingly as a helper so long as they keep their full independence from her authority, unlimited sovereignty, and complete liberty of action. They would abandon the domain of conscience to her so long as she leaves politics to them and recognizes the social efficacy of modern ideas, generally known as the principles of 1789.

He sets this up as a contradiction.

Many generous minds are seduced and do not understand how such moderate proposals could be rejected. Some separate themselves from the Church, imagining the absurd—that she truly requires the sacrifice of progress and liberty. Others, not daring to deny the virtue of the modern formulae, make laborious efforts to convince the Church to accept the proffered reconciliation. Full of good will, they are satisfied that apart from a few nuances the principles of 1789 are pure Christian principles, and that it should be easy to adopt them and gradually lead them to recognition and blessing by the Holy See.

The government, for its part, giving one hand to the new Right and the other to religion, and believing these two supports necessary to its solidity, has neglected nothing that might bring them together, or at least prevent them from quarreling with and weakening one another.

Who, even among Catholics, has not participated in these well-meaning but sterile attempts? Who has not signed his own little treaty with the champions of the new ideas in hopes of preserving religion? Who has not dreamed of a free Church in a free state? These are powerless remedies, palliatives for a day, good only to cover the wound that saps our strength, but without force against the invincible logic of events.

Indeed, what are these chimerical essays in reconciliation? They are a pretext by which the enemies of the Church pursue her ruin. With a miraculous accord that should suffice to open the eyes of all men of good will, atheists, pantheists, rationalists, indifferentists, Jews, Protestants, and St.-Simonians unite their efforts (if only for this) to chip away at the keystone of Catholicism. Having vainly tried the frontal assault of a forceful revolution, today they prefer ruse to violence. Adopting an air of sincerity and generosity much more dangerous than open persecution, they content themselves with demanding the secularization of society and the separation of Church and state. They are so certain to attain their goal this way that even the most impious declare themselves Catholic and ready to kneel before Jesus Christ, provided the Church abdicate the temporal part of her sovereignty in their favor.

This circle of subterranean enemies has gradually tightened its noose around Rome and the Holy See. The new Right, so moderate in France, has shown its true colors in Italy. Materially the stronger, it summons the papacy to submit to it.

Having arrived at this decisive moment, modern society dares not go all the way. We are ill at ease protecting the pope any longer against what we believe to be progress and civilization, and yet we are not quite sure that the Piedmontese unity really is progress and civilization. Hesitant and troubled, we should like to keep a scrap of territory for the pope. We should still more like to assure his tenure. We pray, we beg: let him grant the least concession, even if it be only to remain silent. What could be easier than not to speak?

And now, at the risk of irritating those who protect him and who might extinguish him with a mere gesture, the pope tears the veil and declares that society is mistaken, ill, and in peril. No more equivocations, no more contradictions, no more temporizing. In our interest, the pope wants his protectors to understand what we are protecting in Rome. While we still have the right to his gratitude, he tries to acquit himself by opening our eyes to the abyss yawning at our feet. The pope extracts from the thoughts, writings, and actions of the day the spirit of error that has inspired them. To the insinuations and reproaches of his enemies, to the advice and prayers of his friends, he responds by clearly and solemnly proclaiming what the Catholic conscience affirms for the good of man and nations, and he forces the modern conscience to formulate its faith, if it has one. The political powers and liberty of the day offer a place to the Church in the shadow of their protection, and Pius IX declares that neither this power nor this liberty is certain of its future, and that there is no hope for either save in accepting its place in the bosom of the Church.

All sides cry that this is an open rupture. The pope responds to civilization's advances with a formal and categorical condemnation of what we hold most dear, that is, the principles of 1789.

The principles of 1789 are mentioned neither in the encyclical, nor in the *Syllabus*. Like all vague formulations, they have only the value ascribed to them. Now, what are they in the minds of their partisans? If they are no longer what they once were in the minds of those who wrote them, that is, progress and liberty built on the ruins of the Church, it is incontestable that they are at least progress and liberty outside the Church. We should very much like to be reconciled with the Church and to live in peace with her. Yet we do not want at any price to recognize her absolute truth, or the sovereign beneficence of her authority, or her political and social preeminence. Thus, the principles of 1789 serve as the standard of those who call themselves injured and condemned by Pius IX. In reality, these principles are the received and current formula of the naturalist doctrine that opposes Catholic doctrine.

The Church is far from condemning the large and generous hopes that so clearly point out the superiority of Christian times to pagan antiquity. Yet what she cannot do is relinquish her place at the head of this great movement of liberation. She alone has been able to awaken in man's heart the desire for universal good. She alone can satisfy it.

Strong in her faith and her eighteen centuries of existence, the Church proclaims that men and nations—tending towards evil from the day of their birth—need her help and authority in order to sustain themselves and to progress in the temporal order as well as the spiritual. She protests against that political and social naturalism that pretends to organize governments and societies according to reason but outside all positive religion, and which even contests the Church's right to influence political authority and denies the state's duty to protect and defend Catholic truth. She declares that this disastrous separation will necessarily end in the triumph of brute force, the unbridling of material desires, and the loss not only of the Faith, but of all civilization and liberty. To her eyes, socialism and communism, which menace family and property, are but the logical consequences of naturalism in politics and ration-

alism in theology. Only Catholic truth with the fulness of its rights
and liberty can stop the rapid decline of the nations.

On the other hand, reason, proud of the conquests that it believes
it has made without the Church and which are protected by the
state, misunderstands the threats to this fragile work. Reason sup-
poses itself capable of attaining truths of all orders and of governing
the affairs of this world unaided and independently. The secularization of politics, science, industry, and work is its goal and what it
proclaims as the precondition of progress and true civilization.

Now we see that the Church and modern society are fundamentally opposed. What for one is the essence and guarantee of liberty
is for the other its negation and ruin. It is impossible to be more
clearly and more radically in contradiction, and this about the vital
question for humanity.

This is the burning question raised by the encyclical and the
convention. On it all our attention is concentrated. The faith of a
great number of souls—even of society as a whole—depends upon
its resolution.

If we look for the source of this antagonism, we will see that, as
always, it begins with the reality and consequences of original sin;
from there the debate moves to the necessity of the Redemption,
and thence to the divinity and sovereignty of Jesus Christ and His
Church. The encyclical condemns innumerable errors that are
linked in their common denial of the dogmas of the Fall and
Redemption. The moderate rationalism that wants only to secu-
larize human science and society and the virulent pantheism for
which Jesus Christ is a dangerous myth have the same origin and
same end: to destroy the royalty of Jesus Christ and the preeminence of His Church under the pretext of liberating reason. Thus,
Catholicism as a whole is at stake, as we see in Renan's *Vie de Jésus*.[7]

A secret instinct whispers that truth cannot contradict itself.
Religion, philosophy, politics, law, and natural science can only
form a harmonious whole. Where we find happiness, liberty, and

[7] Ernst Renan's *Vie de Jésus* (1863) openly sought to persuade against belief in the divinity of
Christ.

269

progress for all, there also must be religious truth; and, reciprocally, when we find religious truth, we may be sure to find rushing forth as from a spring the most effective remedy for all that ails humanity.

Thus, from the true and divine Church we require political and social teachings sufficient to assure both our earthly destinies and the salvation of our souls, and teachings capable of reducing to silence the pretensions of human wisdom. Furthermore, we require a religious truth that will make moral progress march with material progress and win an incontestable triumph over ancient Catholicism.

Let us give thanks to Pius IX, for his encyclical puts an end to our sorrowful uncertainty. Far from forcing us to renounce the progressive emancipation of all men and nations, it forces us to ask who will best fulfill these legitimate hopes: the Church or modern reason?

In fact, if the Catholic, Apostolic, and Roman Catholic Church was truly founded by God and is directed by God living in her, then she should be invested with full power with regard to nations, princes, and individuals. The torch of justice and truth, she can be opposed neither to the discoveries of science nor to the conquests won by civilization and liberty; and, furthermore, she alone is capable of directing and controlling them and making them truly serve the well-being of all. Societies are as free to be skeptical and rationalist as they were to be pagan and heretical. The Church will not teach Catholics living in them to revolt. But the moment when nations or governments seek the road to well-being and liberty outside of her authority, she cannot let these peoples or governments believe that they are still Catholic. She cannot let them believe that they will ever succeed in finding true liberty. For she knows what is in store for them: moral, intellectual, and material decadence; the obscuring of the most simple notions of law and natural justice; and the unbridling and mutual antagonism of material appetites that brute force alone can curb. Not to proclaim this, above all in a time when the desire for riches and independence is so ardent and when men are so quick to seek these outside of Catholic truth, would be to make herself an accomplice of the illusions and myths that afflict so many nations and souls.

Let me be plain. If the modern principles invoked to justify the convention should make men and nations thrive and bring about an indefinite era of power, enlightenment, and true felicity, then Jesus Christ will not be God, the Church will not be His spouse, and the pope will not be His vicar. Then the Church and her incomparable doctrine will be a mere human institution, responding to the needs of certain times and certain souls, but also dated, eclipsed, and refuted by modern science and reason. The pope and the Church will have been falsified, and their intemperate protests will soon subside, like a far-off murmur, amidst the harmonies of a new civilization.

The choice is between these two sides. On which side is the truth, not only theological, but political and practical? Is it with that Catholic and pontifical infallibility that so many enemies have attacked and contested without discouraging it and whose eternal standard the encyclical has brought again before our eyes? Or is it with those mysterious oracles of 1789, of whom the whole world speaks without knowing and fears without having considered, but whose prestige can vanish under impartial examination? It is worth the trouble to examine the question. But let it be said at the outset: we must be Catholic with Pius IX while discarding the illusions of our time, or cease to be Catholic by maintaining these illusions.

Now, if one must be with Pius IX to remain Catholic, then it is not enough to submit oneself and accept the truth with eyes closed, without dreaming of ever studying or applying it. The adherence of a Christian is not an abasement, still less an abdication of reason. For him, the word of the Church is a sun that all at once illumines new horizons where his mind feels a thousand times easier, freer, and stronger. He is pleased to find in one splendid vista the truths he seeks. At the same time, his duties become clear, and certitude brings strength and joy to his conscience.

The encyclical is not a last protest against incurable ills or irrevocable deeds. No such wounds are incurable but those to which one does not dare to bring the iron and fire of truth. If the pope spoke at the risk of inciting our passions, he did so that we might escape the danger. We must now act so that the warning cry of the supreme pilot be not a fruitless admonition, lost in the tempest. We have spent ourselves in vain efforts to save the boat and must now submit ourselves to his direction. If we are resolute, salvation is within our grasp.

Pius IX shows us the lessons of history, our present obligations, and our future hopes. His words and our elders' examples will teach us to be not rebels or retrogrades, but the men most useful to our countries, the citizens most loyal to the ruling power and true liberty, the most peaceful proponents of the common good, and, above all, the most zealous defenders of the poor, the weak, and the oppressed. We shall prove and be proof to dubious governments that the Church propounds the principles necessary to the existence of all authority; to liberal champions of the rights of man that only the Church can strengthen and consolidate these rights; to all that Catholic doctrine is not an apple of discord or an instrument of despotism but the salvation of a thriving soul. For there is no true union except in the truth, and no possible liberty except among men united by the same truths.

In this way, we will see the practical consequences of the encyclical as the application of the laws of nature and reason and as the ideal towards which we must ceaselessly strive. "The spiritual and temporal sovereignty of the pope will be for us an impregnable fortress. In it reside all justice and all truth. From its ramparts the supreme guardian perceives from afar the hidden reefs and ambushes of our enemies."[8] Now, it does not suffice to have a vague notion of this magnificent vista. We must attain the clear, simple, and reasoned view. We must prepare ourselves to respond to all objections and to convince all men of good will. Only thus will we accomplish the duty set before us.

[8] Keller again quotes the Declaration of Bishops of June 9, 1862.

For their part, let the partisans of the modern principles make ready to examine them with us. We will show them the motives for our faith. They should not think themselves dispensed from proving their own. When the Divine Word respects our reason enough to furnish decisive arguments for it, by what right could the human word excuse itself from this obligation? 1789 must justify its doctrine, its origins, and its results as well as its promise for the future.

It is a characteristic of truth alone that the more one explores it, the more one finds hidden strengths and riches. Error, on the contrary, is seductive at a distance but soon vanishes, like will-o'-the-wisps that extinguish themselves under a traveler's feet. We shall see that such is the ephemeral spark of modern ideas. The masses, starved for justice and progress, have followed this deceitful light for a long time. Even now they make a last and supreme effort to attain the goal that escapes them. It is a vain hope. As it is approached, the flame will disappear, leaving the people in dark shadows, shackled more than ever in the servitude they believed themselves to be fleeing.

What is surprising in this? Disdainful of the lessons of history, of the needs of the human heart, and of the last rays of good sense as much as of the dogmas of the Faith, these strange liberties, under the pretext of better attaining religious, social, and political truth, are the negation and ruin of all religion, all government, and all society. They serve only the passions and interests of a few Liberal barons who skillfully make them dazzle the eyes of the crowd and who, in the name of progress, lead us to the old traditions of pagan Caesarism.

Discontented with the bitter fruit it picks, democracy does not share the enthusiasm of its exploiters. Following Proudhon, its unique and incomparable logician, it rejects the bourgeois formulae that have produced nothing for seventy-five years. To its eyes, the Convention of September 15th was but a fleeting truce between irreconcilable doctrines. It knows that we must either seek a more radical remedy for its sufferings in the pitiless deductions of socialism and the definitive suppression of all authority, or return to the complete solution offered by the encyclical. Here is the abyss of social revolution; there, amidst the wreckage, is the unshakeable rock of the papacy. On the one hand, the unknown, absolute negation, powerless to affirm anything; on the other, a clear, precise doctrine, immutable in its perfection. For all disinterested and far-seeing men, and for the nineteenth century as a whole, we may either respond to the pope with violence and folly, or satisfy our legitimate aspirations and throw ourselves into the arms of the Church.

THE ENCYCLICAL OF THE
8TH OF DECEMBER (1865)
CIVIL LIBERTY OUTSIDE THE CHURCH

Capitalism ✗ *(An intelligent argument against it ☺)*

Exhausted by the fight, many good people have renounced
involvement in politics or religion. They have come to believe
that to have the worst of constitutions and the poorest of creeds
is better than change after change. They conclude that to maintain order and tranquility all we need do is suppress discussion,
as if we could forestall the course of events with silence. They
are like fish who think that safety is found by hiding their heads
under a rock. Yet events march onward whether we speak of
them or not, for the people thirst insatiably for truth and persist in seeking it and hoping to apply it in all things. And
behind the political and religious questions of the day, the social
question on which these depend is forced upon us by the logic
of events.

bad monarchy is better than instability + disorder

    Where is the civil liberty based on the equality of citizens and
the suppression of privileges that should console us for the
slumbers of our political liberties and make us patiently await
the completion of the edifice? Far be it from me to think mali-
ciously of France, or to fail to recognize the generous instincts
and charitable devotion that seek the betterment of the worker's
lot and are a powerful counterbalance to the dangerous effects
of the revolutionary utopia. Yet the more admirable the energy

of French and Catholic sentiment, the more severe we must be on the economic illusions that hold it in check.

Just as in 1789 religious liberty was inaugurated by the most bloody persecution, national liberty by the disdain of treaties and general war, and political liberty by insurrection against the established powers, so also was civil liberty begun by confiscating the common and inalienable goods that assured families, trade guilds, and associations a patrimony and common resource. In the name of individual equality, these precious reservoirs—already more or less dried up by the fiscal measures of the old monarchy—were emptied and absorbed into the great reservoir of the national wealth, to which each of us, we were told, had the same right.

Was it not just that all might fight with equal weapons in the tournament of fortune? Was it not just to give to each child a part of the wealth saved from the work of prior generations by abolishing those private institutions that made some privileged and rich before their birth and others pariahs, condemned in advance to poverty and dependence? Was it not urgent to assure public services requiring each to contribute to national expenses according to the measure of his income and by calling everyone according to his capacity to positions and honors until then inaccessible to the vast majority?

Bewildered by such grand promises, we never dreamt that the protected wealth we believed to be an obstacle to general activity were instead the most sacred, most pure, and most useful of savings, and, in the end, the only effective remedy for the weakness of individuals.

Far from benefiting the country, these goods were sold at the lowest prices, and the pittance they raised was soon rendered meaningless by the shortfalls created by stoppages of work. These properties fell to the share of those few clever men well placed to take advantage of the crisis to seize the spoils of the clergy, nobility, and corporations. The Revolution, meanwhile, devoured a hundred times more money than the value of the nationalized properties.

Thus, excepting that of a bold handful who made their fortunes overnight, the condition of the country and each of its members was singularly worsened, and that part of the national wealth which was supposed to return to each citizen turned into contributions, forced loans, and requisitions to meet the needs of a ruined treasury.

The savings of the past having been squandered, men had now to return to work with a blank slate, as unlimited individual liberty replaced the excessive and tyrannical regulation of the Old Regime. The vital jolt that this violent shock gave to general activity and the development of wealth is incontestable. But like all unlimited liberties, this inevitably led to the triumph of the strongest and to the oppression and exploitation of the weakest. The poor, and the state itself, found themselves at the mercy of capital, which had complete license to sell, to buy, to speculate, to charge fees, to retain funds, or to lend at high rates.

The newly emancipated wealth was quick to refuse those free services that hitherto had been regarded as an honor to render to the country. In confiscating the goods of the clergy, great care was taken to leave to the state's expense, and thus to the nation's, the provision of education, charity, and worship that the Church had originally provided. In return for a small payment, the wealthy were exempted from military service, which hitherto had been their special mission. While with one hand they pushed away the work of pure devotion, with the other they grabbed the best ranks, offices, and functions that the nation dispensed. It was said that access to these was open to all, but the entrances were private and carefully guarded by the favored, the wealthy, and the clever.

Finally, to crown their privileges, the rich found a way, in the name of economic science, to avoid all taxes and levies on their own active and invasive capital. While the farmers, their land cut up into small parcels and irrigated with their own sweat, paid an amount equal to a large portion of their harvests, the capitalists, concentrated masters of commerce, industry, and even the soil, painlessly accumulated large revenues free from all public taxation. The only service that they would still consent to render the state was to advance money at a large profit. Heartless and unpatriotic, these rich would have emigrated at the least threat.

The country now has the obligation to pay a triple army of soldiers, employees, and creditors, an army that grows each day and whose general staff is drawn from a small circle of favored families. Thus, in place of a great reservoir of national riches on which each could draw, we have a public debt of ten billions, and each infant gains at birth the right to pay about fifty francs each year for his part of the debt. Thanks to this predominance of material interests, the aristocracy of devotion, virtue, talent, military honor, judicial integrity, and municipal patriotism is everywhere eclipsed by the aristocracy—or better, by the feudal barons—of finance, the basest and most self-serving of all.

+debt

One more step down the road of free exchange, free speculation, and free commerce, one more conquest of the superstitions of a bygone age: let us abolish the law prohibiting usury, and—to listen to you happy bourgeois—we will have found our Eldorado. Perhaps so, but you forget that outside and around you, behind the gold panels and plush hangings by which you limit your horizons, there is another people lacking a patrimony, gnawing at bones, and asking whether this is the fruit of seventy-five years of revolution, sacrifice, and suffering. You can no longer blame the Church lands, for you have stolen them; or the monks, for you have chased them away; or the guilds, for you have sent them packing. What have you put in their place? Have you achieved the good of the masses? Are their rights respected? Are they truly sovereign? In destroying respect for religion and political power, what have you given to the man who has nothing but hunger and misery?

so scathing!

Far from destroying the proletariat, the Revolution created it. The Revolution created, and still pursues, the division of society into two classes: on the one side, those who have nothing and who, never being sure of the next day's bread, live from day to day on their work; on the other, those who hold the capital, the instruments of work—the land, money, and machines—and are thus at once independent and the masters of the worker's lot.

In France, where this transformation has been going on for more than seventy-five years, and where the industrial and economic changes have occurred especially after 1815, the proletariat and the centralization of capital are still far from being the general fact that they are in England. At the same time, in the countryside the Faith resists the attacks of an impious and corrupting press, and the small farmers retain their common sense in the face of the spread of luxury and softness and against competition from machines and large capital. But it is no less true that in a few years the number of proletarians has increased by some three millions, while the number of farmers has diminished by the same. The evil therefore mounts, and, with the rapidity that social evolution takes today, with the growing attraction that detaches men from the earth and the plow and piles them up in cities, the evil is such that, from this day forward, we should be seriously worried about it. There is an even worse prospect for the diminution of family property, a decrease that the luminous work of M. de Tocqueville has shown was already great before 1789. The tragedy of our day is the reconstitution of large capitalist properties and the ruin of small patrimonies.

Amidst the mounting tide of poverty, the people of Paris, formed of the most intelligent and skilled workers, appeared first in line as the perfected type of the proletarian, imbued with modern ideas and detached from all patronage and authority, given over defenseless to the provocations of frenzied lust and the contagion of political and social utopias. Not only did this immense Parisian mass exert a direct influence on the destiny of the entire country during the days of our great commotion, but it is at all times the guide of opinion, fashion, taste, and public spirit, in a word, the model that the rest of France strives to resemble. Thus, it is among the proletarians, who multiply in our sight, and especially among the workers of Paris, that we must study the fruits of contemporary economic doctrines.

that's a YACHT, stretch. is that you?

Listen to this worker. Do not fool yourself: he is intelligent. His logic is flawless, and the questions he poses to modern society are categorical. Is it just that after six thousand years of labor, inventions, and progress, a great part of mankind is born disinherited, without any part of the treasure amassed by his elders? In the condition of inferiority in which the proletarian lives, what good to them is freedom of opinion or political equality? What good is it to them to vote for a municipal counselor or deputy who will not make them more rich? Why not attack the evil at its root? An article has been added to the *Declaration of the Rights of Man* to the effect that the right to property is inviolable and sacred. It was the property-owners who made this false inference and thought up this contradiction to save their own fortunes. Since neither religion nor political power is sacred, why ought property alone have this privilege? If it is true that the people are good, that they become bad only through poverty and ignorance, and that at bottom it is their right to make laws and determine all things, will not the first use of their sovereignty be to distribute more equitably the goods of this world? Are there not things to be done other than to seek a better interpretation of the Bible or to add a cog to the parliamentary machine? Property owners, take heed: at stake are your lands; capitalists, your rents; speculators, your profits. Of you it is now said, and with good reason, all that you once said of the Old Regime which you put on trial and then replaced. What do you have to say in response?

But, you cry, this is to misunderstand the most evident progress and to reject unlimited liberty, which today gives everyone an equal chance to become wealthy. There are no more masters and journeymen, no more monopolies and prohibitions. Each is free to pursue an education and to learn, free to borrow capital lent at a low rate, free to make profitable investments, free to make his fortune and to dispose of it at whim. Free? Yes, on one condition: that he is already rich.

In truth, what does liberty amount to for the one who has nothing? Education, the best of all tools, is only truly accessible to men in proportion to their leisure. Under the empire of necessity, the child of the proletarian is wrenched from his mother's breast to be cradled by administrators at a daycare center; then he moves to the kindergarten, where his education often ends. Put in school prematurely, he leaves it the moment he might profit from it, and the primary instruction offered him by society is an insult, since in order to live he is condemned to waste his vigor, health, intelligence, and character in workshops in which the wages do not meet his needs. Is not his hunger greater than his salary? Thus he comes to be a marked man, useless for military service, or a weak woman, a stranger to her housework; soon a new generation follows, growing on less sap than the one before it.

Once he is grown, is the worker truly free to choose a trade and to succeed in it? Each trade requires professional training, a time of study and apprenticeship, which in turn requires a parental investment that is impossible for the poor. It is even more difficult to become independent, to work for oneself, to buy a store, or to start a business. When a man has arrived at that point through the strength of his sacrifices and has enough to pay for his workshop, materials, tools, permits, and advertisement, a powerful manufacturer comes to the same street, armed with capital and machines, as sure of overcoming his petty competition as a battery of cannons in a battle against savages, and all in the name of liberty. Not only can he centralize and divide the work, but, like a captain who does not hesitate to sacrifice a part of his forces in order to win the high ground, he can sell at a loss until he is master of the market, then raise his prices and enrich himself on the ruin of his neighbors, who are reduced to asking him for work and a salary in order to fend off starvation. This is no imaginary war. Everywhere the large stores and large factories devour the small: we are lucky if we do not see, as in England, vast machine harvests supplanting the small farm, that sacred nursery of the independent man.

Even well-intentioned industrialists today find themselves incapable of improving the worker's lot. In spite of domestic competition, they take extraordinary profits from the public. To remedy this, commercial treaties have subjected them to international competition. In order to lower their prices, the manufacturers are almost all forced to lower salaries; thus it is at the expense of the worker that they compete against foreigners. AMEN!

We believed that we could lessen the problems of unlimited liberty by making that liberty universal. But if this liberty gives birth to a few barons of industry in one country, how shall we prevent it from leading to the triumph of the strongest and largest capitalists who pay the least possible for labor and craftsmanship in others? The cotton produced at the lowest prices by slaves in America and Egypt will always win out over the linen and hemp cultivated with our own free hands. One day the rich factories of England will force an entry into our market by cutting prices below our minimum, and we will be inundated with their iron and fabric.

Given this war to the death, in which we dare not let our industry succumb, how can we raise salaries, prohibit child labor, better the lot of women and the elderly, and reconstitute family patrimonies? When we chased the English from France, was it time to free the serfs? The Jacques Bonhommes believed it, and we had to carve them into pieces.[1] It is the same today with the emancipation of the proletariat. No one dreams of it in the midst of this race in which the palm goes not to the one who makes his worker happier, but to the one who knows how to exploit him more cleverly so as to produce goods at a lower price than his rivals.

We are told that credit makes capital, and thus machines, available to all. It is as if money asked only five or six percent from the worker who accepts its services. This is magnificent in theory. But in practice, to whom do we lend? There is a proverb for it: to the one who has much, more will be given. Suppose you have a million. Within an hour you will raise three or four more to begin your project. But suppose you are hungry and unemployed. Only with

---

[1] Keller alludes to the peasant rebellion of 1358. Jacques Bonhomme is the French equivalent of John Doe.

much difficulty will you find a week's loan at fifteen, twenty, or fifty percent.

We now treat as a superannuated prejudice the religious belief that condemns this infamous exploitation. What, says the economist, do you want? Interest must be proportionate to the risk undertaken. It is very risky to lend to the one who has nothing, and, if of two debtors only one can repay the loan, there is not even a profit at an interest rate of one hundred percent. Therefore, the borrower pays more the poorer he is. For him, capital is never a bargain, unless, by rare good fortune, he has some savings as collateral. Then the wealthy turn against him and diminish by as much the small reserve that he would have succeeded in gaining.

There are, I know, credit unions that seek to remedy this cruel inequality by lending to workers. But however ingenious the calculations, money cannot be made from nothing. For loans to be made to those who have nothing, first there must be either pious gifts, or capital that through charity exposes itself to the possibility of default, or, more dangerous because potentially unlimited, subventions given by the state. Even with these resources, credit will never be anything to the poor but negative property. Whatever is done, the one reduced to borrowing will be less free and less the master of his future than the one who owes nothing to anyone. To anticipate and sell one's future will always be a form of servitude. Only a patrimony gives true independence, and so long as the proletarian has no house, no provisions, and no savings for difficult times, he will be at the mercy of capital.

There remains as a last resource, or rather as the supreme chance for those who have nothing, the freedom to speculate, to buy today and sell tomorrow, to predict the rise or fall, and to play double-or-nothing on the stock market. It is a dangerous game. The news is known in advance by several colossal financiers who keep current with the affairs of the whole world. Following from afar the roll of the great waves of commerce, these vigilant navigators always know how to avoid the tempests. When they give the signal to return to port, there is no time left: the little boats that want to follow them break up on the shore, and others are already in the deeps laying their hands on the staves of broken ships. Poor men! You tried so hard and always came too late. You are sure to buy high and sell low. Whether the news is good or bad, you will always bear the cost.

To sell at a loss in order to ruin a neighbor less rich than oneself, to borrow on false guarantees and lose the money of others in crazed undertakings, to exploit information one is privileged to know: these are but ways of stealing from one's neighbor. This kind of larceny, trickery, and cheating merits the galleys. Yet how are we to prevent them? Are these not the inevitable consequences of unlimited financial liberty? He who speaks of liberty without limits speaks of the use of all human force, the triumph of the most audacious and clever, the ruin of the lowly, and the oppression of the weak. Under this regime, machines, steam, telegraph, and credit, instead of doubling the general well-being, become engines of domination in the hands of the financial barons who enjoy their monopoly.

Capital is just as centralized as work, and the larger it is, the greater its profits. Moreover, it tends to accumulate in only a few hands. The situation is reversed with the worker. The one who is most hungry, and therefore content with a morsel of bread, will be preferred to the others and ruin them by accepting a lower salary. Just as the large fortunes dominate and absorb the middling ones, so the most miserable dominate and absorb those less miserable. Thus does society divide itself—to the great detriment of well-being, virtue, and liberty—into two classes separated by an abyss: the rich, who enjoy more and more without working, and the proletarians, who painfully earn their bread each day and whose most determined labor fails to gain their release from this semi-servitude.

The social problem is far from being resolved, and it rightly preoccupies those with the sentiment of true fraternity who understand the age. Yet the most generous minds have wasted their time in theoretical disputes.

We see clearly how the evil is to be understood. On February 20,

1864, the electoral manifesto of the Parisian workers summarized their complaints with great moderation:

> We have reached our political majority through universal suffrage, but we still lack social emancipation. The liberty that the Third Estate conquered so vigorously must be extended to all citizens of democratic France. An equal political right necessarily implies an equal social right.
>
> We are tired of hearing that there are no more classes, that since '89 all French are equal before the law. But we who have no other property than our arms, we who daily submit to the conditions of capital, be they legitimate or arbitrary, we who live under exceptional laws—such as the law against coalitions—that harm our interests and injure our dignity: we find it most difficult to believe this affirmation.
>
> We who have the right to select our representatives do not always have the means to learn how to read. We who lack the power to unite or freely to associate are powerless to organize professional training. We who see this precious instrument of industrial progress become the privilege of capital cannot stand by this illusion.[2]
>
> We whose children often spend their earliest years in the demoralizing and unhealthy atmosphere of the factories, or under apprenticeship, today hardly better than domestic service, whose wives are forced to leave the home for hard work contrary to their nature and destructive of the family, who lack the right to make ourselves heard in order peaceably to defend our salaries and insure ourselves against unemployment: we affirm that the equality written in the law does not exist in

[handwritten margin note: political power requires that certain rights be established + met]

---

[2] The allusion is to the Le Chapelier law of 1791 prohibiting workers' associations, which, with various modifications, remained in force until 1884.

society's habits, and that it is far from being realized in fact.

Those deprived of education and capital, and who cannot resist the self-serving and oppressive demands of capital through liberty and solidarity, must submit fatally to the domination of capital. Their interests remain subordinated to other interests.

We will see a financial aristocracy constitute itself. The middle class, like the workers, will soon be no more than servants.

Thus far all is clear. The uncertainty and error begin when they propose a remedy. Thinking only to enlarge the path we are already on, the workers and economists carefully remove any religious principle from their program. They persist in placing themselves under the patronage of 1789, and demand that to the freedom of the worker be added the right of association, to political liberty the representation of all interests, and finally, to liberty of conscience primary instruction open to all. There is in this threefold formula, as in all modern ideas, a vague and generous instinct for the truth. Yet we do not see all the contradictions and impossibilities it contains. We forget that in creating individualism, the proletariat, and Unitarianism, the Revolution itself killed association, representation, and popular education. And in charging liberty alone to heal the injuries it has made, to satisfy the aspirations it has proclaimed, we condemn the most effective means to radical powerlessness.

Let us examine, one after the other, these three solutions of free association, the representation of the working classes, and, finally, free education for all, and let us see whether these reforms—the supreme end of current science and liberalism—could be achieved under the rule of our modern maxims.

There is nothing more simple than to permit workers to unite themselves and meet in order to discuss their interests and salaries. By number and solidarity, they will be as strong as their employers, and equilibrium will be reestablished. The application of the new law on coalitions arrives in time to give us the measure of the right that the workers really possess, and to let us see, in a striking picture, what always happens between the workers and their employers. In truth, what good are these coalitions? What do the workers require in order to be able to strike, or, what amounts to the same thing, to dictate their conditions? Must they be poor, underpaid, and unjustly oppressed? Not exactly. The strike is a means, or rather a privilege, reserved to the small number of those who have savings to spend, or who, in other words, earn more than they require. This weapon will be still more strong in their hands when they will have made further economies. The day on which they have spent all their savings is the day on which they will once again be at the mercy of capital—whatever be the justice of their demands. As for those who really do have such low salaries, and who work day and night to succeed in barely feeding their families, they are effectively prevented from going on strike for a week or even a single day.

Thus, instead of creating an arbitration able to end the conflicts and arrange equitable conditions of work, we have almost created a permanent war in which victory goes to the one who has the most money to spend. And we flatter ourselves for having inaugurated the reign of equality! True inequality was not in rights. It was, and still is, in wealth. If each worker has nothing, then together they will be no more wealthy, and thus no more free. In order to demand a higher wage, one must be able to wait; that is, one must have something to eat. However short the walk-out is, those with the most savings will have their hand forced, not by the employers, but by those who have saved nothing and need to work in order to eat. The manufacturer who employs a thousand workers is necessary to each of them, but each worker represents an insignificant portion of the manufacturer's production. He can fire whom he pleases without difficulty, or sell the plant and realize enough to live on for the rest of his days, while the workers could at best live three or four weeks

[margin annotation: complete equality comes via an equal lack of freedom]

if they pooled their resources. If, in the presence of this profound inequality, they give in to the temptation to use violence, they will then face the police, the gendarmes, and prison, in a word, the state, obliged to maintain public order at all costs.

How then is freedom of labor to be created unless the workers are guaranteed an individual or collective patrimony? How are they to be united without peril to public peace unless they are given enough to live on and are inspired to virtue and moderation sufficient to keep them from abusing their power? This double difficulty, economic and moral, was resolved by the Church, but has baffled the champions of unlimited liberty.

It is the same in politics. As long as the proletarian is not socially emancipated, common rights will give him only an illusory liberty. When a man is unsure of tomorrow's bread, can he dream of exercising independently the rights of the citizen? In the great cities, the means of forming opinion—speeches and journals—are in the hands of a small oligarchy, which calls itself democratic but dominates the masses far more than it represents them. In the countryside, the workers are at the mercy of the manufacturer. On election day, each foreman leads them in groups to the voting table, where they cast their votes under the boss's eye. Universal suffrage thus puts hundreds and thousands of voices at the command of several wills, and so the workers may indeed say that they are not truly represented.

Let us see whether modern society at least respects the inviolable sanctuary of the worker's conscience. Can the man with neither a speck of gold nor a patch of land reserve part of his sustenance for his mind and heart? It is said that we will achieve this by free and compulsory schooling, given not by the Church as in the Middle Ages, but by the state. Man will no longer be a slave or brute lacking the barest notions of morals and common sense. Society will no longer be permitted to shirk its obligation to distribute such knowledge freely, and the father of the family will find a time set aside for the education of his children that is guaranteed by law and enforced by penal sanctions.

+ the problem of free education

This argument is specious and has been often refuted. It is easy to see that because the state has nothing and its coffers are filled by taxes on work, the poor will pay for the instruction that we give them as a gift and the rich will cease paying for their own. Furthermore, neither fines nor prison will enable a miserable father to find the resources or time to allow his children to go to school, for he is only too happy to find a little leisure so that he might spend some time with his children.

In this way, free education, independent of any religious direction, is powerless to free man from ignorance and poverty. Still less will it succeed in emancipating his mind and conscience. Indeed, we must consider the issue from this higher perspective. It is not only the child, but also the father, the mother, and the elderly who need time set aside by law and the public conscience so that they might rest their bodies, recollect their minds, and broaden their souls. Without rest of this kind, the worker is but a beast of burden in the service of those perpetually at rest, and education is but another lie and arm of oppression for the few who are privileged.

Now the free thinkers, who would cry tyranny if forced to work with their hands for even one day a week, make religious liberty consist precisely in the suppression of the Sunday rest prescribed by the Church and necessary to religion. What would follow were the law revoked?[3] The poorest and greediest would hasten to work on the seventh day, and capital, which measures salaries by the strict needs of those who accept them, would profit by requiring seven days of work from all workers in exchange for their weekly bread. By this means, disdain for the natural law is enshrined in public law, and the Paris worker must now work on every day of the year.

It is not sufficient to provide education during childhood and then bind adulthood to interminable labor. In the name of religious liberty, this instruction will be made to conform to the image of the state, which has nothing to do with religion. A question of morals must be applicable to Protestants, Jews, and Rationalists. Histories

[3] Sunday rest had been abolished by the Revolution and was restored in 1814.

will speak with the same respect for Jesus Christ as for those who cru-
cified him, for the popes as for Luther and Calvin. The most able
teacher cannot succeed in playing this impossible role, cannot always
speak without betraying his true convictions. Even granting that he
were to make himself completely impenetrable, what would our children, with their instinctive clairvoyance, conclude? If the state, its
bureaucrats, and its approved writers can treat all religions equally,
they also must have the right to the same indifference and disdain.

Thus, under the pretext of leaving the conscience free, we will fail
to nourish it. The Faith, which is its life, is fatally undermined in
the child's heart by the teaching that should confirm and strengthen
it. Soon it will completely disappear in the whirlwind of an adult life
in which religion no longer has a day or hour reserved.

To the young men and women who have so great a need for the
living God, for the tender and compassionate Lord, always ready to
console, nourish, and strengthen them, Jesus Christ will soon be no
more than a statue of antique marble—just as Renan would like—
or a moralist lost in bygone ages. But Bacchus and Venus are there
in flesh and blood on every street corner, calling their victims and
multiplying the snares and seductions around them. Amidst these
perils, only the rich man can preserve his faith and his children's
virtue. By the most monstrous and intolerable of inequalities, the
worker's son—save by a miracle—is condemned to indifference and
skepticism, his daughter to dishonor and premature loss of beauty.
Then these miserable people, so well described by the former representative Corbon as carelessly drinking in the venom of the newspapers, impassioned and embittered against the priest whom they
know only through calumny, and detesting the Church, which
alone can make them happy, are angered against the rich and the
powerful, desire an ideal that they see nowhere, pursue it in
debauches and revolutions, and expend their lives, health, and souls
in deception, violence, and torture of all kinds.

What then becomes of the family, the last refuge of liberty and
moral dignity? Here also, under the guise of liberty, misery exerts its

(Family)

tyranny. Deprived of all patrimony, of all individual or collective saving, the poor are no longer able to fulfill the charge of raising their children. The rich cry out with Malthus that the poor's numbers must be limited and, as if this gave them the right to do so, attempt to lower their salaries in order to keep their families smaller. Not only does the lowliest Parisian worker no longer have Sunday, but if he has more than two children he is indigent. The natural temptation is to sterilize the marriage, and then not to marry at all. The indissoluble and fruitful bond dictated by the natural law and consecrated by religion gives way to inconstant and selfish unions. Where faith and piety are lacking, the state has only the false and powerless formula of civil marriage in the battle against Malthusianism and promiscuity, and this will soon be found dispensable. As morals go, so does respect for women. Thus, by a system as inept from the economic point of view as it is guilty from the moral point of view, the population—the foundation of wealth—will slowly decline. Indeed, the education of children is the best-placed capital, and the one thousand or twelve hundred francs which each costs will be nothing compared with what they themselves will produce when grown. A land reduced to refusing them the light of day because it cannot afford this small investment will be, by its shameful thrift, more base than the American planter who enriches himself by breeding his black slaves.

For the man with nothing, equality under the law, social liberty, political liberty, and religious liberty are mere decoys. His body is condemned to fatigue, his mind to ignorance, his heart to misery, his home to solitude, and his rare children to skepticism or seduction. If, happily, it is not this way everywhere, it is thanks to the virtues and traditions that are completely independent of this so-called civilization. The evil is of course greatest in the bosom of the capital, where it exerts all its influence. We may therefore say that the *laissez-faire, laissez-passez* abdication of Church and state profits only a new aristocracy, no less absolute and no less exclusive than the preceding ones.

It is not only today that unlimited liberty produces such fruits. The old feudalism, armed in iron, went about fighting under a similar banner when it delivered the land to pillage and opened a career for all ambitions. For the kings, it was fitting and popular to suppress the political and military liberty that these turbulent lords invoked and abused. Later, liberty of thought gave birth to an aristocracy of the reformers and sectaries whose excesses and disorders soon forced the government to suppress that liberty. Today, we have financial liberty, an absolutism of capital freed from all laws—human and divine—and dealing mortal wounds to the social liberty it claims to have founded.

To distract the multitudes and turn their attention from the exorbitant privileges they enjoy, these newcomers cannot cry out enough against the abuses of the past, the dungeons, and the convents. Do not look so far afield. They are the true Old Regime, right here, living at our expense: the bankers who pay no tax and levy a tithe on all new enterprise; the manufacturers for whom the worker is but a cog the upkeep of which they restrict to bare necessity; finally, the journalists—too often in the pay of the rich—whose worn-out liberalism monopolizes publicity.

Doubtless there are bankers, manufacturers, and journalists animated by the best intentions, just as in the Middle Ages not every lord was an anthropophage. Yet besides these generous exceptions, who are powerless against evil, the others dream only of exploiting, peacefully and with great gusto, modern liberties, modern progress, and modern civilization. For seventy-five years we have made our fortune with the principles of 1789. What is their intrinsic value? The bourgeois does not ask; he has merchandise for sale. During the Revolution and the First Empire, he began by gorging himself with the wealth of the clergy, nobility, and conquered lands. Then, to save his wealth, he bet on the rising market the day after Waterloo and voted for the fall of Napoleon I. He then liberally invaded the public offices and constitutional machinery of our two parliamentary monarchies, only to abandon both at the first sign of danger. At last, he sacrificed liberty just as he had earlier sacrificed glory, our franchise as he had our conquests, in order to protect his own privileges. He had been by turns Voltairian, Jacobin, Imperialist, Royalist, Orleanist, Republican, Reactionary. He had betrayed and sold all, beginning with his soul, to continue to enjoy his gold and dividends. He alone, however, is the man of progress, the man of '89, the true liberal, treating all the governments, grandeurs, and glories of the past with the same disdain. Pygmies, let these great men sleep in their tombs: you would have kissed their feet had you seen them living. While you pretend to be brave against the disarmed dead whom you evoke to cause fear in the credulous masses, what really takes courage is to denounce you, the feudal aristocracy of the day, you who confiscated the Revolution. It is not back to the old, but onward to the new absolutism that this aristocracy leads and will fatally bind us.

Indeed, when this nefarious band has bought up all the wealth of the clergy and corporations, the lands of the crown and the great families, the concessions of mines and railroads, the present and future wealth of nations, and, as in England, there remains only a minority of property-holders amidst a growing multitude of proletarians, who will prevent the angry people, so long incited against the shadow of the Old Regime, from turning against those who have excited, beguiled, and tricked them? After the political and religious truths have been dismissed, how shall property avoid being put to the question? Is not property more imperfect, an institution riven with abuses, varying with time and place, modified each day by laws and taxes? Is this not the key to the problems that weigh so heavily on the nineteenth century; must not each citizen have an inviolable home, and each family a patrimony whose independence is guaranteed if equality under the law and liberty for all are not to be but vain words? This is the result of the emancipation from all religious authority and the abdication of the state in economic questions. Here is the profound evil that the most generous efforts will only attenuate and delay unless an effective remedy is found.

Thence comes—and think deeply on it—the inevitable menace of war and social revolution, the mere specter of which froze the bourgeoisie in terror in 1848. At the end of these violent struggles came the no less lamentable necessity for a new centralization, a new absolutism of the state on the economic terrain.

The liberals pushed for it just like the others. From the moment their privileges were threatened, they found it easy to invoke the arm of the state in deportation and firing squads. At the least scare, they demanded the help of the government. Steal a cabbage from them and they demand that the fields be garrisoned. Incapable of doing anything in their own defense, they require a bureaucrat everywhere. Thus, little by little, everything tends to concentrate itself in the hands of the central power, an abstract being, a mysterious but omnipotent divinity, who will always incarnate itself in one or two men—intelligent, devout, and naturally without excess. The elective or hereditary aristocracy will cede place to a new aristocracy of directors, subdirectors, inspectors, and controllers, all well-paid bureaucrats who fulfill their functions with the moderate zeal that one has for other people's business. The country will resemble a giant railroad company, incapable of managing its own fortune, hardly knowing those who are chosen to represent her, and whose hearts, minds, arms, and fortunes will be at the mercy of several braided helmets, at once all-powerful and irresponsible.

It is an act of cowardice for the rich to sell their conscience and liberty to the government, which promises to grow while preserving what they enjoy. But what do those who have nothing stand to gain from this new despotism? What will the laboring masses gain? When, through the impossible, property will no longer be hereditary but will become completely elective and put entirely at the disposition of the state, capital will be no less demanding, no less pitiless towards the worker. The most radical laws, attempting violently to divide actual wealth, will only destroy it and end by encountering a power infinitely greater than its own. Under the pretext of emancipating the proletarians, this final application of the principles of

1789 will place the seal on their economic, political, and religious servitude.

In all times and under all regimes, the only way to be free is to have something of one's own. The Revolution created only the unlimited liberty of the property-owner, that is to say the absolutism of those already free, and it could not touch wealth itself without injuring it in its source. How shall we escape this vicious circle? Where is the moral force capable of regulating the use of the goods of this world without destroying them, to distribute them more equitably without violence, and to assure to each a portion sufficient to guarantee the life of his family, the exercise of his civic rights, and the independence of his conscience?

We have taken note of the principle of death that was unchained by unlimited liberty. It is time to find the principle of life that can give association, representation, and serious instruction to the workers, and rally into one common bundle the isolated forces and devotions that confusedly agitate for their emancipation.

THE ENCYCLICAL OF THE
8TH OF DECEMBER (1865)
SOCIAL TRUTH, THE PRINCIPLE OF SOCIAL LIBERTY

It is easy to spend or waste the savings of the past. When we wish to preserve or increase them, whether we wish to make millions or grow a single head of wheat, then the dreams of the imagination are succeeded by the severe and inexorable, strong and yet fertile laws of reality. The smallest bit of happiness, even merely material, is born only from man's submission to these laws. General prosperity and liberty result from his free adherence to them.

Work is indispensable to the progress of wealth, but it does not create it alone. It only develops it, and for this it needs a first wealth, or capital. It needs tools, buildings, land, seeds, livestock. Thence the division of profits or revenues between those who provide their work and those who furnish the material or instruments, or, in other words, between labor and capital.

In the treaty they conclude, however, the conditions are far from being equal. For the one who has nothing works regardless what salary is offered to him, whether constrained by slavery or hunger. Yet capital is free to dictate the terms, to wait if it pleases, and if it needs to, it may live on itself. If one tries to take it by force or even disturb it, it flees, emigrates, or dies.

Even the earth, which seems too easy to seize, disappears between the hands of the one who takes it, and wherever despotism comes, there the peasants, beasts, and fertility of the soil disappear. Indeed, capital is the stronger of the two, and it lives only on the condition that it be free.

The first favor to obtain from this power is for it to wish to preserve itself in the hands in which it is found. Thence comes the necessity of giving owners to existing wealth, to make a certain number of landholders who are willing to keep it and to preserve it from pillage, while waiting for the whole world to become such. In barbaric societies, the strongest are the only masters of the soil; force is the only means to acquire and defend it. Here progress beyond the savage, who does not know how to respect his own livelihood, can already be found.

Inheritance, which transmits a patrimony and which is only possible with the maintenance of the laws of the family, is at once a lively stimulus for thrift and a first distribution of fortune among the children, who did not earn it by their work. This is progress, accomplished by the free choice of those who possess wealth. As for those who do not, they are condemned to respect property in spite of the abuses it contains and to submit to inequalities and injustices, all the more striking and irremediable when the moral level of society is lower. It is useless for them to revolt. They would be the first to be punished. Their ambition should be to arrive in their turn at economic liberty, that is to say, at the peaceful possession, rather than the destruction, of wealth.

It is neither by scientific formulae nor by violent revolutions but by virtue, freely and courageously practiced, that the worker will one day gain his independence. And first, instead of seeing work as a hateful yoke, let him accept it with love as a duty full of grandeur and dignity. Whatever his salary might be, let him find a way to save a part of it and let the incredible power of the economy—the growing return brought by compounded interest—be as powerful for building a fortune as it is for destroying it in the hands of the improvident. Finally, let him cultivate that fraternal devotion and patriotism of the guild, ingenious for dividing the burden of ill-fortune, for charging the keep of widows and orphans to able-bodied men, and for setting aside wages for the unemployed.

This is not all. Capital, given over to its egoism, can render these efforts and sacrifices useless. Giving the laborer only enough to avoid dying of hunger, the owners forever prevent him from winning his share of property. Here again it belongs to moral force to oblige the conscience of the rich not to abuse their superiority and not to profit from the misery of others. Instead of considering their fortune as if made for their personal enjoyment, they should see it as an office created for society and the common interest, a serious and heavy charge that, far from dispensing them from work, obliges them to give free services to their country in proportion to their revenues. In the inverse of the pitiless economic law that raises interest rates for the poorer debtor and lowers the salary of the hungrier worker, the moral law teaches that it is a crime to charge interest to >Leviticus the one who has nothing, and that the more miserable people are the more it is necessary to extend an open and generous hand to help them reconstitute their patrimony. The rich should see each worker as an equal before God and a brother among men, not as a machine that must be made to produce as much as possible. They will be the workers' patrons, that is, their responsible protectors. They will watch over them with constant solicitude. They must assure them the possibility of raising their families in a dignified manner, and to breathe freely on the days of rest that are even more necessary to the soul than the body.

Finally, it does not suffice for the moral power of which I speak to have penetrated our consciences and then to pass into the customs and legislation of the people. To fight the native egoism that always leads the rich to exploit the poor and makes them find a thousand clever ways to elude or paralyze the law, this force must be organized and permanent, and it must add the eloquence of leadership by example to its doctrinal instruction. We must oppose the bad rich men with an army of voluntary poor who give all they possess to relieve great sufferings and to re-create a heritage for those who no longer have one. No matter how much we preach thrift to the poor and humanity to the rich, there will always be a gulf between them created by luxury, greed, rapacity, and improvidence. How shall this gulf be filled—today when it is growing ever wider—if intelligent men do not throw their lives, minds, activity, and fortune into the breach, not seeking their own rights, but sacrificing all personal interest, occupying themselves entirely with others?

If any property is sacred, it must be that which is given up for the good of the poor, to assure charitable works for children, the sick, and the elderly. If there is a liberty that can and should remain unlimited, it is the liberty to devote oneself to their suffering, to unite and to associate in order to serve them under the protection of a common rule. Next to those temples of debauchery where so much wealth is consumed in pure waste, the establishment of asylums that throughout the ages have been the support and last recourse of those who have no other cannot be prohibited. The ground of modern industry must be cleared as once were the forests of Germany, and to the pagan political economy and the ancient feudal lord, who both treated man like a beast of burden, it is time to oppose the peaceful competition of generous endeavors which have as their sole end making work moral, loaning to the poor without interest, helping workers' associations advance, and opening well-paid workshops for fathers of families and widows burdened with children. Far from humiliating the weakest, devotion will honor itself by lending them a hand, while being the sole effective and legitimate means of keeping them from succumbing to the oppression of the strong.

What will ensue if this path of the virtues is not freely chosen? The law of social necessities will exert itself in all its rigor with its heavy penalties. Without great and heroic sacrifices, the natural virtues soon diminish. If capital does not spontaneously consent to improve work conditions, to raise salaries, to encourage thrift and family life, then wealth will be concentrated in the hands of a financial feudalism, as bitter and hard as that of the Middle Ages. If the worker does not succeed in reconstituting his property through savings and association, he will remain at the mercy of capital. In vain will he seek a remedy in the illusion of socialism. The socialists' insane schemes will only end in the destruction of acquired capital, the disorganization of work, the reconstitution of slavery under the form of a proletariat, and, on top of these wounds, the cancer of ancient caesarism.

Social liberty is thus above all a moral problem, and it is founded uniquely on respect for social truth. Wealth is consumed, destroyed, and wasted by the sterile experiments of error; it can only be produced, even in the smallest amounts, by the assent we give to truth. Error leads us to servitude, the just chastisement for our pride and cowardice. Truth teaches us to conquer, through virtue and sacrifice, the free tendency of our strength, intelligence, and activity. The sum of social liberty enjoyed by society is therefore measured by its moral health.

We urgently need to know who will give us the doctrine capable of teaching this truth, to produce these virtues and devotion. *Philosophes*, men of letters, bankers, and noblemen of all kinds, even Catholic ones, favored by fortune, can sleep in their wealth. Forgetting these questions, which are questions of life and death for the majority, they amuse themselves by believing in systems that caress their vanity but which threaten neither their honor nor their revenue, and leave them free to drift on peaceably in their soft existence. This is the easy path. It is not thus for the masses, who know misery intimately. What they need, and what interests them, is not the academic and sterile fight of contradictory religious and political systems, but the true religion and the true political system, which, instead of exploiting them, will give them their dignity and independence.

In pursuit of this ideal, the man of the people is not moved by the narrow idea of his personal enjoyment. Holding neither to the money he earns painfully, nor to the life which is his only wealth, he is always ready to give his savings or throw himself into the fire to save someone in danger, and his greatest joy is to sacrifice himself for the public good, for the well-being and emancipation of those who suffer. An easy, comfortable, and pedestrian life does not satisfy him. He is more poetic than this. He is artistic and chivalrous, just as our fathers were. He must do great things. If he cannot find great things to do and his hopes are dashed, he will consume himself in extravagant dreams, excessive pleasures, or even throw himself into adventures, dramas, and revolutions, struggling against the government and even God Himself when it seems that he can no longer occupy himself with the great interests of the world. He is still French and knows nothing of Cartesian doubt, freethinking, the balance of powers, or the principle of nonintervention, in a word, of aristocratic or bourgeois indifference under its thousand different forms. He wants to know what is true and to believe it, what is beautiful and to love it, what is good and to do it.

Animated by this generous thirst, will the people find religious truth, the first source of social truth? The question is not as difficult to resolve as one might think. Man can so little go without religion that each economic system hides one from him, and the different schools that captivate our minds on social matters are in reality the economic manifestations of different beliefs that struggle for the command of souls. Only Catholics have founded and can still found corporations based on the free union of capital and labor. Beside them there is the schismatic or aristocratic school of centralizing lawyers, in power since Philippe-le-Bel. Without denying original sin, they pretend that its cure lies in their power through the regulation of commerce, industry, capital, work, and instruction. Then there is the Protestant school, or the camp of financial feudalism, whose dogmas are the free expansion of individual forces, the absolute dominion of capital, the exploitation of the worker, and speculation and usury in all their many forms. Finally, there is the revolutionary school, more logically and openly denying the

Fall, on which ~~doctrine inequality and social injustices have been~~
~~supported.~~
~~✗~~ ~~Today the choice lies between Catholicism and the Revolution.~~ ~~✗~~
The latter has passed sentence on the aristocracy and feudalism that
have exploited us down to this day. In their place it has proclaimed
the infallibility and omnipotence of popular reason as the absolute
master of public and private fortunes.

Yet, as we have seen, this supposed sovereign reason only lives by
abdicating and then incarnating itself in one or more men. In its
name will soon reign an aristocracy of bureaucrats, a *de facto* government exerting unlimited authority: this is the path to caesarism,
the worst of tyrannies. In political economy as in so much else, the
Revolution had the great advantage of passing sentence on intermediate solutions. By putting us in the grip of the logical consequences
of rationalism, it forcefully brings us back to Catholicism as the
only refuge against all the perils that menace us, the only instrument
of civilization in a position to respond to popular aspirations.

Yet if the Church possesses social truth in her religious truth, will
she not in turn exercise an unchecked despotism over worldly
affairs? No, for then she would no longer be the truth. Nor will she
invoke either an absolute regulation incapable of restraining the
nature of things, or an unlimited liberty powerless to correct itself
in its vices. Today, as at her origin, in social questions as in all others,
she only sees coercive force as a secondary and purely defensive
weapon against evil. For her primary weapon, she has persuasion
and man's free adherence to truth and virtue: to truth, in order to
accept social necessities and to create stability; to virtue, to render
these necessities less harsh and to create progress. Here is the whole
economy of the Catholic system: let a moderate and reasonable regulation, accepted by opinion and the public conscience, repress the
manifest violations of natural justice, the shocking assaults of
cupidity and exploitation; let unlimited liberty be left to the good,
that is to say, to pure devotion, which voluntarily consecrates itself
to repairing the inevitable misfortunes, relieving and dressing

the wounded on life's battlefield. In this way the Church claims to realize for everyone the best and only possible liberty.

First, the simple expansion of Catholic life and Catholic institutions will spontaneously produce a love of work, thrift, the virtue of family life, and the spirit of association in the worker. The egoism of capital will thus be confronted with a charitable competition that will cause the sentiments of justice and brotherhood to penetrate our customs and laws. At length, by thrift and association on the one hand, and by the generosity and reserves of charity on the other, we will see the patrimony of the proletarians reconstituted as the true coronation of social liberty.

There is doubtless nothing better than to encourage the savings banks and mutual help societies that we already possess. Nevertheless, by itself this is not enough. We would multiply its power tenfold were we to organize them by trades and permit the corporations to create collective and inalienable reserves to meet the needs of their members. Here Rome offers us living models, much closer to true liberty than the corporations of the Old Regime. Follow this example: strengthen these associations by a religious bond, allow them to have schools, churches, hospitals, and feasts of their own, and you will give them a healthy life with none of the shortcomings and dangers of the revolutionary groups. To aid them and to give them examples, supports, and assistants, let the religious orders consecrate themselves to the service of the workers, and devote to the task of resolving the problems of industry that perseverance which the children of Saint Benedict employed to cultivate our wastelands. Finally, let us renew and develop on a Christian basis the practice of free loans to workers, dowries to poor girls, aid to widows and mothers of families, and other such works that cannot be sustained by a mere philanthropic urge.

Here is the role of individual liberty in the social order. Now, what intervention of the civil power is necessary to protect it? What are the laws, the protective measures, that are in harmony with the public conscience and the needs of the nineteenth century? One *marriage and family*

would be wrong to think this a delicate issue that requires certain parts of the truth to be carefully hidden from view. On the contrary, here the superiority and triumph of the Church shine forth. In all ages she prides herself on having diminished the rigor and number of necessary punishments, the violence and arbitrariness of power, and to have limited and restrained the use of coercion. It could not have been otherwise, inasmuch as she creates the greater part of the laws of order and morals by her persuasion and support for virtue.

This general rule is easy to verify in its applications. If opinion were to support the efforts of the Church and to brand as infamous, as they deserve, illegal schemes, speculation, and usury, this would suffice to apply legislation with vigor. Let us allow the vigilant eye of justice to scrutinize business affairs down to the smallest detail. Let us maintain the legal rate of interest and the prohibition against speculation in futures, measures that today have been beaten down by the blows of license and almost fallen into disuse. Without serious innovation, we will succeed in repressing the abuses of the sovereignty of capital.

As to the dignity and independence of the worker himself, sensible economists agree that it does not exist without a family, and that there is no family without respect for marriage, education, and Christian Sundays.

Indeed, what sanction can the wisest civil law bring to marriage, and how will it make this union desirable and fertile, if the spouses do not freely and generously accept the duties God imposes on them? Since the law is too often powerless to repress disordered morals, what good is achieved by attacking them in their most pure source by taking the place of the priest and usurping his right to unite the spouses? What good does civil marriage serve that is anterior and superior to religious marriage?

So, you will say to us, you would return to the priests the registers that the Revolution took from them, and, by abolishing civil marriage you will deny a man's natural and inalienable right to unite himself with a woman, a right man enjoyed well before Christianity? No. The Church merely affirms and consecrates this primordial right/Yet, when it is not done in the name of God as witness to the parties' promises, and when the conditions of the marriage are not examined and weighed, one of two things will happen: either those who believe themselves united were not in fact able to be so, in which case civil marriage has merely placed these wretches between a guilty bond that they are no longer free to break and the voice of their conscience that tells them to separate, or they really were able to unite themselves, and then civil marriage, not being able to make them understand or respect the holiness of their vows, is a vain promise and a slippery slope between the religious bond and concubinage.

This having been said, it would be a simple matter to leave the registers to the state and the ceremony to the priests of each cult, and thus reduce civil marriage to what it can be in reality, that is, the certification that a religious marriage has taken place. In practice, since divorce has been abolished, this question involves many fewer difficulties than once thought. If civil marriage had attempted to establish itself independently, by giving itself its own laws and proper conditions, it would never have been able to penetrate a Catholic people. Thus, only furtively, by minutely copying the rules of the Church and by reducing Jews and Protestants to Catholic marriage in spite of their freedom of conscience, has it succeeded in insinuating itself in modern society. It has followed that civil marriage very rarely creates bonds that conscience cannot later recognize. On the other hand, even amongst those who are at first appearance the least pious, a man thinks himself dishonored not to marry in a Church, and he receives with a knowing smile the mayor's benediction that Jules Simon[1] hopes in vain to surround with greater majesty. The immense majority would thus be unaffected by any modification, against which at best only a few lawyers and freethinkers would revolt. Since there is so little to do, why persist in maintaining a state of things that is false in principle, which

[1] Jules Simon (1814–96) was a parliamentary leader in the Radical or anticlerical party.

attributes to the law a right it does not have, which changes nothing in the morals of the countryside, but create in the cities a sort of intermediate morality that leads rapidly to scorn for the Faith and family? What is the good of encouraging fleeting unions by a legal consecration that the wind will soon blow away in spite of the legislator?

Certainly it cannot be a question of imposing religious marriage on a nation that would oppose it. Yet, under the pretext of liberty, such a nation might wish the systematic weakening of the family, and from the state of nature that might be invoked, she will gradually fall well beneath nature into the most shameful vices. On the contrary, by giving religious marriage the place it merits and drawing morality from its true source, the law will certainly see diminish, by the sole means of the public conscience, all kinds of disorders, the growing numbers of which now rightly alarm serious minds, and which coercive punishments are powerless to reduce.

The family once constituted, education is both the first duty and sacred right of the parents. Now, unless we would hand over the younger generation to doubt and incredulity, it is indispensable that religion be the basis of all primary, secondary, and even higher education, and that the children of each cult receive completely separate instruction. There is here, for the state, the strict obligation to respect the faith of all and carefully to avoid, especially in history, philosophy, and political economy, lessons given in its name that inculcate the worst of religions: atheism.

The Church has always proclaimed and respected more than anyone the liberty of parents to raise their children in their own beliefs, even if they be erroneous. She has shown herself, and still shows herself in Rome, much more tolerant than any other society, religious or civil. If from century to century an example like the one of Mortara be produced, this exception has the advantage of noting in a solemn manner the limits that the truth has traced and the infinite precautions with which she has surrounded the rights of parents. More free in Rome than in many other lands, the Jews there enjoy the right to divorce; they are, in a sense, at home there, and in many instances they govern and judge themselves. All the same, it is forbidden them to take Christian servants, and in any case sincere Jews are the last to do so. Moreover, it is severely prohibited to Christians to baptize a Jewish child without the consent of the parents, except in case of imminent death. If, in spite of these precautions, little Mortara[2] became Christian—in some sense, in spite of the Church—baptism, which is not a vain ceremony, gave him the right to a Christian education and the full knowledge of the truth. At this time, he is a child of the Church, and the pope would have given his life rather than to have voluntarily abandoned a soul for which he had become responsible. Yet, I repeat, this is a unique case, in which the right of erring parents gives way to truth's superior right.

All the while, in infidel states, whether heretical or schismatic, thousands of souls are violently wrenched from the truth, and in rationalist states the government, under the pretext of impartiality, condemns all youth to skepticism, that is to say, to organized servitude on the largest scale.

Let us cease to educate Catholics in the same grade schools and high schools as Protestants, Jews, and the Muslims of Algeria. This promiscuity is one of the disgraces of the nineteenth century. Education cannot be separated from religion. United to religion, it will never be too developed or too widespread. Let it be free for the poor, not through forced contributions taken from their labor, but through the voluntary gifts of the rich! Let it be obligatory, addressing itself to children truly freed from premature work, and not competing with beings lessened by fatigue and misery! This was the desire of the councils of the Middle Ages; it will always be that of Catholics. If under the eye of religion, education can be free of

---

[2] Edgar Mortara (1851–1940) was born to a Jewish family in Bologna but was baptized a Catholic in 1852 when his Catholic nursemaid feared for his life. In 1858, the maid told the archbishop of Bologna what she had done, and the boy was subsequently made a ward of Pius IX. He was ordained a priest in 1873.

charge yet obligatory, and also accord with the right of the parents; if handed over to rationalist and faithless instruction, it becomes a yoke of despotism. In this regard we are, fortunately, far from the tendencies of the Revolution. The law of 1850 opened the way, and all that remains are improvements easy to put in place.

Finally, Sunday rest is the basis of the intellectual and moral life of every family and every man, no matter what his age. One of the first concerns of a serious legislator should be not to lead to the churches by force those who are not disposed to go, but instead to prevent the supreme liberty of the soul from being taken from anyone. For by being constrained to work endlessly, men are reduced to brutality and servitude. The Catholic countries are the only ones where passion and antireligious rage went so far as to deny the importance of this primary law, which England and other Protestant countries have the good sense to respect as the basis of their political and social health.*

Thus, first of all, let the state, which should set an example, suspend its work on Sundays and leave its workers, employees, soldiers, and bureaucrats the time to accomplish their duties and breathe for at least several hours with their families. Then, what could be easier than to put such a clause into the regulations of all the great enterprises given government privileges, such as canals, railroads, mines,

*On this subject, we may cite as a model of wisdom and the dignity of man rightly understood the resolution recently adopted by the association of journeyman printers in Berlin.

Considering: a. that rest of body and mind after an earnest six days' work constitutes an urgent need for all workers; b. that activity interrupted only by the indispensable amount of sleep weakens the strength needed for work and denies the worker any elevated moral tendency, for which it also renders him incapable; c. that the salary for work of six days should be sufficient for the worker's livelihood, and that experience proves that the lot of the worker is not improved when he works seven days; d. that the establishment of Sunday work as a means of competition is absolutely reprehensible; e. that the "free" worker cannot and will not remain below the slaves of antiquity and of the present day; the association of journeyman printers of Berlin declares that Sunday labor is prejudicial to their material and intellectual prosperity and must be absolutely rejected from the point of view of morals, and invites, by making reference to earlier efforts in this regard, all the societies of workers as well as all benevolent employers to publish similar declarations and to act as they can against the damaging practice of work on Sunday in the workshops. [*author's note*] and the like? On the request of the employees of commerce, who are all interested in having a day of liberty, why not grant them, as in England, the closing of shops? By becoming universal, this measure will harm no one and will give the employers themselves the leisure that competition denies them. Finally, if the workers recognize the incontestable utility of this, why not make a common rule for the numerous workshops? Why not fix on this day designed by nature the reunions, lessons, or lectures that are the public and intellectual life of the worker?

Let us note well that this is not a question of forcing an unwilling people to keep holy the Lord's day. If we had the pious desire to do so, we would still fail. Such laws must be demanded, sanctioned, and upheld by the public conscience and our habits, and when this force leaves them they fall into obsolescence by themselves. Yet if, as in France, a minority of strong minds work together to discredit Sunday rest and a minority of capitalists or bureaucrats make it impossible for those employed in the great public works projects, it is a grave wrong. We are fools to let them do this. The people must be shown that this so-called liberty leads straight to servitude, that it only results in creating bands of slaves to be exploited, without home or altar, gradually stripped of the last vestige of dignity and independence. It must be proven to the worker that to obtain real social, intellectual, and moral liberty, his first step must be to decide to respect Sunday rest. This is the only way to make possible and easy, through the free initiative of men, a great deal of progress that today appears illusory and revolutionary violence and economic for-mulae will never achieve. Finally, by thus elevating the moral level of society, we are certain to diminish the crimes and offenses that society is so often obliged to punish. In a word, Sunday rest is the best way to increase the share of liberty and to restrain that of repression.

Thus, freedom of religious marriage, freedom of religious instruction, freedom from work on Sunday, freedom of religious associations and corporations, in a word, the freedom of the

Church, which is nothing other than social truth rooted in religious truth, and which, by the free virtues and free devotion of men alone can widen the field of social liberty: here is the whole program of Catholics. Let the state openly favor the expansion of their activity. Let it rid itself of the impediments that paralyze the Church. Let it protect her against the perfidious passions that attack her. And let it content itself with repressing the grossest abuses of the power of capital. It will thus exercise the easiest and mildest of interventions, instead of throwing itself into some kind of despotic and futile imitation of pagan caesarism, and it will assure the intellectual and moral life of those masses whom the Revolution tends inevitably to reduce to the miserable situation of ancient slavery.

RENÉ DE LA TOUR

DU PIN

ON THE CORPORATE
REGIME (1883)

The principle of the corporate regime seems to us to consist in the recognition of the equal rights belonging to each member of an association, to the association within the state, and to the state with respect to the association.[1]

This is the principle that governed the social organization of the Middle Ages. . . .

Let us first speak of the rights of each individual member of an association. The recognition of these rights was so characteristic of and fundamental to the society of the Middle Ages that it can be seen long before the great age of the guilds. It appears even in the life of the serfs. The serf attached to the glebe . . . has been much exploited by those who allege that our past was barbaric. Yet in reality the serf's attachment was that of a laborer to the soil or an artisan to his workshop. It was the same reciprocal attachment desired by the socialists who say, "The land to the peasant, the tools to the worker." This attachment was infinitely superior to that seen in the days of modern liberties in the world's most free countries. Consider this example: the Italian government seized 470 small farms in a single township, age-

[1] The first several pages of La Tour du Pin's essay have been omitted because they pertain almost exclusively to the activities of the *Oeuvres des cercles* in 1883.

old homes of humble families, to be auctioned off in the presence of the unfortunate people, who were expelled so that the government could collect overdue taxes.

To return to the corporations of arts and trades: each of the members, whether apprentice, journeyman, or master, had his own right guaranteed by the statutes of the organization and protected by its directors. He truly had that "possession of an estate" whose name has remained in our current jurisprudence more often than has its substance, and he could not be deprived of it except by legal judgment.

Today, under the liberal regime, where is the right of the worker that guarantees fixed conditions of labor for today and the future? Not a single patron will—or, under current conditions, can—recognize such a right. This is the true obstacle to the propagation of our ideas among the leaders of industry: they do not want to hear the rights of workers spoken of.

Tomorrow, under the socialist regime, what will become of the rights of the patron? For in the end there will always be an owner, or at least a director of the enterprise. Yet how will he have possession of his estate, and what will be his guarantee, his security?

No, only the corporate regime can secure the right of each individual, not a single right for all, inasmuch as people have different functions within the association, but an equal respect for differing rights. This is the foundation of any social order worthy of the name. These rights were combined in such a way that they were not the weapon of one group against another, but a protection of the interest of all, joined in harmonious solidarity, just as a sound constitution does not arm citizens as enemy parties, but unites them by making the public good truly the common good.

After the guarantee of individual rights, the defining characteristic of the corporate regime is the guarantee of the rights of the association. This is not, as in our day, a purely private society having no tie to public things. It is a social institution holding a determinate place in the organization of the city, and more or less directly in that of the state.

At this point the question arises whether corporations should be free or obligatory. Yet neither kind can exist without the corporate state. The free corporation cannot exist if it has no protection other than the common law from the unlimited competition of the free market. Nor can the second exist if it is created by decree, for then it would be a bureaucratic mechanism rather than a spontaneous organism.

Obligatory corporations have nowhere been attempted. Free ones have nowhere succeeded. What the Austrian legislation has done is to give the force of law to preexisting free corporations, in order to protect their freedom to work and to prevent them from being snuffed out by competition that is often dishonest. We can only hope for the development of free corporations if they be given this privilege, for they have never existed without it. This privilege is not a monopoly. It is only the exercise of jurisdiction over competition to keep it within the limits of justice and the interest of society. Thus it is that from having begun as free, which it must in order to be born, a corporation becomes obligatory by the nature of things, and obligatory it must be if it is to exercise a political function. Instead of speaking of abstractions, let us consider whether it is not always thus in practice!

The third essential characteristic of the corporate regime is the place it gives to the rights of the state. The corporation is like the township, a state within the state, that is, it is bound to the state by a moral contract that includes reciprocal rights and duties. The public authority does not dictate its rules, but it approves them in order to keep them within the bounds of a corporate utility that does not injure the public utility, while at the same time it protects their application against material difficulties and outside oppression.

Because we must not only preserve but also promote the corporations, the actions of the government must be full of solicitude. Its current role should be that of the vigilant tutor, who supplies by his own ability what his pupil cannot and thus provides for the pupil's future. When the pupils have attained maturity, the government

[handwritten margin note: Naturally free, but needs laws to function as a system and survive.]

will only act by the promulgation of laws that coordinate these new autonomous forces with the whole ensemble of social and political institutions.

In truth, there is a great difference between administering a country and governing one. A country should never be administered, rather, each of its elements should administer itself within a structure furnished by laws. Now, the respective spheres of national legislation and administration cannot be determined in the abstract. Their reach depends on the morals and circumstances of the people. What is crucial is that these two notions not be confounded by those who treat social questions, so that in their laudable aversion to bureaucratic centralization they not forget the role that legislation plays in every civilization. Christians can live under pagan legislation, but they will never form a society with Christian morals while under it, and alas, this is as true today as it was under the Roman caesars.

The state has an interest in supporting the interests of the working class that, far from being opposed to the humanitarian considerations evoked by those who support the free market, are actually inspired by them. On this view, it is a duty of government to protect these interests against foreigners, not by means of a tariff war, but by agreements that fix the rate of tariffs at the point necessary to protect both the market, considered from an economic point of view, and national labor, considered from a social point of view. Thus the power that imposes restrictions on industrial profits for the sake of the well-being of the working population should direct its foreign relations in such a way that the inhumane profits from competition that it prohibits at home do not weigh upon her from abroad. We have often waged wars to open a market to a harmful product, just as opium is physically harmful to China and numerous European products are morally harmful to primitive countries. Would it not be more Christian to wage wars only to protect humanity where it is unjustly exploited by the cupidity of the few? There is a white slave trade just as there is a black one. It is found just beyond our borders, where women work as beasts of burden in the mines, as in Belgium, or where the working day lasts sixteen hours, as in some factories in Moravia, or where the salary of women is absolutely insufficient to procure their strict necessities, as in England, or, finally, where certain members of the working class are so miserable that their very humanity is degraded, as in Germany.

Here would be a far more noble war for a Christian prince than those wars of the Revolution that overturned the face of Europe in order to spread antisocial ferment. Here would be a political program the generosity of which would merit the people's favor, whose condition it would improve at the same time as it protected the-mand their interests. Moreover, it can be pursued without violence, as shown by our neighbor Switzerland, which by an ensemble of laws and tariffs has been able to protect a relatively large and flourishing industrial population.

It seems that we have strayed from our goal, which is the examination of the principle of the corporate regime. Yet this is a necessary preliminary, for the solidarity that it would create among workshops cannot exist without national solidarity, and it would exist more perfectly under Christian solidarity.

We have laid out above what we take to be the fundamental principle of the corporate regime, that is, the recognition of the rights of the individual as well as of each of the classes that cooperate in production and each of the social bonds that exist between these elements, from the corporation to the state. Now we must examine the fundamental practices that these rights make possible. We shall keep ourselves to the essential points, leaving aside questions of application specific to this or that form of work.

The fundamental practices seem to correspond to the three essential aspects of a corporation:

- The existence of a common property that receives a share of the profits of the industry;

• The acknowledgment of the professional capacity of the entrepreneur as well as the worker;

• The representation of each interested part in the government
of the whole.

We shall examine each of these in turn.

The existence of a corporation is so tightly bound to that of an
indivisible and inalienable corporate patrimony that this first practice would require no further explanation were it not for the difficulty of creating this patrimony. This is an urgent matter, for if the
creation of this communal property is indispensable, and if its quantity must be sufficient to provide for all manner of needs, including
stoppages of work, pensions, insurance, and professional schools,
then it must not be left entirely to caprice. An optional institution
requires only optional measures, but a necessary institution requires
regulated contributions.

The most logical way to provide these contributions would be by
a sum levied on production. This is because the benefits of such a
patrimony are the result of the enterprise's commercial action, and
also because these benefits should be considered as payment for part
of the cost of production. When the accounting is done, it will be a
simple matter to make management and labor bear equal parts of
the burden, both parties making their contribution, the one of
tools, the other of labor. We might even measure this contribution
by an amount of time, as for instance by the uniform production of
half a day per week.

Whatever the process may be, it exists so that the corporate fund
shares in the profits of the industry. This kind of process is already
being applied in a number of agricultural enterprises, where the permanent workers receive a certain percentage of the harvest. What is
required is to capitalize this sum rather than to distribute it to individuals. In industrial joint-stock corporations, the fund could be
created by reserving a certain number of shares through a reduction

from the normal salary (which is always easy to evaluate in terms of shares), provided the worker be bound by a contract or not participate in the fund until after a certain amount of time. We should note in passing that it would be wise to retain this means of evaluating work in terms of capital, because it could be the basis of a number of arrangements tending to substitute a social contract between ownership and labor for a mere labor agreement, and it also allows satisfaction of workers' needs without damaging the legitimate interests of the owners.

We will not here attempt to describe each of the many different ways that the various factors of production already cooperate. It suffices to note that the proceeds required to create a corporate fund over time do not need to be invented, but simply employed in a more constant manner and for a particular end, namely, that of leading the worker, who can but with difficulty obtain individual property, towards the attainment and maintenance of the advantages of holding collective property in a secure manner.

This is mere justice. If property is to be considered as one of the bases of society, it is upon the condition that it be accessible in one form or another to all social classes, and this requires us to put an end to the division of society into property-owners and proletarians that has been created by the modern regime.

Capital is not the only form of property from which a man can legitimately draw advantages in virtue of his own right. The possession of a career or a trade can also be seen as having the character of property when it is guaranteed by the law. That is to say, it constitutes a right belonging to the one who has acquired it when it gives him a privilege that can only be taken away by legal judgment.

Now, we believe that this characteristic can be found in a certificate of professional capacity, given according to certain rules to each productive person, be he engineer or worker, and without which no one can be an active member of a corporation, nor raise himself above the lowest rank of the professional hierarchy.

The laborer, that is, the simple unskilled worker, does not strictly speaking possess a trade. He employs his strength, not his ability. The number of such laborers tends daily to decrease with the progress of machines that provide strength and require only human direction. As soon as a man has acquired an ability, whether it be to lead a harness, to stitch together clothing, or to carry out a trade, he truly possesses what was formerly called an estate, and this estate should be guaranteed to him by that assemblage of institutions that we include under the designation of the corporate regime. Moreover, he should be able to raise himself within that estate as far as his ability and good conduct allow, that is, from journeyman to master, with all the degrees in the estate being acknowledged by a certificate assuring him certain advantages independent of his current employment.

These same principles apply to the engineer. At the same time as the industrial corporation, for instance, employs only those engineers with the proper certificate, it also opens access to that career by means of professional schools, if not to the simple laborers, then at least to their children, thus offering the most humble members a healthy and legitimate hope of improving their social rank.

All of this was practiced for a long time in our country and all of Europe, and it is now starting to reappear. Thus, in Austria, where the legislature has reestablished the corporate regime for arts and trades, he has also reestablished the requirement of the masterpiece, or, what is its equivalent, a certificate of professional studies, in order to be able to direct a workshop. Moreover, it seems that this measure should be extended to other industries beyond the trades, even to purely commercial ones. In fact, the honor of the profession and the security of the clientele both require that the merchant no less than the manufacturer understand and be responsible for the quality of his wares.

In places where the corporate regime does not exist, but where nevertheless one does not desire to abandon everything to the struggle of individual interests, as for instance in Prussia, certain private enterprises of great interest to the nation, such as mining and forests, can be directed only by certified engineers, who must submit their annual plan of work for administrative approval. There is a similar measure in place for the great agricultural properties of Hungary, because the poor care of these properties would be ruinous not only for the owners, but also for the country.

In closing, let us note that our examples of state intervention, which might appear abusive, are taken from those countries where it has become necessary in spite of the existence of free corporations. This kind of intervention would disappear in an obligatory corporate regime. Only there, contrary to what is often said by those who have thought little about it, are the corporations truly open to whoever fulfills their conditions. Free corporations, conversely, are necessarily closed, and for that reason it becomes difficult for the state to grant them the exercise of a more extensive jurisdiction.

This word "jurisdiction" should be the object of special consideration because it corresponds to a fundamental idea of the corporate regime. A society does not include all the conditions necessary for its independent existence until it possesses within itself the three powers that, according to Montesquieu, constitute the mechanism of government: legislative power, judiciary power, and executive power. To put it another way: the corporation decrees its own rules, judges conflicts among its members, and administers its patrimony through delegates chosen from among its own numbers.

Once these principles are admitted, it must then be acknowledged that they do not receive their correct application until all of the elements of the association participate in its government, not according to their number of individuals, but according to the order of their social functions. The association will not be a perfect society unless it includes all the elements that contribute to its end. Now, the end of an association of labor being production, all the agents necessary to or immediately concerned with production must be present. The application of this principle will differ according to the nature and conditions of the work in question.

Thus, in large industries we easily distinguish three kinds of agents: capital, generally formed by a group of shareholders, management, represented by a certain number of directors and employees, and labor, the workers. In agriculture, we generally see the same three kinds of agents: the landowner, the farmer (whether a steward or a sharecropper), and the laborer. In the arts and trades, at first glance there seem only to be two, corresponding to the old names of master and journeyman. Yet if we consider the present transformation of the market, we see that the trades have not been able to resist the competition of industry except when they work for a client, and not for the open market, as happens generally in the clothing and building industries. Thus we can say that this clientele acts by its demands in a way similar to the shareholders in a joint-stock corporation: that is, it provides the capital. Thus, the clients can legitimately and usefully be represented in the corporate organization. At any rate, we have admitted this fact in our first attempts at restoring the old corporations, insofar as the committee of honor, as we call the group of benefactors formed to protect the initial stages of our foundations, is an indispensable part of our program.

As to the reciprocal role of these three elements in the council that governs the corporation, we shall surpass all that has recently been presented elsewhere as plans for the reorganization of corporations by reestablishing the "vote by order," with each order being represented by only one vote.

Much more could be said under this heading, but now, having seen the vital principle and fundamental practices of the corporate regime, we must hasten to explore its advantages.

We should like to see the corporate regime replace our current regime, the regime of the freedom of labor. The advantages that would follow from the corporate regime are these: the end of economic decline, brought about by honest competition and the prosperity of the trades; the end of moral decline through the preservation of our homes and the return to family life; the end of political decline through the reestablishment for each person of the possession of his estate. We shall attempt to describe these advantages.

The freedom of labor, otherwise known as capitalism, exhausts both man and nature and endangers both the producer and production. Capitalism is the system today practiced throughout our social economy. It tends to one end: to increase the return on capital by decreasing the costs of production. It does this in two ways: by procuring the best possible price for labor and materials and by employing in production the least possible quantity and quality of each. Here is how our social problem, reduced to a simple sketch, plays out every day. A skilled and conscientious manufacturer makes a good product. A commercial house buys it and thus gives him publicity and a sufficient profit. Yet as soon as the price is set for the public and the costs have been recuperated, either a rival house or the same house itself has but one goal: to obtain a product of similar appearance at a better cost by employing labor and materials of lesser quality. Then, if the manufacturer wishes to preserve his good workers and the honesty of his manufacturing, he is lost, unless, having foreseen the necessity, he had raised his prices in advance or had set aside enough to live on for several years.

Competition is said to be the soul of production. Yet it existed just as much in the past, even with the corporate monopoly, which, on the one hand, did not permit a price above the just price because the public authorities watched over it, and, on the other, did not tolerate the decline of the product because the masters kept control over it. There was competition between the masters of the same corporation, competition to see who could offer the best product while paying the same wages and costs for materials and charging the same price. Everyone gained from this: the client was well served, and the worker and the master both had a secure livelihood. This regime did not pose limits to the freedom of labor as much as it did to the freedom of capital, which is even more tyrannical today towards the manufacturer than it is towards the laborer, who feels only its consequences.

Has the system of unlimited freedom of capital improved our production, as is claimed, or has it diminished it? The latter, for it has allowed production to die out on our national soil by allowing it to emigrate to wherever it can find labor and material at better prices. When we argue about the economic decline of France we should pay attention to this fact: our annual imports exceed our exports by a billion francs, that is, we consume a billion francs more than we produce. Who pays for this excess of foreign production, unless it be the profits of French capital that has left to make fruitful other fields than our own? Our commercial houses often sell the produce of foreign nations under French trademarks. A large part of those things "made in Paris" are actually made in Germany, and by this double trick of capitalism even our export statistics are often falsified. Thus, recently a rich Viennese landowner who had ordered some rugs in France had workers from his own city recognize their own work. The Parisian house had ordered the rugs from Vienna and had thus exploited the misery of the Viennese worker and also the good faith of the consumer at the expense of the reputation and industry of France.

Let us consider the consequences of this system. The multiplication of the paths of exchange will soon lead to its logical conclusion, and we will only see on the market those goods produced by the most miserable of peoples. The Chinese will become the world's best workers because they only require that their animal needs be met. Later, the worker, the engineer, the salesman, and the banker himself will be purchased on the open market. Then the banker of London, Paris, or Vienna, having made himself rich by putting his capital to work in China, will in turn face an unequal struggle against the Chinese usurer, who will not give himself the luxuries of a princely palace, teams of horses, parties, and the life of the rich. An irremediable decline awaits the economic order of the civilization of the West at the end of this path of freedom of labor, a path down which it is led by the teaching of the philosophers, the science of the economists, and the power of the capitalists.

The corporate regime is no less necessary to avert decline in the moral order than in the economic order, for the regime of freedom of labor has been, in the first place, the regime responsible for the destruction of the worker's family life. Let us consider the book recently published by the abbé Cetty on the disorganization of households and corruption of morals in the manufacturing centers of Alsace, so famous for the flourishing of its industry and the sacrifices and philanthropic efforts made by its industrialists on behalf of its workers. Worker cities, property given for homes, insurance agencies, cooperative purchasing societies, libraries, schools: all that charity can do for the worker has remained powerless to stop the moral decline that follows from the insufficient protection of morals in the regime of freedom of labor. This will be repeated as long as conservatives refuse to see the evil as it is or seek such powerless cures in face of such a vicious organization.

The organization of the family cannot resist the disorganization of workshops in which each of its members works in conditions that take no account of the rights and needs of the household. The workshop in turn cannot be reorganized with a view to respecting and maintaining the organization of the family except by the common agreement of all the agents of production and under the aegis of laws. Laws would no doubt suffice to make Sunday rest respected, to prevent the abuse of the employment of women and children, to curb seduction, and so on. Yet they will not be able to make reign that moral discipline that rests, first of all, on the respect of hierarchy in the family and the workshop. Only the corporation can maintain the father of the family in his dignity while assisting him in his charges, and the mother of the family in her household by keeping her there, and thus preparing a shelter under which the influence, morals, and practices of religion can reign. That is, without a corporation, only heroic efforts can do this, and these will always be rare. These are the very words of the abbé Cetty. If one requires more than the word of a priest to treat this aspect of the religious question, we can invoke the memory of Monsignor Ketteler, the bishop of Mainz, and his *The Worker Question and Christendom*.[2] It is not without emotion that we read these lines that preceded by fifteen years the Catholic movement in favor of the reestablishment of the corporate regime: "May God in his goodness soon raise up men who will bring this fertile idea of associations of production onto the soil of Christendom, and there make them prosper for the salvation of the working classes!" Here he aptly traced the mission of the *Oeuvre des cercles*:

> In the past, the Church saw the sacrifices of the nobility give birth to the greater part of its large monasteries. It seems to me that nothing would be more Christian or more pleasing to God than a work having as its goal the creation of Christian associations of production in those places where the sufferings of the workers are the worst. Yet first of all it is necessary that the idea of these associations and the manner of founding them be examined and become clear in all its connections. When everyone recognizes their importance for the working classes, when the working classes themselves are reached and the greater part of them have a lively conviction of the benefits they offer, and at the same time we know under what form and by what means they are to be established, only then will we be able to hope to see the attempts to found them multiply.

Do we want to know what the great bishop thought of the attempts to resolve the worker question by other means? Here is what he said about the popular banks, the most celebrated of such attempts, whose promoter, Schulze-Delitzsch, recently died after having seen three thousand of these societies arise in Germany, societies with no other bond than a financial interest: "Many more Schulze-Delitzsch banks will appear, proclaiming salvation to the

---

[2] Wilhelm Emmanuel von Ketteler (1811–77) was the pioneer of Catholic social thought in Germany. His *Die Arbeiterfrage und das Christentum* (1864) helped to shape Leo XIII's *Rerum Novarum*.

working classes, before the last tower built by the last of them will fall in on itself and the poor worker has had his hopes dashed and abandons the sad role of dupe."

After having seen that the corporate regime is the only possible means to stop economic and moral decline, we must now show that it is also the only way to stop political decline, through its promise to provide a basis for social reorganization with its principles of the possession of an estate for all and the representation of all interests.

It goes without saying that in order to make the people conservative, we must first give them something to conserve. Now, this is exactly the opposite of what liberalism has done in suppressing the social organizations in which each had his own right and secure estate. Since then our discontent has been permanent and our revolutions chronic, because a stable political order cannot be built on an unstable social order, the former being but the coronation of the edifice formed by society within the limits of a nation. Elsewhere we have insisted on the fundamental distinction between state and society. Here we must consider their connection: the state functions only for the preservation of society. Yet if society itself is troubled, if its members do not wish to preserve it and thus render it untenable, then the mission of the state becomes impossible to fulfill, and, because it is the exterior form of society, the people become discontented, begin to hate it, and seek only to overturn it.

This is the result of a century of liberalism in the governance of the ancient states of Christendom. The discontent of the people mounts in inverse proportion to its promises and in direct proportion to its progress. All the beautiful catch-phrases in the world cannot prevent the realization of this historical fact, nor retard the social evolution that will make the world pass from the anarchy of the liberal regime to the despotism of socialism, because these are the two terms of one and the same illness that invades the world from time to time, most recently in 1789. Liberalism has given birth to socialism by the logic of its principles and by a reaction against its practices. This evolution is far more advanced than is generally thought, and we no longer need to stop the first phase of the development, but the second one.

The corporate regime, taken as the basis for social reorganization, is not the middle way between the two, as has often been said, because it takes neither its principles nor its forms from either one. Nor is it Christian socialism, for the conjunction of these two words in our language is but nonsense, since socialism is taken in the pejorative. In fact, it is social Christianity; but this is redundant. It is Christianity. It contains the seed of social well-being in that instead of the principles of the Revolution, it truly incarnates those of Christianity, for it has been solely by deduction from the doctrines of the Church that we have been able to recognize these principles and appreciate their power.

Yet for this seed to develop fully, the corporate regime must receive its complete application. It must be applied not only to manual labor, but to all social activity, because it contains the only truly conservative principle of an order that is democratic in its basis and aristocratic at its summit, that is to say, the natural order.

These ideas are not original to us, nor are most of those here addressed, for they were proclaimed in years gone by in the memoirs of Prince Metternich and in the manifestos of the count de Chambord and in the publications of the republican Mazaroz. So strong is the agreement between our various sources, who speak such different languages, that a foreign statesmen who came to our conference told me that he saw this as a powerful sign not only of the truth of this doctrine, but also of hope for the future.

We must conclude. If, as I have attempted to show, the corporate regime rests on a principle so eminently social, if its fundamental practices are acceptable and its advantages are many, then to call for its reestablishment must be an excellent way to combat the Revolution.

We will show that to call for the complete establishment of the corporate regime will give the Catholic movement a program with regard to the social question, and then will open political action to it by forcing parties to announce either their support or their opposition, and finally will hold in check the revolutionary forces both outside and within the nation.

It must first be said that to call for the complete establishment of the corporate regime is by itself a program for the social question. In truth, its destruction was the consequence of a program that was neatly expressed in one line by the author of the law of 1791: "It should not be permitted to citizens of certain professions to assemble for their so-called common interests. . . . [I]t belongs to the nation to furnish work to those who need it to survive and aid to the infirm." It is immediately evident that this is a program, the program of the Revolution. The secretary general of the *Oeuvre*[3] had only to recall it when on the 12th of June he mounted the tribune of the Chamber of Deputies to lay out the opposing program for the worker question and explained that it does not belong to the nation but rather to the corporations to organize work for the benefit of the workers. To corporations, that is, with a determinate constitution, corporations that should be established with special privileges in order to pave the way towards the corporate regime.

In order to see that this would give the Catholic movement in France a social program for the first time, it suffices to say that every time it has been proposed, the Catholic legislators in the parliament have remained mute and have voted with the liberals, with the sole exception of our confrere Monsieur Keller. Why this sad state of affairs? It comes from the very source of the matter, as the count de Mun has explained:

> The social situation [created by the abandonment of the corporate regime] has been given a name: it is individualism. This is the wound that troubles our society from head to toe. Yet no one has suffered more cruelly from it than the worker, because no one is more in need than the weak, *for whom the social question almost always becomes a question of subsistence*, and no one has more

[3] Albert de Mun.

> need to be protected and to find some compensation for
> his sufferings in social institutions.

This was not the least of the many courageous acts that adorn the
life of our friend, to have taken up, against the current of opinion
of almost all Catholics this side of the Rhine, the thesis set forth by
this memorable opening line from the writings of the famous
bishop of Mainz, the first to have seen the worker question in its
true light: "The worker question is essentially a question of subsistence."

In the fifteen years that have passed between the words of
Monsignor Ketteler and those of our friend, Catholics were at first
content to say that the worker question was essentially a question of
virtue on the part of the workers, and to await its solution through
the development of religious outreach to the workers, that is to say,
those efforts of the few priests or laymen devoted to the exercise of
a special apostolate towards the rare workers who would speak to
them. Then we saw that it might also be a question of virtue on the
part of the owners, and one of them, our dear Léon Harmel, called
them back to their Christian duties with the eloquence of his fiery
tongue and his still more admirable example.[4] Yet if neither the
former nor the latter charitable actions made great strides towards
relieving the state of the worker, it is because the spirit of charity is
the final condition of this relief, while its first principle must be the
spirit of justice. This spirit of justice is that of a social order that will
reestablish the organic relations of the reciprocal rights and duties
of the three agents of production: the capitalist, the entrepreneur,
and the worker. The corporate regime must cast a fine net so that it
catches not only the last two, but also the capitalist, for labor
without capital is like a fish without water. Therefore the regime
must be constituted by public law, and it cannot merely be optional
and, out of respect for the liberty of capital, leave the weakest
depending on the good will of the strongest.

[4] Léon Harmel (1829–1915) was a pioneer in the communal organization of the workplace
at his textile factory in northern France. He was also active in the *Oeuvre des cercles*.

When his own affairs are at stake, His Majesty the Capitalist has succeeded in replacing the Christian religion with the worship of the golden calf. Anyone who reminds us that the doctors of the Church taught a doctrine about the role of capital other than that it was free to make money pour forth at will is labeled the most extravagant utopian or a dangerous socialist.

Until now, the teachings on political economy that have been promulgated by Catholics, even by fervent ones, have too often lacked clarity and conclusiveness, because Catholics have not dared to vindicate the principles of the Church and to base themselves squarely on this ground. They have not yet sufficiently departed from the liberal school to create their own school, nor have they broken with common opinion nor even convinced their own audience, that is, the youth educated in Catholic schools. This is why it was neither a lawyer nor an economist but a military man, as we know, who told his country the truth that "for the worker, the social question is a question of subsistence," and who pointed out its solution in the corporate regime.

While Count de Mun thus emulated Counts Blome and Belcredi and the Princes Liechtenstein,[5] who were the first in our time to make such language be heard in a parliament, he was far from being supported by public opinion or the workers. He mounted the tribune almost alone, having in support of his motion only the signatures of thirty-two of his colleagues and several thousand members of the *Oeuvre*.

We must admit that his language is the expression of the thought of a mere handful of men, whose efforts over the past eleven years have been neither followed nor understood. We can say that we have at least given the Catholic movement in France the beginnings of a program, but we cannot say that it has made this program its own. We have staked out a position for it on the battlefield where the destiny of our country will be decided. We can say that we have carried the very banner of Christian civilization. They must rally to

[5] These were the leaders of the Catholic social movement within the Austro-Hungarian Empire.

it. And it is the responsibility first of all of those who teach to detach themselves from liberalism in political economy as in all else, and to make shine those words spoken in the Vatican: "Science is a gift that must lead us back to God."

The day when French Catholics frankly devote themselves to a program for the social question will be the day on which they will find action open to them in the field of politics. What is more, they will have prepared their supremacy if their program is a just one, for the triumphs of error are not eternal. It must also be the right kind of program, for a social evil requires a social remedy. Society knows what ails it, and it is tired of politicians who each offers his own medicine, whether it be Empire, Republic, or Monarchy, without saying anything about the regimen of treatment that the medicine requires.

In France there have always been Catholics convinced that the source of all the fundamental truths of the social order is the doctrine of the Church, but their number has been decreasing constantly since the days of the League, when they saved national unity. The successive errors of Jansenism, Gallicanism, and finally so-called Catholic liberalism, errors which have infiltrated the clergy, have so weakened the party that from our youth I was told not of Catholic statesmen, but of Catholic writers, from Maistre, Bonald, and Blanc de Saint-Bonnet to Cardinal Pie, Keller, and Louis Veuillot. The Catholic party, for the League was none other than that, has always decreased with the weakening of Roman doctrines and the triumph of liberal doctrines in religion, politics, and social economy. And, we note in passing, this is the response that should be given to those conservative Protestants who reproach the Church for having lost so much ground in face of the Revolution: alas, she lost less ground from the attacks of her enemies than from the abandonment of terrain by her own children, by those who call themselves and still wish to be her faithful, but who no longer are faithful in their hearts and minds.

The Catholic party was so weakened that we have only recently seen her reborn in the wake of a national disaster, and her first truly characteristic action was the national vow to the Sacred Heart. The Church blessed it and encourages the flowering of works and all signs that point to this renaissance, among which we have the privilege of citing the *Oeuvre des cercles catholiques d'ouvriers*. Yet the Catholic party still refuses to give battle against the Revolution other than by protesting against its mounting attacks. The protests against the dispersion of the religious orders and against the secularization of public education were the expression of this negative politics, which does, however, at least allow the Catholic party to remind the public of the existence of rights other than those outlined in the so-called "rights of man."

In this first period, the Catholic party only interested itself in the rights of the Church. Political rights, the most complex of all and the most easily misunderstood, require a more solid education in order to be rightly understood, and this cannot be done by a youthful party. Social rights also seem to be difficult to grasp and to demand. Yet as these are demanded from all sides, we must now pass from the period of criticism to that of affirmation, and, with respect to social questions, we sense that the *Oeuvre des cercles* is slowly drawing the Catholic movement towards the third period, when a program of action will be formulated.

The actual extent of this progress is difficult to determine, especially by those who are themselves a part of the movement. Yet the observer finds a characteristic sign in the sentiments expressed at one of the most recent regional Catholic conferences. The program of the congress bore this heading: "On the Resistance to the Anti-Christian Action of the Secret Societies." The commission given this charge made this pronouncement: "The only way for Catholics effectively to resist the anti-Christian action of the secret societies is to work by political means to take away the civil power that these societies have gained and to turn this power into the hands of a Catholic government." It also expressed the desire that "Catholics more deeply study social questions and thus prepare the complete restoration of the Christian social order by first reestablishing in themselves, and then communicating, the complete idea of it." From most fitting prudential considerations, these desires were not submitted to the sanction of the entire congress, but the words were no less spoken for that, and subsequent meetings should follow this direction or they will fail from lack of interest. The world is on the march, and after having marched for our adversaries for many years, it now marches against them, whether it march under the banner of socialism or under our own.

Moreover, we should note that this movement does not recognize borders and that France has been preceded in it by many other Catholic peoples. We like to cite this example, taken from our own stock, from an electoral program in Canada: "A whole and entire adherence to Roman Catholic doctrines in religion, politics, and social economy should be the first and principal qualification that Catholic voters should require from the Catholic candidate. This is the most solid criterion with which to be able to judge men and things."

The day is not far off when French Catholics, taking their inspiration from the social program whose beginnings have been so brilliantly set out by the count de Mun, will no longer have to fear being compromised by their subjection to a political party. On the contrary, they will accept the allegiance of those parties that are able to follow them, and they will become a daunting foe of the Revolution. No less than this did Monsieur Lockroy, the speaker for the majority in the Chamber, say in response to our friend's motion. Let us consider his meaning without being moved by his words, which were those of an actor rather than a statesman:

> The Honorable Monsieur de Mun has come before us today under the pretext of social order and liberty in order to defend the working class against the exploitation of the republicans by placing their interests in the hands of the patrons and leaders of the *Oeuvre des cercles*! Under the pretext of liberty and social order he has

just demanded that we dismantle one by one all the barriers that the Revolution had constructed to defend us
against the encroachments of the aristocrats. And it is
this pretext of liberty and social order that he uses, and
that has always been used, to promote the undertakings
of political reaction and clerical domination. *Never has
an undertaking of this kind been more eloquently defended
and more skillfully conducted; never has one been more
dangerous for* [revolutionary] *society.*

Although there is much more to be said, we are content to bring
these considerations to a close with these words that escaped from
the mouth of an anxious revolutionary. . . .

We, on the contrary, proclaim: return to the people the just guarantees that they are owed, and reconstruct on the basis of these
restored rights the whole edifice of social and political law. Our program is Catholic in its source, which is why we see it grow without
any apparent bounds in those countries that are tired of being
exploited by the Liberals and have no confidence in the rule of the
Socialists, wherever, in a word, the Revolution loses ground. And it
loses ground before our eyes. Let us take courage! The political parties that have raised the social question will perish by it. The future
belongs to those who know how to resolve it.

A final word. Why, when we come bearing the rights of the
people in hand, have we not yet made our appeal to them? Why
instead have we made our appeal to the devotion of the class that
has most greatly lost the notion of these rights? Because it was in
this class that the revolutionary society was formed before it
devoured the people, and because one must crush the head of the
serpent, not its tail. It would not be difficult for us to play Prince
Kropotkin[6] and to speak to the workers of rights to be reconquered

---

[6] Prince Peter Kropotkin (1842–1921) renounced his title to become a popular advocate for
the Russian serfs.

while we are still not yet the masters of those rights and able to give them away, for we are less "bourgeois," according to their language, than those who exploit them in one way or another. Yet this is not what our Lord and Master Jesus Christ did. He did not preach revolt to slaves. He told the great that the little ones were their brothers and that we must give each man his due. From this was born, and will be born again, if God wills it, the Christian social order.

SOURCES

François-René de Chateaubriand, "De Buonaparte, des Bourbons, et de la nécessité de se rallier à nos princes légitimes, pour le bonheur de la France et celui de l'Europe" [30 mars 1814] in *Grands écrits politiques*, tome I, ed. Jean-Paul Clément (Paris: Imprimerie Nationale, 1993).

Louis de Bonald, *Pensées sur divers sujets, et discours politiques*, 2 volumes (Paris: Adrien Le Clere, 1817).

———, *Mélanges littéraires, politiques, et philosophiques*, 2 volumes (Paris: Bloud et Barral, 1882).

Joseph de Maistre, "Réflexions sur le protestantisme dans ses rapports avec la souveraineté," in *Écrits sur la Révolution*, ed. Jean-Louis Darcel (Paris: Presses universitaires de France, 1989), 219–39. The edition is reproduced from *Oeuvres inédites du comte Joseph de Maistre* (Paris, 1870), 509–48.

———, *Du Pape* [1819], édition critique par Jacques Lovie et Joannès Chetail (Geneva: Droz, 1966).

Frédéric Le Play, *La Réforme sociale en France, déduite de l'observation comparée des peuples européens*, 2 volumes (Paris: Henri Plon, 1864).

Émile Keller, *L'Encyclique du 8 décembre et les principes de 1789, ou, l'Église, l'État, et la liberté*, deuxième édition (Paris: Veuve Poussielgue et Cie., 1866).

René de La Tour du Pin, *Vers un ordre social chrétien: jalons de route, 1822–1907* (Paris: Éditions du Trident, 1987).

N.B.: Authors' footnotes from some of the original documents were omitted so as not to impede the flow of their arguments.

ACKNOWLEDGMENTS

Joseph de Maistre would smile upon learning that this book, like his Soirées de St.-Pétersbourg, was the fruit of a conversation among three friends. It was under the venerable branches of the Jacobite Oak that my colleague William Fahey raised the topic of the French counter-revolutionaries, knowing that Jeff Nelson had been wanting to publish something of their works and that I had been working on them. Let me, then, first express my warm gratitude to them both, and to Jeremy Beer, also of the Intercollegiate Studies Institute, for making a long-standing interest of mine grow into something more substantial.

I should like to testify to the helpful advice about the craft of translation that I received from Robert Wilken and Kenneth Whitehead, and, in an earlier stage of the project, from the Reverend Michael Keating and Mark Henrie. What grace is present in them I owe to the influence of my wife's fine ear for English style. I do not, however, wish to implicate any of these persons in whatever errors or lapses of judgment that may remain in them.

For my knowledge of the French language and culture, my thanks are due especially to my mother, my first French teacher, and my father, the generous patron of my travels and studies abroad.

For their helpful suggestions about the text of the introduction, I should like to thank Michael Aeschliman, William Fahey, Charles Glenn, the Reverend Michael Keating, and Jonathan Reyes. For the generosity of their support over the years and for the wisdom of their conversation, I am grateful to, among others, Anthony Andres, Michael Brown, Warren Carroll, John Cuddeback, Bradley Lewis, the Reverend Marvin O'Connell, Phillip Sloan, and Constantine Soutsos.

Finally and most importantly, I thank my wife Kathleen and dedicate this volume to our son, John Louis.

INDEX